'*Fit Mind* is a journey from the head to the heart. On this journey, Pat encourages all of us to learn to listen deeply, building trust and connection with ourselves. Through this engaging process we discover how inner strength is found in our vulnerabilities and shadows.

This book has helped me to return to what nourishes my 'base' and polish my lens with simple yet powerful practices that deepen attention and awareness in a distracted, noisy and burned-out world. This is a powerful invitation to come back to the heart.'

Dr Easkey Britton, surfer and author of *Saltwater in the Blood*

'*Fit Mind* can help you rewrite your inner story and reclaim your power. Pat Divilly has created a transformative guide that can help anyone who is looking to make a serious change in their life.

Mental and emotional fitness is the next frontier. This is crucial work that can not only help the individual, but can positively impact society as a whole. Pick up this book if you are ready for deep growth.'

Yung Pueblo, *New York Times* bestselling author

'They say that you should never take travel advice from someone who has never left home; Pat Divilly is a man I would take advice from 365 days of the year. He is erudite, vulnerably honest and empirically practical: this is a man who lives his philosophy, and that is a rare gem indeed.

I believe that *Fit Mind* will change your life for the better, and if you are in a dark place it could save your life. Highly recommended.'

Geoff Thompson, BAFTA-winning writer

FIT MIND

Pat Divilly is the host of the hugely popular *Pat Divilly Podcast*, as well as an author, speaker and health and wellness coach who has fast become one of Ireland's leading authorities in that area. In sharing tools to support physical, mental and emotional wellness, Pat's goal is to provide practical, accessible perspectives and initiatives to promote long-term health in both body and mind.

FIT MIND

8 WEEKS to CHANGE your INNER SOUNDTRACK
and TUNE INTO YOUR GREATNESS

PAT DIVILLY

GILL BOOKS

Gill Books
Hume Avenue
Park West
Dublin 12
www.gillbooks.ie

Gill Books is an imprint of M.H. Gill and Co.

978 07171 9132 1

Designed by Bartek Janczak
Edited by Jane Rogers
Proofread by Esther Ní Dhonnacha

Printed by Clays Ltd, Suffolk
This book is typeset in 12 on 18pt Minion Pro

The paper used in this book comes from the wood pulp of
managed forests. For every tree felled, at least one tree is
planted, thereby renewing natural resources.

A CIP catalogue record for this book is available from the
British Library.

5 4 3 2 1

To Ryan Johnson. Thank you for the encouragement and love you and your family showed me in my late teens. It changed the course of my life forever.

In loving memory of Eric Coleman, Chick Gillen and John Creaven.

ACKNOWLEDGEMENTS

To my parents – thank you for your sacrifices, your love and your support throughout my life. Aine, Colm, Liam, Wayne and Barry, thank you for always being there for me and for accepting me as I am.

Rod Boothroyd, Madeline Hand, Emma Murphy, Natasha Vavasour, Josh Connolly, Niall Graham, Jason Best, Brenda Tuite and Owen Fitzpatrick – thank you for your input, feedback and love throughout the writing of this book. On the days when my inner critic was loud, thank you for making me feel so supported.

Elaine Wall, Aoife O'Halloran, Carla Savio and Aisling Gordon: thank you for doing your best to keep me organised in supporting those we have worked with!

To all those who have listened to my podcasts, attended seminars or retreats, been a part of my meditation or men's groups or picked up a copy of this book, thank you for allowing me to do what I do.

Mary 'Sky' O'Sullivan and Declan Hammond, thank you for your mentorship and guidance on what can sometimes feel like a lonely path.

Thank you to the sea, and to all of the people who joined me for swims in the cold Galway waters over the last two years, especially Gill, Danielle, Yvonne, Jonathan, Roger and Robbie.

Michel Durinho, Ben and Indra Davis, and everyone at Shaolin MMA and Point Blank Submissions who I've trained with on the jiu-jitsu mats over the last few years – thank you for the mat therapy!

To the men I've sat in circle with as part of my learning and development, particularly those from BaseCamp, Amakooshi,

TRIBE, the ManKind Project and MALE's Ireland: thank you for your vulnerability, courage and acceptance, and for being a mirror to the parts of myself I couldn't yet see.

To the countless teachers and mentors I have learnt from and continue to learn from, thank you for your courage, wisdom and your willingness to walk your own path, notably Ram Dass, Anthony DeMello, Timothy Leary, Stanislav Grof, Joseph Campbell, Debbie Ford, Byron Katie, Geoff Thompson, Udo Erasmus, Louise Hay, Gabor Mate, Carl Jung, Michael Singer, Paul Chek, Robert Bly, Julia Cameron, Diego Perez, John and Julie Gottman, Marshall Rosenberg, Viktor Frankl, Tony Robbins, John DeMartini, Richard Schwartz, Mihaly Csikszentmihaly, Jamie Wheal and Steven Kotler.

East Forest and Alan Doherty (Aldoc) – thank you for your beautiful music, which served as the soundtrack to the writing of this book.

To all the team at Gill, especially Sarah, Rachel and Teresa. Thank you, guys, for your support and patience throughout the writing of this book.

It is in writing the acknowledgements to this book that I realise how supported I have been and continue to be on my journey. Listing everyone who has played a role in my life would be a book in itself, so if you aren't included but have played a part in my story, thank you for being there and thank you for being you.

CONTENTS

INTRODUCTION
Inner Exploration

This is a book about the stories we tell ourselves about ourselves and about the world, and the impact those stories have on our health, happiness and overall experience of life.

We speak to ourselves more than anyone else in this world. Thousands of thoughts, beliefs, stories and assumptions run through our minds every day. For most of us these stories and thoughts go largely unquestioned; we take them as gospel and blindly believe them, often with little or no evidence to back them up. With so many thoughts and beliefs going through our minds all day, every day, we might assume we are 'thinking'. In truth, we are often just remembering old internal narratives played on a loop. These old stories or beliefs are the lens through which we see the world and serve as the 'script' or 'blueprint' for the story of our lives.

We walk through life with this largely unconscious blueprint, a collection of ideas and expectations about how things 'should' be in order for us to be happy. We then quickly make judgements about our experiences in life, labelling them 'good' or 'bad', 'right' or 'wrong', depending on how they match up to this unconscious script or blueprint of expectations in our minds. These beliefs or stories that make up our blueprint of how the world should look are shaped by our environment, our past experiences, the society and family we've been raised in, what we see in the media that we consume and what we've been told either implicitly or explicitly by others.

We have stories about how our bodies 'should' look, how our partners 'should' communicate, how we 'should' or 'shouldn't' feel given our circumstances and countless other stories about what we need to experience in life in order for us to be happy. The tighter we cling to these stories, the more conditions we set up for our happiness and the more conditional we become in our love for ourselves, for others and for life itself. It's rare that we think to question or challenge these stories that run our lives and thus we can begin to feel that life is happening *to* us rather than *for* us as we see the same difficult cycles and patterns repeatedly showing up in our lives.

If we think of this one precious life we've been given as our very own movie, are we playing the role of the scriptwriter and director, creating the film and making it our own unique masterpiece, or are we the actor with no creative control who's playing out a script written by others?

We often think that it's the events or circumstances of our lives and relationships that cause our stress and problems, when in fact it's the stories we tell ourselves about these events or circumstances that are so often the source of our suffering. The stress or suffering we associate with our relationships, our health, our finances or our career are really a result of the disconnect between how things are and how we think they 'should' be. As a result, day-to-day life can feel like an emotional rollercoaster and we can spend much of our lives trying to change the outside world to match the pictures and expectations we have formed in our heads.

When we begin to become more aware of our stories we can find appreciation, gratitude and freedom from our expectations and can be with life as it is rather than life as we feel it 'should' be. There are a great number of things outside our control in life and all too often our attention is focused on those things we can't control. Taking responsibility in life involves bringing our attention back to the controllables – our thoughts and our actions.

In my younger years I had stories playing over and over in my head about not being enough, about not fitting in and about not being of value. I had stories about who I needed to be to be loved, stories about what I needed to achieve to feel successful and countless other stories and expectations – for myself and others – that made living with myself difficult and exhausting. It might surprise you when I tell you from the outset that all those stories that I used to live with still go through my mind frequently. The soundtrack is still there; the difference is that now I don't believe everything I think and I have a simple toolbox that helps me quickly find perspective in times of stress or suffering – to help me change my internal tune.

This toolbox not only enables me to question or challenge the stories, thoughts and beliefs that surface in the present, but also to look back on past experiences and become aware of the origins of my beliefs and stories. It also helps me to see that thoughts and emotions I previously deemed 'negative' are actually where many of my lessons and much of my potential lie. I have learnt through the consistent practice of the tools in my toolbox to go from identifying with my disempowering thoughts to instead being aware of those thoughts, recognising the impact they have on my feelings and

actions and then choosing whether I'm going to blindly believe the
difficult thoughts or take some time to explore their purpose and
origins. I have also learnt to accept and work with the 'negative'
thoughts and emotions I once tried to dismiss.

I look forward to sharing this toolbox with you in the coming
chapters.

Self-care has become a real buzzword in recent times. It is often
used in the context of looking after yourself through diet, meditation,
exercise, or lighting some candles and having a bath. There's merit
in all of these, but I can't think of any greater act of self-care than
actively choosing to improve the way we speak to ourselves.

We improve our relationships with ourselves, not by achieving
more to fill voids or wounds that we feel within, but by accepting
parts of ourselves that we've yet to accept, by coming to more intimately know and understand ourselves, our fears, our values and
our drivers.

How we talk to ourselves matters the most.

As a kid I'd often arrive home from school and announce that
I was 'stupid' or that I didn't 'fit in'. Without skipping a beat my
parents would quickly challenge these stories by shifting the perspective to things I was doing well or to the groups I did fit in with.
You've probably done something similar with your own kids or your
friends, helping them to find perspective beyond the narrow lens
of their inner story.

This book invites you to begin challenging the thoughts, stories,
beliefs and assumptions that are causing you dis-ease in life, and
it arms you with the tools to do so. Alongside concepts, ideas and
new perspectives, I will share an eight-week practical programme
of journalling, meditation and self-enquiry techniques that offer a

chance to immediately begin implementing these new ideas and practising mental and emotional 'fitness'. I encourage you to pick up a journal that you can use alongside this book as you go through the eight-week self-enquiry programme. You can also find guided versions of the book's meditation exercises, along with other bonus material, at **patdivilly.com/fitmind**.

Despite the comforts of the modern world, there's an overwhelming collective experience of disconnection, isolation, addiction and depression. Our connection to others starts with our connection to ourselves and so it's in the work that we begin to do in this book that we improve every relationship in our lives.

In the coming chapters I will share how you can:

1. Become aware of the meanings you are giving to your external experiences.
2. Learn to go from believing your difficult thoughts to finding perspective and choice.
3. Recognise how your memories and origin stories influence your current worldview.
4. Understand the 'characters' in your head that seem to want to hold you back.
5. Implement a simple daily practice for improving self-talk and emotional awareness.

I look forward to going on this journey with you and helping you 'take back the pen'.

Grá mór,

Pat

PART ONE

From Patterns to Presence

The Conditioned Self

'Give me a child until he is seven and
I will show you the man' – ARISTOTLE

GOLD BENEATH THE CLAY

The tale of the clay Buddha sets the context of the origins of our own internal narratives.

In 1957, at a monastery in Thailand, a number of the monks decided it was time to move a giant clay Buddha that sat outside. The statue stood over ten foot high, so the monks needed a crane to move it. As the crane began to slowly lift the giant clay Buddha, a small crack appeared in the statue and it became apparent they had underestimated its fragility. They quickly instructed the crane operator to gently lower the statue so that they could rethink their plans. Worried about damaging the statue further, they decided to defer relocating it to the next day.

That night, one of the head monks came outside with a flashlight to inspect the statue. As he scanned the Buddha with his flashlight, he saw, in the crack, reflected light shining back at him. Intrigued, he got a hammer and chisel and began to chip away at the covering of clay. As he worked, he began to see bright gold light shining back at him. Over a number of hours, as he continued to chip away, he came to see that what he'd thought was a clay statue was in fact a golden statue that had been covered in clay.

Historians believed that the golden Buddha had been covered in twelve inches of clay three hundred years earlier when the monks in Thailand (Siam at the time) got word that the Burmese army were set to invade and attack their monastery. Eager to protect their beloved statue, they covered it in clay to hide its value and beauty. During the attack by the Burmese all the monks were killed and it wasn't until years later that the clay Buddha was discovered and assumed to be just that, a clay Buddha, the gold hidden for so long that it had been forgotten about.

This story of the clay Buddha serves as a metaphor for our own experience of life, the gold representing our potential and wholeness and the clay being the layers of stories, masks, fears, defence mechanisms and beliefs that we have built up in our unconscious efforts to 'protect' our gold, the authentic self.

This clay is what prevents us from connecting honestly and openly with ourselves and with others and prevents us from allowing our potential to shine brightly in the world. As the years pass and we continually add layers of protection, it isn't surprising that we sometimes forget the gold beneath and see ourselves as the collection of ideas we have accumulated, not the golden potential we once were.

The more stories we build about who we are and how we fit into the world, the smaller our world seems to get and the more limited our options in life seem to be. Our labels and judgements put us in a box that seems to get increasingly smaller. The tighter I cling to who I have decided I am, the more I limit myself in who I could be. Rather than look inward in our efforts to reclaim our gold we often go outward and look to gain external achievements and validation largely based on societal conditioning and other people's dreams.

Take the example of a child who comes into the world with pure potential but develops a belief as a young person that they are flawed in some way. In their efforts to find acceptance and approval, that person might go on to chase material success to prove to themselves and the world that they are 'good enough', forgetting in their chase that there isn't anything actually missing. This person might achieve every goal they set their sights on in life, but they unknowingly hold on to the clay exterior, the belief they are in some way inherently flawed. Our efforts to accumulate more or be given external approval for our achievements or position in society are based on the belief that there is something missing within us, and as a result many of the things we seek and efforts we make to 'improve' ourselves come from a place of wounding rather than a place of worth.

When we become aware of the stories and beliefs that cover our gold and come to see that our potential and wholeness lies beneath the clay exterior, we can begin to approach life with the aim of seeking fulfilment and authenticity rather than trying to compete with or challenge others in a game we can never win.

When I achieve the thing I thought I wanted and am left unhappy and unfulfilled it is likely I have come from this place of wounding and wanting to prove myself to others. When I find my flow in life and experience fulfilment in the journey, I am coming from a place of worth and living a life that is authentic and true to myself.

The golden Buddha in our story represents the full expression of ourselves that is born into the world open and judgement-free, full of potential, hope and possibility. The clay Buddha is akin to our ego or conditioned self, who has learnt who we think we need to be to survive and win acceptance based largely on the information we received in our earliest years. As human beings we enter the world pure gold, without fear, expectation or worries about being judged for who we are or what we do. Watch a carefree young child dance and play without any fear of judgement, happy to be the centre of attention and admired in all their glory.

At a given point something changes. The child whose dancing was once a source of entertainment and affection is now ignored, shamed or frowned upon. The child is told to grow up, and gaining approval and love isn't as easy as it once was. Acceptance and love become conditional, it seems, at least through the eyes of the child.

In subsequent years we see that same child begin to collect countless implicit and explicit messages from their parents or primary caregivers as to who they need to be in order to receive love and acceptance and fit in within their family structure. Certain emotions, behaviours, hobbies or beliefs are frowned upon, shamed or criticised while other emotions, behaviours, hobbies or beliefs garner praise and acceptance. Of course as children we do not have the ability to understand context or find perspective and thus we often misinterpret our experiences and come to the false belief that we are in some way flawed, not good enough or not deserving of love.

Though we come into the world curious and open, our ego begins to emerge as we form judgements about ourselves and others and judgements about what is 'right' and 'wrong' in life, largely as a result of what we learn at home. When the young child follows the rules at home and meets the expectations of their parents they are labelled a 'good' boy or girl and are given praise and approval. When they don't follow those rules or meet the expectations, love is temporarily removed, a frightening experience for a young person completely dependent on the support of their parental figures. This conditional love leads to the child editing, filtering and conditioning themselves to act in certain ways and repress or deny other parts of themselves which have been deemed unacceptable.

Imagine a child is scolded when they refuse to eat their vegetables at dinner. As grown adults with perspective and logical understanding of the importance of eating healthy foods we can see why the parents insist on the child finishing their dinner. However, through the naïve eyes of the child their interpretation of the same experience is perhaps that love is removed or withdrawn when they say 'no' and refuse to meet their parents' expectations.

When the child goes to school they encounter a new set of conditions as to who they need to be to gain and maintain the approval of their teachers and peers. Slowly, the carefree, spontaneous, expressive child becomes self-conscious and ashamed of the aspects of themselves that others deem unacceptable. Now they wear a collection of masks in order to fit into their environment. Maybe when they are laughed at because they stumble over their words while reading from the textbook in front of the class the child comes to the belief that they 'don't fit in with their classmates'.

Taking just these two examples – a child coming to believe they aren't supposed to say no to their parents and that they don't fit in – you can start to see how our earliest memories and the meanings we give to our experiences start to shape how we see ourselves and how we think we 'should' act in life.

As children we are like sponges absorbing implicit and explicit messaging from our family structures, society, teachers, friends and other influences. Certain judgements are implied, while others are explicitly spoken. Of course, at this time in our lives we don't have the tools or the capacity to find perspective. Because we aren't responsible for anyone else and because so much of our world centres on ourselves, we tend to make things all about ourselves. We don't understand that our parents are tired or stressed after work and we take their lack of engagement as a withdrawal of love. Harsh words said (or kind words unsaid) by others when they are stressed or overwhelmed can be internalised and taken to heart, further shaping our identity and adding layers of clay above the gold, limiting our potential and possibilities.

It is said that every inner voice was once an outer voice that has become internalised; the voice in our head that tells us we're not good enough emerged from something we perceived or heard from someone else in our younger years. Maybe when you think of your own 'inner critic' it reminds you of a voice from your youth?

Acceptance over Authenticity

Public speaking is often said to be one of the greatest fears that people experience in life. It isn't the actual speaking that is scary, of course; we do that all the time. It is the fear of judgement and potential rejection.

Growing through our childhood and into our early adolescent years, after we have passed the stage of feeling unconditionally loved, we do all we can to avoid rejection and negative judgements. As a result we all experience the battle between the desire to express ourselves authentically and the desire to be accepted and stay connected

to those around us. As young children who are completely dependent on the care of others, in this battle between authenticity and
acceptance the desire and need to be connected, supported and loved
by others usually wins. This means that our authenticity takes a back
seat and we begin denying, repressing or filtering parts of ourselves
that are deemed unacceptable by the 'tribe'.

In years gone by this tribe will have been relatively small. In the
modern world, social media and larger communities have opened
up a much larger audience whose acceptance we hope to win and
maintain at all costs – the ultimate cost, in fact, when we reject
ourselves in the pursuit of acceptance from others.

Our stories and beliefs about who we need to be in order to fit
in, be accepted and loved accumulate over time and the more conditions we collect about who we need to be, the further we can feel
ourselves drift away from our authentic selves and our potential.

Defence mechanisms and roles we have taken in younger years
to keep ourselves safe from abandonment can bleed into our adult
lives and, like the clay on the statue, we can feel fragile and unstable,
forgetting that at the core we are pure potential, masked by self-
doubt, fear and stories. We see glimpses of the gold, our authentic
self, at times – when there is a crack in the clay and we temporarily
forget the story about who we need to be to fit in. It might be in a
moment of play, connection, love, joy or even grief, when we 'lose
ourselves' and show up in the present moment without judgement.

Watch a group of grown men cry and embrace as they watch
their favourite football team win the championship for the first time
in years, or a stadium full of people singing along without shame
or self consciousness, losing themselves in the moment of watching
their favourite band. Notice moments of vulnerability, when the

hard edges of how we see ourselves and others begin to soften and allow us to communicate from the heart (love) and not the head (fear).

Outside these glimpses of our potential, we often quickly revert back to protecting ourselves and steering clear of being judged negatively for being seen in all our glory. As a means of protecting ourselves from hurt, abandonment or disconnection, we continue to cover our gold in layers of clay in the form of further evidence that protects our limiting beliefs, societal masks and fears.

PLAYING OUT PATTERNS

The tens of thousands of thoughts we have every day throughout our lives would perhaps more accurately be described as 'remembering', as we form this fixed identity and conditioned self with a rigid perception of who we are and how we fit into the world.

In my own life an early experience of bullying led me to believe I didn't fit in. 'Being an outsider' unconsciously became a part of my self-image and it was something I believed for years as I replayed the same thought in my head without ever questioning it, repeatedly finding evidence that backed up my existing belief. In efforts to avoid further rejection from other social groups I became like a chameleon in school and college, drifting away from my authenticity and changing aspects of my appearance, personality or attitude to win the approval of others and avoid risking further rejection. This craving for acceptance from others often led me to abandon my own internal voice and self and go on a relentless and exhausting journey of 'achievement' to prove to others I was lovable. Needless to say, this self-abandonment had a dramatic effect on my self-esteem. It led to a journey of looking outside myself in pursuit of anything that would bring about validation from external sources that I hadn't found internally.

This can start to point to the importance of exploring some of the meanings we gave to our earliest experiences and how those early experiences have shaped us.

- A young boy who is told that 'boys don't cry' becomes the man who cannot connect to his own emotions or be vulnerable with others.
- A child who rarely sees their parents because they are always out working becomes a grown-up workaholic and struggles to be present with their own family.
- A child who is not allowed to make their own decisions has a hard time expressing their needs or putting down healthy boundaries later in life, as they have been implicitly taught to place the needs of others above their own.

From my early teens to mid-twenties I read every personal development book I could get my hands on in an effort to find the secrets to success and happiness. I learnt lots of strategies on time management and goal-setting, but I found nothing that explained why, irrespective of my accomplishments, I never felt good enough. I wasn't ever going to find a book that would show me directly how my own early years had shaped my unconscious blueprint of the world which was running my life in the present.

There won't ever be a book written that does this work for us. Personal responsibility is required in doing the work of shining a light in the dark, a process described by Swiss psychiatrist Carl Jung as 'making the unconscious conscious'.

By becoming aware of our stories and beliefs, we allow ourselves to show up as the capable, mature, brilliant adults that we are.

However, when these stories stay in the dark, we often feel ourselves reverting back to the scared child within, irrespective of our current age. In the work that I'll introduce in this book I will invite you to walk back to earlier life experiences with a new perspective and adult eyes to see if you might come to a more empowering understanding of experiences you may have previously resented or deemed negative.

CLEANING THE FILTERS

My own personal work in recent years has been to slowly chip away at the clay exterior and protection I have built up over many years to fit in and be accepted. By going back to my past and exploring the meanings I gave to my early experiences and how those meanings have played out since, I've been slowly able to reclaim aspects of my natural state. Revisiting childhood experiences and viewing them with a new perspective and through adult eyes has allowed me to understand and override much of the conditioning I lived with for many years.

It's important to note that the nature of conditioning is that our past experience affects our present and our present thoughts and actions affect our future. In my own experience we cannot outrun these emotional blocks and sticking points. We must face them head on rather than continually looking outwards for the answers that are within. As adults looking to excel in different areas of our lives, we are often quick to try to 'overcome' or banish the inner critics or voices in our heads that seem full of negativity and self-doubt. What if, rather than trying to overcome this voice, I befriended it, saw at what point in my life it tried to protect me, and then allowed it to be in my life but not running my life?

As an example, when a voice in my head tells me, 'Don't put yourself out there, people will ridicule you and you'll be rejected,' I become curious. I know this story is part of my 'conditioned self' and not my authentic self and so I look back and see where that voice may have originated in my life and how it might have tried to protect me. Maybe after the hurt of being bullied as a kid that voice looked to keep me safe, and maybe it did a good job at the time. I can thank it for that, but let it know it isn't needed right now.

By slowly chipping away at that clay and bringing awareness, compassion and context to our past we begin to reclaim some of the gold we haven't seen in a while and we begin the process of true self-acceptance.

Life is too short to spend it over-analysing every childhood experience and what we came to believe about ourselves and the world via the meanings we gave to our experiences. However, if there are painful or disruptive patterns and cycles playing out in my life repeatedly or I find myself stuck in rumination and incessant thinking, it is worth exploring the origins of these patterns and working on finding perspective and freedom from the unconscious stories that keep me stuck.

MEANING-ATTACHING MACHINES

The meanings that we give to our experiences in life ultimately become our experiences. What I mean by that is that from the time we are kids we begin making judgements and giving meanings to everything that happens in our lives. These meanings will be based on our conditioning and thus our memories, assumptions and beliefs play a large role in how we show up in the present.

This ties to the idea that there are always two triggers in the context of us forming stories about our experience: the external trigger and the internal.

- The external trigger is what actually happens without any judgements or emotions placed on it.
- The internal trigger, then, is the meaning that we give to what happens.

Only by becoming more aware of the internal triggers and separating our stories from our experiences can we take full ownership of our lives.

Take, for example, three people going for a job interview and all three being told, 'I'm sorry, we don't think you're the right person for the role.'

This external trigger – the situation – is the same for all three candidates. The internal trigger, the meaning each candidate gives to what's happened, will dictate how they feel and act in response.

One candidate might see this as a great learning experience – they got to practise their job interview skills and they'll be better prepared for their next interview. The second candidate may have seen the interview as a wake-up call – perhaps this isn't really the type of work they want to do. The third candidate may attach the meaning that they've been rejected.

Here we have the same experience, with three very different meanings attached. These meanings or stories the candidates tell themselves will dictate how they feel and act going forward, and their resulting actions will dictate the course of their lives. Here lies the power of the meanings we attach to our experiences and the stories we tell ourselves.

We can go back in time and explore our past experiences, such as the childhood examples shared earlier, but it is perhaps easier as a starting point to work with any current stressors we may be dealing with in life.

Before encouraging you to get into the practice of separating the external and internal triggers in your stressful experience I would like to share a few examples.

Book in the Bin and no Love on Social Media

It's May 2016 and I'm presenting an eight-hour workshop in Dublin to a full room of eager attendees. The 'discovery day' session is centred on setting goals and putting a game plan in place to attain them. About two hours into the day I head to the bathroom while the group complete a journalling exercise from the workbooks they'd received upon entry. After I've washed my hands I throw a paper towel in the bin and out of the corner of my eye see that the last thing to go in that bin was a copy of one of the workbooks I'd given the attendees.

My heart sank and my head went into overdrive. What had I said or done to prompt someone to leave an eight-hour workshop within the first two hours, and to have not even wanted to bring the workbook home with them?

Walking back to the room, I did my best to shrug off the anxiety and self-doubt I was feeling 'knowing' that someone had been so bored or upset at the workshop that they'd left within the first two hours.

- What must everyone else in the room be thinking?
- How am I going to engage a room of people who must be bored stiff for another six hours?
- Will there be anyone left by the end of the day?
- What ever made me think I'd be a good public speaker?

Around 6 p.m., as we wrapped things up, a friend who had helped me with registration that morning congratulated me and told me it had been a great day.

'I'm not so sure,' I said, and I told him about the workbook in the bin.

He burst into laughter and told me that an attendee had spilled a cup of coffee on her workbook at the registration desk that morning and he'd given her a new one before dumping the old one in the bin in the men's bathroom.

I asked him to confirm he was telling the truth before breathing a sigh of relief, feeling a weight lift off my shoulders and feeling my heavy heart soften.

I shared this story at a corporate event two years later and a sceptical attendee, with their arms crossed, said, 'Maybe your friend was just saying that to make you feel better and maybe someone did throw your book in the bin.'

That could be true too, of course, but recognising the conclusion I had jumped to and hearing that it might not be true reminded me that the meaning I had given to the situation was evidence of how quickly I make assumptions with little or no evidence to back them up. The feelings my assumptions had created within me were a reminder of the power that my thoughts hold over me.

Our 'negativity bias' will often send our focus to what's not working, or where we're falling short, as had been the case with the infamous 'book in the bin'. The 'negativity bias' is our natural tendency to focus or dwell on negative thoughts or experiences rather than on the positive. Rather than judge ourselves for being 'negative thinkers', it is worth remembering that our brains are wired for survival, not for happiness. As such, it is essential that our brains are always looking out for possible threat, danger or difficulty.

Only a few weeks after the 'book in the bin seminar', I shared the story with an audience in County Kerry, where I spoke about how our minds quickly come to conclusions and attach meanings to situations with little to no evidence to back them up.

How often in life does the future rewrite the past when we receive new information that changes completely the story we had previously believed? Have you ever not heard from a friend, family member or new love and built stories in your head about what you've said or done to upset them, only to later find out that they'd just been busy, had a break from technology or sent you a message that didn't deliver?

A man at the back of that room in Kerry shouted, 'It's all well and good you talking about us telling ourselves stories, but my family don't like me and that's not a story.' I was taken aback at first, unsure how to respond and in admiration of his willingness to just say it in a room full of people. When I quizzed him about how he knew his family didn't like him he said, 'They never like any of my social media posts.' The audience quietly laughed, but he was very serious. I did my best to help him challenge his thought that his family didn't like him and invited him to look at the situation in different ways, but he wasn't convinced. A few months later I smiled from ear to ear when I received an email from that same man over the Christmas holidays: 'The stories we tell ourselves. I get it now.'

To cut a long story short, the man had a young son whose godmother, the man's sister, lived in Australia. Disappointed she couldn't get home to see her godson for Christmas, she texted her brother and asked if he could post a picture on social media of her godson with his Christmas presents so she could see him. The man responded that he would, but in the back of his mind he knew she wouldn't engage with his social media post because she never did.

Twenty-four hours after posting the photo of his son with his Christmas presents no one had engaged with the post. When his sister rang on Christmas Day to ask why he hadn't posted the picture he was enraged. He said that he had posted that picture against his better judgement and knew she wouldn't acknowledge it because she never took an interest in anything he was doing. His sister calmly asked him to take a few deep breaths and to log on to his Facebook profile to check his settings. It turned out, whatever way he'd set up his profile, that he and only he could see any of the posts that he was uploading. No wonder his family weren't engaging with any of his content. They couldn't see it! 'Maybe my family do like me after all,' he wrote.

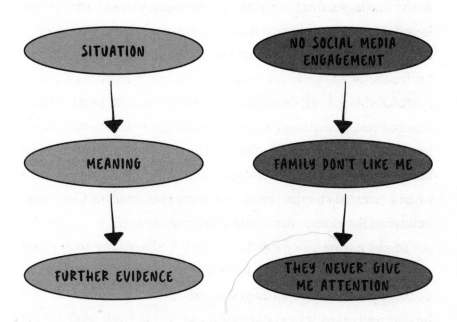

Now, this example might seem funny, but it was causing the man a lot of stress and, with our stories serving as filters to the world, it impacted on all aspects of relationships with his family. The belief that they didn't like him led to feelings of resentment, sadness and anger, which led to him pushing his family away, and thus it acted as a self-fulfilling prophecy.

Imagine for a moment Christmas dinner in that man's household. Someone doesn't think to pass him the gravy and suddenly in his mind it's not an innocent mistake, but a spiteful way for them to show yet again how little they like him! Again, we always experience two triggers, the external and then the internal. The external one here would be someone not passing him the gravy, which in itself is a neutral event. The judgement comes from the internal trigger, the meaning that he gives that situation based on his beliefs about the world. The beginnings of our freedom therefore lie in our ability to create a space between what is happening in reality and the story or assumption we have jumped to about what is happening.

MAKING THE UNCONSCIOUS CONSCIOUS

All this being said, it is our job and responsibility to clean our filters, by challenging our painful and limiting stories about ourselves and the world.

This can start with simply separating our 'activating event' – what has happened – from our belief or story about what has happened. For example:

Activating event: No likes on social media accounts.

Belief: 'My family don't like me.'

From the time we are kids our minds get to work on attaching judgements and meanings to different situations and experiences.

Life is so fast-paced that we often fall into the trap of taking our judgements and meanings as gospel and never questioning or challenging them. Now, if I've got a judgement that supports me and makes me feel empowered, this doesn't cause problems. However, if I've attached a meaning to something that disempowers me and is causing me stress and anguish it's important that I create the space to question it, particularly in areas of life where I see the same difficult themes or experiences recurring.

Our negativity bias is there to act almost as a protective mechanism to help us identify and avoid potential threats and danger. At its core the purpose of our brain is to keep us alive. As a pattern recognition machine it works to keep us alive by recreating the patterns that kept us safe yesterday rather than by stepping out of our normal routines.

'Positive thinking' would have killed our ancestors if they spotted a wild animal and thought, 'What a beautiful animal, I'm going to pet it and be its friend.' On the contrary, they would have used negativity bias to identify that wild animal as a potential threat to their safety and lives.

One of the greatest threats to our old brains living in these modern times is the threat of standing out from the tribe. In years gone by it was essential that we fit in with our tribes as we were reliant on collaboration and protection to survive. Those tribes might have had fifty people, a world apart from the worlds we live in today where the internet and big cities open us up to a world of thousands. Our need to fit in with our ever-expanding tribes has led to us becoming invisible.

The term 'waking up' refers to the moments in which we see beyond our judgements and come to see that life isn't happening *to* us. Life is just happening and we are either reacting to it or responding to it.

CHALLENGING YOUR THOUGHTS

When a child attaches a meaning that they are 'less than' or 'not good enough' in an area of life, a parent or primary caregiver will hopefully not reaffirm the child's negative self-talk or disempowering beliefs. A good parent would be straight into challenging their disempowering beliefs about themselves. They'd find every bit of counter-evidence to disprove the child's assumptions. However, when it comes to the disempowering stories we have about ourselves, we don't think to create the space to challenge these stories and find counter-evidence. Instead, we take our negative thoughts about ourselves as gospel and place them alongside all the evidence of times we've failed or fallen short in our past.

Of the countless self-development and acceptance exercises I've completed over the years I think completing 365 days of journalling where I challenged my most stressful thought of the day had the biggest impact on my overall worldview and wellness. I simply took fifteen minutes a day to write down the biggest thought that was causing me stress and then challenged that thought and found perspective.

Notice I said the *thought* – not the person or situation – that was causing me most stress. Remember, it's not bad weather that makes us feel stressed, it's thinking that the weather should be different from how it is. The stress lies in the thought. The freedom from the stress lies in the ability to find perspective or acceptance of whatever is happening in reality.

We increase our awareness and bring a level of acceptance when we dissolve our judgements and accept reality as it is. When we go from awareness of all that's happening to a focus on what's lacking or missing from the situation, relationship or experience, stress ensues.

Typically in these moments of stress we become reactive and try to get away from what we deem the source of stress, unaware that the stress is the result of an internal reaction, not anything external. If we choose instead to respond to what is happening by checking in with the narrative we have attached to our experience and then becoming curious about this narrative, we can begin to learn from and grow through all our experiences and get away from the idea that negative thoughts or emotions should be avoided.

A/B/C/D Exercise

The A/B/C/D journalling exercise is a simple tool from cognitive behavioural therapy that I used daily for twelve months to help recognise my automatic judgements and find perspective.

As a way to begin recognising the meanings we attach to our experiences and the impact of those automatic judgements I would encourage you to complete this cognitive behavioural therapy-style exercise with pen and paper before going any further in the book.

First, identify an **activating event**, something that has happened which you may be pointing to as a source of your stress. Note what has actually happened as opposed to your feelings or judgements about what has happened. It is an observation and based on facts as opposed to feelings. For example, instead of saying, 'I am upset because my friend turned up late for lunch,' identify the activating event as 'I was due to meet my friend for lunch at 2 p.m. and they didn't arrive until 2.20 p.m.'

Next, we'll look at the second trigger, the **belief**; the story we are telling ourselves about what has happened. Perhaps in this scenario, my automatic internal story is 'My friend has no respect for me or my time.'

Now, having identified the activating event and our belief we want to write out all the **consequences** of this belief. For example, when I believe the thought that my friend doesn't respect me or my time I feel bitter, judgemental and hurt. I am resentful and struggle to be present with them when they do arrive. It has affected my mood and thrown my plans for the day completely off course as it's upset me so much.

Finally, we'll look to see beyond our automatic judgement and **dispute** our automatic belief ('My friend doesn't respect me or my time'). Perhaps I am able to recognise in disputing the belief that this is the first time they have been late, that they were apologetic when they did arrive, that they've supported me a lot in other ways in recent months and that they have had a lot going on in their own life, which may have been the reason why they were late.

This exercise isn't about toxic positivity, making everything perfect, ignoring reality or flicking a switch and removing the responsibility of ourselves or others. It is instead a tool for finding perspective and challenging our judgements to create some space and relief from unnecessary suffering.

Some days when I did this exercise I gained a completely new outlook on a thought that had previously been a great source of stress. On other days it provided me with the tiniest bit of perspective around the thought.

Like anything, this A/B/C/D exercise can be seen as just more information and a nice idea on paper, but if practised consistently it can be a profoundly powerful means of beginning to gain some freedom and liberation from the stories that cause us unnecessary suffering. If you were to close this book now and never open it again, I am confident that committing to this one exercise alone consistently would make a very meaningful impact on your life.

I don't want you to close the book, of course! We are just setting out on a journey that will transform how you see your world, but I do want you to recognise the power of this simple exercise.

As you become comfortable with using the A/B/C/D exercise for small daily stresses you can start to go back in time and use the same exercise on situations, experiences or interactions in your past about which you hold resentment. In finding perspective from our past we create more freedom for our future.

Before moving to the next chapter, be sure to go through at least one A/B/C/D prompt.

The Conditioned Self
– What to Remember

- We come into the world with pure potential and without fear or judgement but begin to hide, deny or repress parts of ourselves in order to be accepted. These repressed parts make up our 'shadow'; the parts of ourselves we accept and embrace make up our 'persona'. True self-acceptance requires healthy integration of the parts of ourselves that we have labelled 'bad', 'unacceptable' or 'wrong'. We can do this by exploring the meanings we gave to early experiences and finding perspective and context in our current stories and beliefs.

- By going back to childhood experience with adult eyes we can begin to find perspective and rewrite some of the scripts that are running our lives.

- While we think we are thinking, in fact our conditioned mind is remembering and playing out patterns based on these early judgements and the implicit or explicit messages we received early on about how life 'should' look and who we need to be to gain acceptance and approval from others.

- We are meaning-attaching machines. Things happen and we give them a meaning based on our own worldview. Many of the meanings we gave to our early childhood experiences have a large bearing on how we see the world to this day.

- Our mind is like an iceberg, with our conscious awareness as the visible part above the water, and the unseen bulk of the iceberg representing our unconscious thoughts, beliefs, assumptions and stories. Our goal in reflective work is to shine a light on some of those unconscious parts, making the unseen seen and the implicit explicit. In doing so we can integrate these unconscious aspects in a healthy way.

React or Respond

*'Having compassion starts and ends with having
compassion for those unwanted parts of ourselves'*

– Pema Chodron

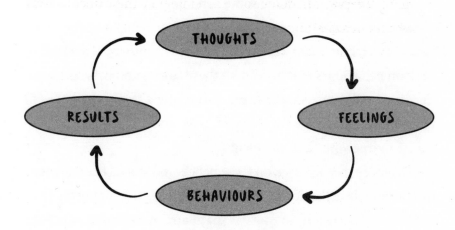

PLAYING OUT PATTERNS

I became fascinated by the stories we tell ourselves during my time
working in the fitness industry. After working with thousands of
clients in a few short years, patterns began to emerge between those

who made incredible progress and those who seemed caught in a cycle of yo-yo dieting and 'self-sabotage'. On the surface all clients were receiving similar plans, similar support and spending the same amount of time in the gym each week – but results varied greatly.

I had always had a love of and interest in fitness, so it came easily to me. But I was creating similar patterns of inconsistency and self-sabotage in other areas of my life. I knew exactly what I wanted to achieve and what I needed to do to make it happen, but I was consistently falling off the wagon and beating myself up for my lack of willpower and follow-through. It was by exploring the areas of life where I struggled and those where I thrived that I began to come to understand the sheer power of identity, stories and self-image. We have all, consciously and unconsciously, built a collection of stories, thoughts, rules and ideas about who we are and how we fit into the world, so our identity becomes the most powerful force in our lives.

My clients who blamed 'bad genetics' or being someone who 'never stayed consistent' for failing to lose weight would always fall back on behaviours that backed up these stories and beliefs. Maybe they'd use willpower to keep them on track for a few weeks, but until the story of who they were changed, they would always fall back to acting in line with their old identity.

The more they fell back on these beliefs and stories the more true the stories felt as they collected more evidence that supported their existing self-image. If my story is that I am an inconsistent person, every time I 'fall off the wagon' I will add that to my collection of evidence of my shortcomings around consistency.

Of course there will be many areas in which we are consistent – we consistently show up for work, consistently shower and brush our teeth and consistently do a hundred other things, but our story of not being consistent serves as a filter through which we see the world. Our attention narrows to find evidence that backs up only our stories around inconsistency while dismissing any evidence to the contrary. And in this way we can become caught in patterns that can keep us stuck for decades.

This is why people generally seem to self-sabotage and struggle to create the very results that we say are most important to us. When there is a disconnect between our self-image and what we say we want in life, we find ourselves experiencing resistance and procrastination in our effort to avoid the fear of change and uncertainty. If we can become aware of the stories of who we believe ourselves to be without identifying with and blindly believing them, we can begin to choose new actions and create new results in life.

Our actions and habits are like the software on a computer; our feelings and stories are the hardware. If we have an old phone or computer with outdated hardware, we can install new software and programs, but they will struggle to run smoothly as they are slowed by the capacity of the old system. Similarly we can buy books, take courses or acquire new ideas that would surely support us in life, but until we choose to consciously update the hardware of our stories and identity we will struggle to run these new programs on an outdated system.

We can know intellectually and on a conscious level what we need to eat in order to look, feel and perform better, but if our 'hardware' is outdated, if we cling to our old unconscious belief that 'I don't ever stay consistent', this new program will struggle to run effectively. We can make new year's resolutions and set goals to begin meditating and spend less time in a constant state of doing, but if our unconscious hardware has decided that busyness is a noble and

selfless act, we will struggle to become consistent with slowing down
and creating space in our lives. We could meet incredible people
and long to connect with them, but if the old hardware has a belief
and understanding that people can't be trusted we will consciously
or unconsciously sabotage this potential to connect with and trust
others.

Cognitive behavioural therapy tells us that our thoughts have
an impact on how we feel, our feelings have an impact on our
behaviours and these behaviours are what shape the results in our
lives. A story that 'I'm not good at networking' will lead to feelings of overwhelm or stress around having to attend a networking
event. Attending a networking event with these feelings of overwhelm makes it unlikely that we will be ourselves and try to meet
new people. As a result, we stand in the corner for the night, meet
nobody new and leave the event having collected further evidence
to back up our belief that 'I'm not good at networking'.

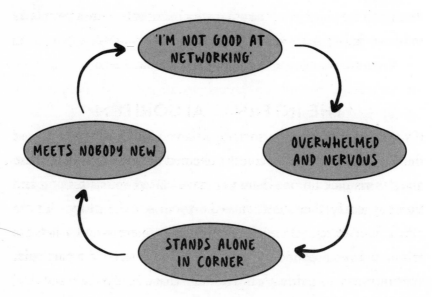

Frustrated by our struggles at the networking event, we could look externally and try to figure out how to change our actions. Maybe we buy a book about how to be a better conversationalist and pick up some great ideas. But as long as that old story in our head is the one that we identify with, it will always impact how we show up and the results we achieve.

Similarly, in relationships we often see the same patterns playing out. The same types of people show up in our lives, triggering certain feelings or stories. If, for example, we have an unconscious belief that we are responsible for the feelings of others, when our partner is in a bad mood we may assume it is our doing. Feeling unappreciated, we might choose to leave that relationship but become frustrated when we see the same pattern emerge months later in our next relationship.

We could spend the rest of our lives going through this pattern and trying to change the external, not recognising that we are projecting our own beliefs and assumptions onto other people. The work that is needed is an inside job. It is easy, of course, to forget that when we point a finger at that which disrupts or disappoints us in life we have three fingers pointing right back at us.

When we change our stories we change our life.

THE INTERNAL ALGORITHM

If you spend any time on social media you'll no doubt be aware of the algorithms that filter content deemed of interest to you. These algorithms pick up on where you have placed your attention and then suggest further content based on your search history. This creates a bit of an echo chamber in which your interests and beliefs are reinforced and amplified. If you have shown interest in a particular type of music or genre of film, an affiliation to a certain political

party or an enthusiasm for content around a given hobby the algorithms will scan the overwhelming collection of content available
online and feed you with what it deems important to you while
dismissing the rest.

In the same way, our own internal algorithm, the confirmation
bias, scans our environment and, instead of bringing all that is happening to our attention, it selects only what it deems most important
to us. In the experiences we deem stressful in life our attention has
generally focused on what is lacking in our lives and we have lost
awareness of what is left. Stressful thoughts will also generally go
from awareness of all options to an attention on the options that lie
outside our control.

When we live busy lives unconsciously and on autopilot our
confirmation bias continually reinforces an identity largely based
on assumptions and beliefs that live in our unconscious. When
we begin to slow down and gain awareness of the stories that are
running in the background we can begin to respond to life with
awareness, creating new results rather than reacting unconsciously
and staying stuck in old patterns.

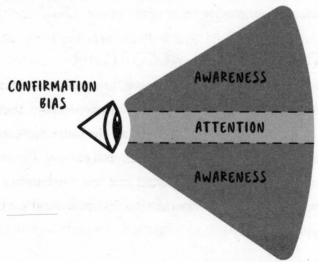

MEETING THE CHARACTERS

I used to see the tens of thousands of thoughts that constantly ran through my head as an unpredictable mixture of inspiration, desperation and everything in between. Some days I woke up with thoughts that made me feel ready to change the world; on other days I woke up with thoughts that made me want to stay under the duvet for ever.

The unpredictability of my mind created an emotional roller-coaster. I was hoping for the positive that would make me feel like a responsive creator in life and hoping to avoid the negative that made me feel like a reactive victim. No matter what I achieved or acquired, certain people, experiences or situations would trigger my fears, insecurities and 'limiting beliefs'. I could go from feeling like a confident, inspired and capable adult to a scared and overwhelmed child in the blink of an eye.

I have since come to see my thoughts as the conversations of different characters in my head, each character with different motivations and drivers based on their memories of the past that, when examined, make perfect logical sense. I have also come to see the people, situations and experiences that trigger or challenge me as providing opportunities to make more of the 'unconscious conscious' and become aware of the origins of feelings surfacing in my body and characters surfacing in my mind.

If we think of our mind like an iceberg, our conscious understandings are what we see above the water; our unconscious beliefs, assumptions or thoughts are out of sight below the water. In becoming more aware of what lies below the water and gaining a greater awareness of where our stories came from and how they surface in the present, we begin to update the outdated hardware and see the world through a new lens.

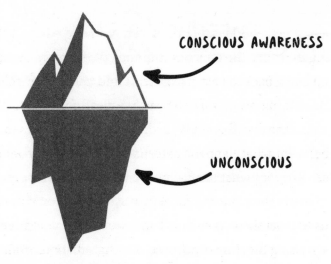

When we update the hardware and go beyond our conditioning we can become present to what is happening in the moment rather than stuck in memories from the past. Then, rather than trying to change the external world to meet our narrow expectations about how things have to look, we can find perspective and freedom from our fixed worldview.

Oftentimes our emotional responses to people and experiences point to that which is unconscious to us. Though these challenging emotions that surface often lead us to become reactionary, fighting for our 'survival' and protecting our ego, the work that we'll do in the coming chapters offers the chance instead to become responsive.

In 2005 the National Science Foundation published an article in which it noted that the average person has between twelve thousand and sixty thousand thoughts a day, and ninety-five per cent of those thoughts are the same thoughts they had the day before.

If we hold a memory of a time ten years ago when we stumbled over our words during a presentation in college, the thought of giving a presentation in the workplace today is likely to trigger the same feelings we had then. We react to a story in our head based on a past perception rather than responding to what is actually happening in reality. Throughout this book we'll do a huge amount of work on going back to past resentments and finding the 'gold in the muck'. By making peace with the past we clear our path for the future.

In the first chapter we brought some awareness to the difference between what happens externally and the story we have told ourselves about what has happened. We saw that all events are neutral in themselves; it is our judgements, based on conditioning, that lead us to label them 'good' or 'bad', 'positive' or 'negative'.

Using the simple tool of separating situations from stories we can start to slow things down when we experience emotionally triggering situations that often result in knee-jerk reactions.

Being able to create this space between the event and our story or interpretation of the event is our first step in becoming aware of our unconscious beliefs, which are always the result of memory and rarely if ever the result of what is actually happening in the moment.

In our reactions based on conditioning, we fight to defend our existing identity. In our willingness to be with our challenging emotions and bring awareness to our unconscious beliefs and assumptions, we allow ourselves the opportunity to learn, grow, heal old wounds and come to our potential. By recognising the aspects of the conditioned self that are showing up in the present moment we begin to chip away at some of the clay that is covering our gold.

How is it that we might go from feeling on top of the world after a first date to feelings of sadness and rejection the very next day when we don't hear from the other person? Yes, it may have been a great date but the overwhelming sense of rejection feels a disproportionate emotional response to not hearing back from someone we've only met once. I am going to suggest that it has little to do with the other person or the experience, but that it relates instead to an internal character. This character shares stories of being rejected based on past memories or experiences that the character has trapped in their mind.

In this scenario we could choose to react to our feelings of rejection, fall victim to our circumstances and 'check out' with impulsive or addictive behaviours. Or we could instead choose to 'check in' and respond by seeing our emotional response as an opportunity to explore and make more of the unconscious conscious. We might ask, 'What memory of feeling rejected has this experience triggered?', and we might notice that it is a younger version of ourselves caught in memory who is triggering such an emotional response. By tuning in to this younger character we can bring compassion to ourselves and self-soothe rather than shame, blame or give in to self-abandonment.

Following on from the A/B/C/D exercise we explored in the last chapter, in which we separated what has happened from the story we told ourselves about what has happened, we could do a similar A/B/E exercise in which we explore the activating event; the belief we have, based on the story we've told ourselves; and our earliest memory of a similar story. This is not an exercise we need to incessantly do for dozens of scenarios. It is most useful in situations where we notice particularly disproportionate emotional reactions to our experiences. For example:

Activating event: I went for a job interview and was told I was not a suitable candidate.

Belief: I am never good enough at anything.

Earliest memory (of not feeling good enough): As a kid I was the last person picked for the football team. I felt rejected and 'less than'.

Using this example, consider that being picked last for the football team will have been a very difficult experience for a young child. Their implicit understanding of and meaning attached to that scenario that they 'weren't good enough' will have driven their behaviours from that point.

This may have played out in many ways, oftentimes in polarised ways. Perhaps it led them to become an overachiever desperately seeking approval, acceptance and validation in life for fear of experiencing this type of rejection again. When someone is being driven from a place of feeling 'less than', no amount of success and approval will ever be enough. The core wound of not feeling good enough remains, irrespective of how much external validation or approval is garnered. Another child in the same scenario may have instead chosen not to bother trying with anything at all. 'I'm not good enough, so why even try?'

Irrespective of this child's reaction to the rejection, this new understanding of the world prompts the child's confirmation bias to collect evidence of other areas in which they 'aren't good enough'. The mind will often overlook the positive and focus on the negative, so that child may spend the next number of years or decades stacking up further evidence that backs up their confirmation bias.

Now, in particularly painful experiences of feeling rejected, the adult self is overtaken by a character who is caught in the memory of those early rejections. It might be a thirty-year-old adult who is thrown off course and overwhelmed with feelings of rejection, but it is perhaps that internal character formed when the child was picked last who is surfacing and experiencing the pain.

By coming to understand this host of characters and work with them I have come to learn that what I previously deemed negative thoughts or limiting beliefs are really just 'protective' beliefs, looking out for my best interests, though sometimes in distorted, outdated and inefficient ways.

PROTECTIVE THOUGHTS

Once we have recognised a character in our mind that often speaks 'negatively' but whose primary goal is to keep us safe, secure or comfortable, we can choose to work with that character rather than against them. Perhaps we have a character who believes that people can't be trusted and will eventually let us down. We find the origins of the character and come to understand that their 'negative' voice is simply trapped in a memory and trying to keep us safe from rejection or abandonment in the future. Recognising that this character isn't actually us, we choose instead to open up to people and allow ourselves to connect and be seen. Perhaps by overriding the character and choosing to act in a different way we begin to form more meaningful and fulfilling connections with those we love.

This is not about transcending or overcoming the character but about integrating them and accepting them as a part of us. Through understanding and integration we can now be aware when it is this protective character that is speaking rather than dismissing our thinking as 'negative' or 'wrong'.

Perhaps after understanding that we are not that character we begin seeing some great changes in our relationships and we feel we have 'got past' the insecurities or fears we had around connection. However someone might then come along and say or do something that leads to the character resurfacing and bringing attention to the evidence that showed they were right all along and that 'people can't be trusted'. These characters don't disappear and thus our dialogue with them must be ongoing. As we come to understand, accept and provide safety and comfort to these different characters we are no longer controlled by them.

As a natural introvert the idea of putting myself out there in the online world as a fitness authority ten years ago led to a character surfacing who would frequently tell me I didn't have the personality to be a motivator and would be better off avoiding any efforts to position myself as an expert. This character was formed in my early years when, after some childhood bullying, I implicitly learnt not to put myself in situations where I would be open to ridicule or judgement. Over time I built a following and gained a lot of support and encouragement in the fitness industry, and that kept that character quiet for a while. But whenever I received criticism or online abuse the character would quickly resurface and point to the one comment in a hundred that was negative.

In these moments we can react to the character and retreat back to the safety of our old identity or we can respond by communicating with them and understanding their role and understanding of the situation. We can begin to identify some of these characters by identifying areas in which we feel stuck in a cycle and bringing attention to the stories we tell ourselves around that area.

In recognising a challenge I had with trusting and connecting with people I identified a story from my past that 'people always let me down'. Of course a story like that overlooks the countless people who have and continue to support me and so I know it isn't true, but is based on a difficult past memory. By naming that character the Lone Shark, seeing how they are trying to protect me and also recognising how they are limiting me, I can begin to notice when it is the Scared Child Pat who is speaking through the guise of the

Lone Shark. This awareness allows me to choose to act from a place
of faith, rather than falling back on this story of fear.

REACT OR RESPOND?

In this new way of thinking of our inner dialogue, and understanding that there are a host of characters who have been driving many
of our decisions and behaviours, we can begin to see moments of
stress, uncertainty or emotional dis-ease as a fork in the road. We
can react with our old patterns or take a breath and respond in a
more conscious and empowering way governed by faith, not fear.

When we find ourselves in a 'fight/flight/freeze' survival state
due to feelings of stress the primitive part of the brain goes to the
patterns most familiar to it in an effort to recreate those patterns
that have kept us 'safe' up to this point. In this fight/flight/freeze
state our efforts are solely aimed at protecting our current position
and so we shut down the opportunity to learn, grow, connect and
evolve. I cannot grab anything new with a clenched fist. In the same

way, holding tightly onto my identity and who I currently believe myself to be by living in reaction is the very thing that stops me reaching my potential.

Being aware that when we slip into this 'reptilian' part of the brain (see more on page 278), we are out of the logical and creative part of the human mind, we will make a conscious effort throughout this book to bring ourselves back to a state of calm. We'll 'rest and digest' through simple meditations and exercises that will bring us to a place of perspective and possibility.

In the coming chapters we will look at how conflict in relationships can actually lead to deeper connection, how difficult emotions can bring us to a greater level of acceptance and self-esteem and how future-based fear can point us to past resentments that offer potential healing, integration and self-love.

For now I would encourage you to continue with the exercise from Chapter 1, creating a space between what is happening and the story you are telling yourself about what is happening. In moments when you feel particularly stressed or get caught in overthinking you could take it a step further and complete the full A/B/C/D exercise, recognising the consequences of this negative thought before disputing it and finding evidence to the contrary.

If you notice the same core beliefs or stories emerging consistently these can begin to point to a character who is making a lot of noise in your head. As you become more familiar with this character you will start to notice when it is them surfacing and pulling you back into old memories rather than allowing you to be in the present moment.

Before getting into the main work of the book in Part 2, just try to notice yourself catching your stories and recognising these characters as they surface in real time. Much like meditation, it is one thing to sit down and be calm in the moment, but the real art is in bringing the practice into the uncertainty of life. I got a laugh recently when a friend's child told me that they were doing meditation classes in school but that the meditation teacher wasn't very calm when she was shouting at them to be quiet!

Sometimes this inner work can be challenging and confronting, but I think it is also important to bring some lightness and humour to the work we are doing. As I come to get to know my characters more intimately, the stories they tell me, which used to throw me off course and into a downward spiral, now have me quietly laughing to myself – 'Oh, there's my inner critic piping up again!'

Exercise:
Meet the Characters

We'll meet a number of characters in the coming chapters, including the Inner Critic, the Perfectionist, the Pessimist and the Mind Reader.

For now, though, I'd love you to take some time to become familiar with some of your own characters and come to a greater understanding of how they operate, what drives them and how they are trying to protect you in life.

Begin by thinking of an area in life in which you've felt caught in a cycle of struggle, challenge or 'self-sabotage'. This might relate to lack of confidence in public speaking, struggles with weight loss, difficulties connecting with others or struggles with accepting parts of your past.

When you're thinking of this area of struggle, try to identify some of the disempowering stories you tell yourself around this challenge. Now see if you can tie that story or belief back to a time in life in which you experienced some emotional pain. Perhaps it was the pain of rejection, abandonment, betrayal, judgement or isolation. Maybe it was something else. Since most of our thoughts are memories replayed in different scenarios, rather than new thinking, our characters are usually stuck in the past.

Looking back on this time, consider that a character will have emerged whose primary objective is to protect you from experiencing this type of pain again. Though this character may have emerged in your earliest years, they have hung on to memories from the past and will stop at nothing to ensure you don't experience this type of pain in the future. It is this character who is responsible for some of the 'protective' beliefs that we may have previously labelled limiting beliefs.

In getting to know this character, reflect on and explore the following questions:

1. Can you think of a name for this character and describe what they look like?
2. What is this character most afraid of in life?
3. Where did this character form and what memory are they stuck in?
4. What beliefs does this character hold and what stories do they tell you?
5. In what situations or experiences or around what type of people does this character emerge today?

Perhaps, like me, you experience challenges in a number of areas of life and you'll choose to identify a number of characters completing this exercise across a few scenarios. I have the Lone Shark character who surfaces when I am afraid of not fitting in or of being rejected, the Mean Girls character who sometimes shows up when

I feel myself getting judgemental towards others and the Ordinary Man character who fears sharing 'radical' ideas, stories or exercises with my clients for fear they will see me as unrelatable. My friend Josh visualises a character who procrastinates as a stoner who just wants to kick back and have a smoke and who says, 'Chill, man, we can do all that stuff tomorrow!'

Have some fun with this one and make these characters visual and memorable. This way, when beliefs or stories you may have previously deemed 'negative' creep up on you, you might find yourself having a little chuckle when you recognise the character who's got the microphone.

React or Respond – What To Remember

- Because our stories impact our feelings and our feelings influence our actions we can often find ourselves in recurring cycles, knowing exactly what we want to do but struggling to make it happen. Recognising these cycles we can look to bring awareness to the disempowering stories that are creating resistance and difficulty in our efforts towards change.
- Our collection of thoughts, beliefs, stories and assumptions makes up our self-image or identity, a powerful drive for our behaviour. Taking new actions that go against our self-image can bring fear, resistance and uncertainty and lead to what we may have labelled 'self-sabotage'.
- Disproportionate emotional responses will often point to core wounds or triggering memories in which we felt rejected, hurt, abandoned or shamed. These emotional responses often point to unconscious material that we can work with in increasing our awareness around the conditioned self.

- The stories and beliefs we have previously deemed 'negative' would perhaps more accurately be described as 'protective' as they look to keep us safe and free from pain. Rather than seeing the voice in our head as one character who has tens of thousands of thoughts daily, it can be useful to recognise different characters and seek to learn where these characters emerged and what they are trying to protect us from.

- A lack of awareness leads to us acting out of our conditioning in patterns designed to keep us safe. In recognising the characters and memories being triggered in different moments we can choose to respond in a way that is governed by faith, not fear.

The ARC Method:
Tools for Change

*'What you are aware of you are in control of; what
you are not aware of is in control of you'*
– ANTHONY DeMELLO

Our goal in the work that we'll do throughout this book is to bring
awareness to the thoughts and stories that we live with every day
and to recognise those thoughts or stories we have identified with
and that might be causing us stress or suffering.

As you go through this book maybe you'll have some insights in
reading through the stories I share from my own life or the lives of
some of the people I've worked with. I've always believed storytell-
ing is the greatest way to teach, so you'll probably have a few 'ah ha'
moments as you read some of the examples that I share.

True lightbulb moments in life or shifts in perspective tend to be
experienced on a felt level rather than a purely cognitive level. These

lightbulb moments are often a result of 'insight'. An insight is a sight from within that is often triggered by seeing yourself in someone else's story. Rather than having to remember or intellectualise the content of this book, trust that the insights that are meant for you at this time will emerge in the parts of the book that resonate most. Maybe, if you come back to the book at a later date, some very different insights will appear for you depending on your life situation at that moment.

The greatest value in this book will come from 'writing your own stories', by implementing the exercises shared at the end of each chapter. This 'integration' aspect is where you'll find the real gold and in practising these simple journalling and meditation exercises you'll effectively become your own coach, taking new perspectives and meeting new parts of yourself every day throughout the eight-week journey and beyond.

My goal in writing this book is to arm you with the tools to question and challenge any difficult thoughts, finding perspective and moving from identifying with the thought to just being aware of it and choosing whether or not you act on it. This means changing from reactionary to responsive, from replaying past behaviours on autopilot to consciously choosing new behaviours that create new results.

Let me share an example of what I mean by becoming aware of a thought without identifying with it. When we live without awareness we often attach to outdated beliefs about who we are and how we fit into the world. So old memories often surface in the present and dictate how we show up in the moment. As we come to recognise our thoughts – which are really just memories – we can choose how we respond to life, rather than constantly living in reaction to life.

Imagine a person who has a very difficult time staying consistent with saving money and feels a lot of frustration around their impulsive spending. Despite having the best of intentions, this person finds themselves constantly self-sabotaging their efforts to save money for a mortgage and in a vicious cycle of consumption to self-soothe when they experience difficult feelings. While the spending might make them feel temporary relief, it leads to feeling further frustration and disappointment when they become convinced that they are addicted to spending money. This person is living in reaction, acting without awareness of the thought or story that is triggering their behaviour. Before they act impulsively there is a feeling that triggers their action and before that feeling there is a thought or story that triggers that feeling.

Without an awareness of this internal story the person will tend to become a victim to that story, blindly believing and acting on it unconsciously and feeling a distinct lack of choice. By bringing awareness to the story they allow themselves choice as to whether or not they act on it.

If this person can commit to checking in with themselves the next time they feel the urge to mindlessly spend money, they can shine light on the story they are telling themselves and choose whether or not they want to act on it. Perhaps their story is something like 'I need a new TV. It's expensive but knowing how much time I spend watching TV it makes sense as an investment.' In the simple act of checking in, the individual will go from unconscious identification with, to an awareness of, their story. Maybe in their story they see a justification for their spending and choose to save their money instead. This awareness is allowing them to separate the external and internal triggers that we talked about in

Chapter 1, the external situation and the internal meaning we attach to it.

Slowing down in the moments of impulse or reaction can help us increase our awareness around our internal narratives. Becoming curious around our emotional reactions too can point to difficult stories that we have identified with. All the people and experiences that trigger stress in our lives are really triggering stories, and thus we are constantly being met with material to work with in better understanding ourselves, our reactions and our potential for growth.

While most of us live in a cycle of trying to change aspects of our lives overnight, relying on willpower without increased awareness, we'll look to take a different approach. With the goal of leaning in, being gentle and bringing a curiosity to our current stories and beliefs I will introduce the ARC method, a way of consciously slowing things down to give ourselves the best chance of creating greater awareness followed by increased choice and sustainable change.

The **ARC** method is as follows.

A – Awareness

By shining light on the dark we become more aware of the fuller picture of life. Imagine you're staying in a hotel and you get up to go to the bathroom in the middle of the night. You shuffle towards the bathroom in the dark, doing your best not to bump into anything, but with the light off in this unfamiliar territory it's a roll of the dice as to whether or not you make it there unscathed. Of course, if you were to flick on the bedside lamp you'd quickly come to see what is in the way and it would make your journey to the bathroom a lot easier!

By switching on the light, you've increased your awareness. When we consider our stories, beliefs and emotions that live in the dark, in the unconscious, we might think about the difficulty of tiptoeing through life afraid of where we might get in our own way and slow our progress or derail our efforts.

If you had the same conversation with a friend every day you'd struggle to learn anything new about them. The same is true of ourselves. When we repeat the same stories and ask ourselves the same questions every day we get the same responses and the same answers. When we ask new questions we increase awareness and make more of our unconscious conscious. In other words, we go from blindly playing out patterns to waking up to and seeing our patterns in different areas.

R – Reflection

Only by making peace with and accepting what we shine light on can we create change. One of the reasons we struggle to sit still and meditate or bring awareness to difficult aspects of our lives is that we've judged and made certain stories, emotions, beliefs or thoughts 'wrong'. The reflection aspect of the ARC method relates to bringing acceptance to whatever we have shone a light on, and reflecting with 'What I can learn from this?'

For example, if we find ourselves constantly self-sabotaging in an area of life, rather than judge and shame ourselves, our goal is to increase our awareness, then reflect and become curious about what we can learn from our 'failed' efforts. Maybe we're taking on too much, maybe we need to find a better plan or maybe we need support. When we judge ourselves or others, we shut down the opportunity to learn and grow, instead opting to stay within our current viewpoint and ego. Curiosity over judgement is key here.

A client who came to a workshop years ago springs to mind.

When he arrived at the workshop he announced that his intention for the night was to come up with a plan that would help him buy a new BMW. After one of the reflection exercises that we completed that night he left with a completely different intention – to improve his relationship with his teenage son. He didn't shame himself or beat himself up when he recognised that he hadn't been there for his son, but instead brought a sense of curiosity to his reflections, allowing himself the chance to create change.

This acceptance piece is key in moving towards choice and change. It is impossible to create meaningful and sustainable change in your life if you are still at war with yourself or your past.

C – Choice

If I go to a nutritionist and am told that I am deficient in some key vitamins and minerals I will have been brought to a greater level of awareness around aspects of my wellness. The nutritionist will have shown me a blind spot and turned on the light around an area that had been in the dark. The nutritionist might help me see some of the gaps in my current way of eating and explain how I might make some simple changes to treat these deficiencies. This allows me choice. Of course if I leave that consultation and continue to live the same lifestyle nothing really changes.

The same is true of the awareness we bring to our stories. Awareness and reflection on their own are not enough. Now we must act on our new insights to support the changes we want. Sometimes we catch ourselves saying, 'I act this way because …' and reference something from our past.

If someone has been through a difficult break-up and developed an unconscious belief that 'people can't be trusted', this story will trigger emotional discomfort and defence mechanisms in the future around the area of relationships. Perhaps after some journalling, therapy, coaching or introspective work this individual comes to see that their belief around not being able to trust people is in conflict with their desire to meet someone new and fall in love again. It feels like there is a lightbulb moment as they scribble out their old belief and replace it with a new belief or affirmation stating, 'I am open to love.'

On paper it all makes sense, but when we feel scared, uncomfortable, vulnerable or under threat our old stories or emotional wounds can quickly resurface. The person who has written 'I am open to love' might feel an old story of 'People can't be trusted' in the early stages of a new relationship. This is where the choice aspect of the ARC method emerges. Does the person fall back on the old story and stay stuck in old patterns or do they choose to lean into the discomfort and growth of a new story?

The choice aspect of the ARC method means recognising that old stories, thoughts and patterns will continue to surface, but we can choose to act in a different way and rewrite our narratives through our actions. When we have choice and a wider perspective we get to pick which story we identify with. When there is only one story we will identify with that story by default. This isn't easy of course, but it is the starting point for creating new results in all aspects of our lives.

Through this process of awareness, reflection and choice we come to find perspective. Hope tends to disappear in times in which we lack perspective and feel we have no choice. Take, for example, feeling trapped in a job that is making us miserable and also feeling as though we don't have any other options. It is easy to see that this is a recipe for hopelessness and suffering. If we can find possibilities and other choices we begin to feel more hope, stepping from a feeling of life happening *to* us to life happening *for* us. This effort to find perspective is our own responsibility. It is not something anyone else is going to do for us.

Of course there are times when we cannot change our situation, but we can choose the perspective with which we look at it. Maybe the job that has us feeling down and out isn't something we can walk away from, but taking the perspective that it is enabling us to save money to pursue a qualification in something that inspires us changes how we see our workplace.

After shining light on and reflecting on our current beliefs, stories, thoughts or emotions we will start to see patterns and look to move from reactive to responsive. This is how true transformation happens.

With the belief that when we change the stories we tell ourselves we start to change our lives, I've used journalling and meditation practices as a means of exposing my blind spots, stepping out of autopilot and bringing awareness to my existing stories and beliefs so that I can rewrite those that are no longer working for me.

If we imagine there's a voice inside us that has perfect clarity on what is right for us in life but that voice has been silenced over time by external noise, conditioning and expectations, think of our journalling and meditation practices as the chance to create some space to allow that inner voice to speak up and guide you on your own unique path.

It's time to practise ARC – awareness, reflection and choice.

JOURNALLING

Over the last ten years journalling has been the single biggest tool that has helped me to bring awareness and understanding to my stories about myself and about the world. It's helped me find perspective, dissolve fears and stress and find meaning and wisdom in my most difficult moments. It helps me move from overwhelm to clarity and from paralysing fear to manageable action. It's shown me my cognitive distortions, skewed thinking and the lies I've told myself about myself and about others. It's helped me set and break down goals, identify limiting beliefs and transform the stories that kept me stuck for years – and it's free.

At the peak of my personal development journey I attended a nine-day retreat that had cost more in money and time than anything I'd attended up to that point in my life. I believed the cost and time commitment involved would ensure huge personal growth and lessons shared by the coach who was running the retreat. On the first day, we were given a blank journal and pen and encouraged to set some intentions for the nine days that we had together. After setting our intentions and doing some introductions, we got some food and retired for the evening.

The next day, as I anxiously awaited the golden nuggets I was sure would be shared, we were given some journalling prompts and encouraged to go and do some writing on our own. I was a little perplexed at first but assumed this was just a warm-up that would be followed by lectures and lessons in which the facilitator would share the secrets of life and success. I was wrong. Each day, we were given more prompts and more time to go and write about our lives. We were discouraged from using our phones or doing any reading and instead encouraged to listen to ourselves while removing any external noise or distraction.

When we weren't writing, we were out in nature for walks or sitting in a circle sharing the reflections that were coming up in our journals. I found it difficult and grew frustrated. At the time I was a personal development junkie, going at a million miles an hour and squeezing in as much reading and listening to other people's ideas as I could, convinced someone 'out there' had the answers to the challenges I was experiencing 'in here'.

What had I paid all this money for? To write about stuff I already knew and then talk about it in a group? Why had I taken nine days out from my busy work life to be in this space where I wasn't learning anything new?

But I was learning something new. I began to trust the process and over the nine days I came to see that I was bringing awareness to aspects of my past and my present that had been completely in the dark, mindless and on autopilot. I was having 'conversations' with myself that I'd never had before. I was learning things about myself that I'd never known before. I was being more honest with myself than I'd ever been before and as I continued to peel back the layers of the onion I became clearer and clearer than I'd ever been before on where I wanted to go in life, and what was holding me back.

We get to know others by taking time for them, being present with them and having new conversations where we listen to them, and the same is true for getting to know ourselves. I know that when I went on that nine-day retreat, I wasn't ever listening to myself – I was always plugged in to external noise. It was no wonder I had a hard time trusting and believing in myself. I valued everyone else's voices above my own.

Consider how we feel when we share a challenge or struggle we are facing and the person we share with doesn't seem to listen or empathise, instead going straight into problem-solving mode, giving advice and telling us what we need to do. It doesn't feel very loving or supportive!

Now consider how many of us treat ourselves in that way. We experience a personal challenge or difficult emotion and go straight to trying to 'fix it' before listening and understanding. The journalling practices we'll look to in this book provide that space to gain a clearer understanding of what's going on for you, before trying to 'change' yourself.

I've had similar experiences since that retreat on mountaineering expeditions when I've spent up to twenty-one days climbing a mountain without any technology or distraction. On the initial days of these trips, it takes some time to adjust to the external silence, which can make the internal narrative feel uncomfortably loud and busy, but this soon settles. Over the course of the expedition what is initially an overwhelming collection of internal noise soon turns to a concise and clear plan and understanding of what I need and where I want to go next.

After each of the eight international expeditions I've completed I've returned to the airport knowing the one change I most needed to make in my work or personal life.

You don't need to go to a nine-day retreat or up a seven-thousand-metre mountain to begin to connect back to your inner voice and shine light on your stories and narratives. It can start by completing the journalling exercises I'll share throughout the book. I would strongly encourage you to invest in a new journal for the 'integration exercises'. This is where you'll get the real value and find the real wisdom – in your words, not mine. Reading this type of book without putting into practice the ideas I share is a bit like reading a fitness plan but not ever setting foot in the gym.

At the end of each of the eight main chapters, I'll provide an 'illumination exercise' designed to help find perspective and increased awareness around the given topic. Each chapter will also include a week's worth of journalling prompts. I suggest you take at least ten minutes each day to write and reflect on each prompt. If you've got more than ten minutes, all the better. There isn't a right or wrong way to journal and it can be the attitude of perfectionism or thinking it has to look a certain way that stops people from getting started.

When asked by an aspiring songwriter about his process of writing songs, Ed Sheeran used the analogy of turning on an old tap that hasn't been used in a while. At first it spits out dirty water, but as you let it flow eventually the clean water comes out. Ed said his songwriting began with letting out the dirty water and writing plenty of bad songs before the good stuff came. In the same way, when you start journalling you may struggle to find much sense or wisdom in your writing but as you stay with it, it gets better and better. The same themes and ideas come up, shining light on your priorities. You learn to trust yourself and listen to yourself, seeing that you already have the answers.

Once you've done some reflection through your daily journalling prompt you might highlight one thing from your writing that you can begin to apply or bring attention to in your life.

It's often said that we learn from experience. I would say that we learn through reflecting on our experience. For me the key piece of the self-reflection aspect of journalling is that we allow ourselves space for reflection, we listen to what comes up for us and then we take some form of action to support our new insight. As we do this we develop confidence, self-esteem and a trust in our inner voice.

Life teaches us lessons but we can be slow to learn unless we pause and reflect. I saw this for years in the fitness industry where people were caught in a loop of signing up to a fitness plan, falling off the wagon a month in and then repeating the cycle the following year none the wiser. If that same person were to sit down and write down why they'd struggled the year before and how they might avoid those struggles or change the plan going forward, they would be able to fast track their learning and pick up the wisdom without the ageing process! This self-reflection would carry more benefit than signing up to ten more fitness plans that promised the world. No one can know us better than we can know ourselves, but we've got to make, take and prioritise the time and be willing to look at our current reality, even when it's a little uncomfortable.

American philosopher Ken Wilber has talked about the 'story gap' – the incongruence between the story we tell ourselves and the story we tell others. These big or small lies can be hugely detrimental to our physical, mental and emotional health and leave us feeling bereft of integrity and struggling to trust ourselves. Our journalling practice offers us a safe place to begin practising greater levels of honesty with ourselves, which in time builds confidence, trust, self-esteem and pride.

I know the daily practice of journalling will allow conversations with yourself that increase awareness, facilitate reflection and allow for great choice and potential.

SENTENCE STEMS

Life coaching, a profession that's gained enormous popularity in recent years, is all about helping people see their blind spots and find new perspectives. This is done mainly through the art of asking great questions. At an early retreat that I attended I watched the coach who was facilitating ask an attendee who was unhappy in their profession, 'What would you like to do for work instead?' The attendee responded that they had no idea what they wanted and had a complete lack of clarity around the area of career. The coach quickly acknowledged their lack of clarity and said, 'Okay, so you don't know what you want to do, but if you did know what you wanted to do, what would it be?' I felt like I was watching magic as the attendee listed in detail and with confidence what it was they would love to do in their work life.

It has been said that the longest distance in the world is that between head and heart. I believe we have a lot more clarity in our lives than we give ourselves credit for, but we allow our minds to override our innate wisdom, heart, gut or intuition, instead looking externally for guidance or validation on what we 'should' be doing with our lives.

Sentence stems provide a means of listening to and reconnecting to our truth before we perhaps analyse, intellectualise and judge that inner voice and inner guidance.

With sentence stems you are simply given the start of a sentence and encouraged to finish it with your first response. An example of a stem might be:

'I would find more consistency in my life if ...'

Your response often points to inner wisdom that you are overlooking or have not yet integrated in your life.

Some other examples of sentence stems:

'The thing I love about myself the most is ...'

'The number one challenge in my life right now is ...'

'I would see massive improvements in my physical health if ...'

'I will feel successful when ...'

Some of the uncertainties and anxieties that we feel in life often come from our gut telling us to change an aspect of our lives but our mind giving us a hundred reasons to stay safe and stay the same. There's a heavy feeling that comes with this disconnect between what we know we want and what we are doing in reality. It is as though we are in a constant internal battle with ourselves.

In our gut we think about leaving a job or relationship which isn't working any more, but our mind quickly gives us a hundred horror stories and justifications for staying. After an exhausting week at work our gut tells us to have a relaxing and recharging day at home at the weekend, but our mind makes us feel obliged to go and meet up with friends. Every time we ignore that inner voice and push it down, we chip away at our confidence and self-esteem. Every time we create space and meet that inner voice with patience and self-compassion we claim back some of that self-belief and trust.

Sentence stems are a great tool that we'll use throughout the book which can help us develop self-trust and understanding. Unlike the journalling prompts, in which I'll encourage you to write and reflect, with the sentence stems I'll encourage you to write the first things that come to you. This is more about connecting with your emotional wisdom than using your intellectual mind. At the end of each chapter I will provide a number of these stems. Of course, you can also come up with your own and become your own coach or therapist. The sentence stems will help you to reconnect to your innate wisdom and will support you in making more of your unconscious stories and beliefs conscious.

They, alongside our journalling prompts, facilitate new conversations we will have with ourselves that can lead to increased awareness, reflection and choice.

MEDITATION

The third tool we'll use throughout the book, alongside journalling and sentence stems, is meditation. Meditation, like journalling, is something that's frequently talked about in the context of self-care. In most corporate or private groups that I work with I'll ask if people have any experience with meditation. Many will have tried but struggled to find a consistent practice. People often say that they know they 'should' meditate but they just can't seem to make it happen consistently. There's sometimes an element of people shaming themselves or feeling bad that they struggle to stay consistent.

Rather than shame and judgement, I'd encourage a curiosity around why meditation is proving difficult for us. In my experience there are two primary roadblocks that people face.

First, there's the expectation as to how it 'should look'. We close our eyes, try to stop thinking, but notice our mind is busier than ever. We question if we're doing it right, we struggle to sit with our inner critic or we wonder why we haven't transcended and become enlightened yet. We perhaps have the misconception that meditation is about emptying the mind and so we wonder why our mind seems noisier than ever when we try to sit quietly.

Second, we don't see linear progress. If I go to the gym today and can do five push-ups when I could only do four last week I can see my progress and I'm encouraged to keep going. But with meditation I don't have that definitive positive feedback loop and it's hard to know if it's 'working'.

I'll ask you, in the context of this eight-week programme, to practise the weekly meditation exercises without any expectation as to how they 'should' look. I'll ask you to trust that the few minutes you take for yourself each day will positively impact the rest of your day. If we remove any spiritual expectations and see the few minutes we take for ourselves simply as a chance to practice 'calm' by slowing our breath, any additional insights or benefits are a bonus. Our objective with meditation isn't to clear or empty the mind, it is to strengthen our capacity to be in the present moment. We do this by noticing when our mind drifts and then bringing it back to whatever our anchor is (sometimes the breath, sometimes a bell or a mantra). Every time we catch ourselves drifting and bring ourselves back we are effectively completing a repetition and strengthening our practice. Meditation is not something you are good or bad at! It is a practice and of course we become more comfortable with anything that we practise consistently.

Sometimes people say that they have tried meditation but didn't like it. Meditation teacher and researcher Itai Ivtzan has said this is a little like saying, 'I went on a date once but didn't enjoy it, so dating isn't for me.' Of course, if this person went on some more dates with different people they might meet someone they did like! Similarly, there are countless meditation techniques and though there is value in them all, the best meditation technique to start with is the one that we enjoy and can stick to. We'll introduce different meditations throughout the book, allowing you the chance to get to know and explore some different ways of practising focusing our attention.

Two metaphors that I come back to time and time again for myself in the context of meditation are the fire alarm and the foot on the brake. I visited a psychiatrist during a particularly overwhelming period in my late twenties and I haven't looked at fire alarms in the same way since. I told her about the emptiness and overwhelm I was feeling despite being where I thought I was supposed to be. I told her how a typical week looked, tried to verbalise my feelings and probably tried to analyse myself before she could.

'We've all got a stress response in the body called fight or flight. It's a useful response, hardwired into us, and there to protect us,' she told me. 'But to me it sounds like your fight or flight response has lost the run of itself and is leading to burnout.'

She was right. I wasn't sleeping, couldn't sit still and constantly felt like life was a race or an uphill battle.

'Think of this fight or flight or stress response like a fire alarm in your house. If there's ever a fire, it's the response of the fire alarm that's going to potentially save your life and certainly keep you safe. However if that same fire alarm starts going off every time you use your toaster, then we've got a problem. Just like the fire alarm, your fight or flight response is there to protect you, keep you alert and clear from danger. If you are under immediate threat or danger it'll give you the hormonal response to protect yourself. However, it sounds like you've got to the point where the fire alarm is going every time you use the toaster. In other words, every little worry or stress is sending you into a state where your body and mind are feeling threatened and endangered.'

When animals experience fight or flight response there's an acute experience of stress – they run or fight, then live or die. The stress response arrives, does its job and then disappears. Their stress isn't a result of them living in the future or the past, it's a protective mechanism designed to help them *in the moment* to avoid or escape real danger from predators or other threats. It's thought that our own stress response in years gone by was similar – acute and short term, doing its job and then allowing us to move into the other part of the nervous system to rest and digest. Here, in rest and digest mode, our body and mind can relax, rest, recover and repair.

However, modern life has shifted things; we no longer experience acute stress but we are in chronic stress, which has a drastic effect on our health, physical, mental and emotional.

The other aspect of the nervous system, the parasympathetic nervous system, is what puts us in a state of 'rest and digest'. This is what tells our body and mind that we are safe, not threatened or in danger, and we can rest, relax and recover.

The second analogy around meditation is a car. The car's accelerator represents the fight or flight response; the brake represents rest and digest. If I always have my foot on the accelerator the car gets faster and faster and I begin to feel more and more out of control, in much the same way as always being in a stressed state makes me experience feelings of massive overwhelm and of being out of control. Eventually the car (or the human) will crash. On the other hand, if I only ever have my foot on the brake I don't go anywhere – and so it's a case of using both the accelerator and the brake. I encourage clients to consider every day the thing or things they are going to do to ensure they 'slow down the car' and get out of overwhelm. This might be playing or listening to music, spending time in nature, doing some yoga or meditation or reading a book. For the purpose of this eight-week programme we're going to introduce some meditation and mindfulness practices that'll allow you to slow down the car every day.

In the context of self-talk and stories, you might question where meditation and mindfulness fit. If you've ever had a poor night's sleep, a hangover, or a sense of overwhelm and busyness, you may have noticed the inner critic and negative self-talk seems a little louder and more believable and you tend to be a little snappier with your judgements, reactions or behaviours.

I'll often ask my seminar attendees, 'When do you get your best ideas?' Answers vary, but they often say 'When I'm in the shower', 'When I'm out walking' or 'Just before I fall asleep'. These are all times in which people are relaxed and in that 'rest and digest' state. At a youth leadership conference in Nepal a few years ago a teenager in the audience made the whole room laugh when he announced, 'I get my best ideas when I'm sitting on the toilet, sir!' When I later asked the audience if anyone wanted to share a dream they had in life he told me he hoped to someday make sure there was a toilet in every home and school in Nepal.

Albert Einstein is quoted as saying, 'We cannot solve our problems with the same thinking we used when we created them.' It might be fair to suggest that we do not solve our problems from a stressed state in which our brain is in 'survival mode'. Our lightbulb moments tend to happen when we least expect them and when we are in a state of feeling safe.

Coming back to the ARC method and the idea of awareness, reflection and choice, this daily effort to 'slow down the car' through meditation and drop into the parasympathetic part of the nervous system is what most impacts our ability to make healthy choices that support where we are trying to go.

When in a chronic state of stress, our body and mind are in survival mode and will always go back to old patterns of the past in reaction rather than responsiveness. By consciously relaxing the body and the breath daily we can send that signal to the mind that we are safe and in a place where we can move on from simply trying to survive to choosing to thrive.

Integration Exercises (How to Use this Book)

If you choose to first read this book all the way through, I would suggest that you then treat it like an eight-week self-awareness journey in which you take a week per chapter to complete the exercises which serve as a means of increasing awareness, learning through reflection and then opening up choice. You'll need a journal alongside this book to keep all the integration exercises in one place.

In these integration exercises we are looking to integrate the parts of ourselves that we had perhaps previously judged or made 'wrong'. This integration is about regaining our wholeness rather than being in a place where we place unfair expectations on ourselves to only allow a part of who we are, while judging the parts we have made unacceptable or unlovable.

Our eight weeks look at:

- Happiness
- Success
- Confidence
- Difficult emotions
- Communication
- Conflict
- Fear
- Purpose

Each chapter introduces new perspectives related to the stories we tell ourselves about what each of these themes means to us.

At the end of each week there are some ARC exercises.

- First you'll see a number of **sentence stems**. Read these aloud or write them in your journal and complete them with the first answers that come to you. Don't filter yourself or try to make it look pretty. This isn't a performance – no one else will see it! It's an exercise in self-honesty and listening to your first responses without a filter or any form of self-censorship.
- Next there is a main **illumination exercise** for the week, which is designed to help you find perspective and awareness through reflection around the given topic. This will usually take the form of a journalling exercise and it is recommended that you give yourself at least twenty minutes to complete it, allowing you the chance to illuminate thoughts, beliefs, emotions or stories that may have been in the dark.
- There are then an additional seven **journalling prompts** related to the chapter and theme of the week. Over the course of the week take ten minutes daily to explore and write about one of the seven prompts.

- Finally, you'll see a **meditation or mindfulness practice** which I'd encourage you to complete every day for the week. This is your chance to 'slow down the car' or 'maintain the fire alarm' and make calm and stillness a daily practice rather than something that you hope shows up at random.

We'll talk a little about behavioural change and habits towards the end of the book, but for now, I would strongly encourage you to decide in advance where and when you will complete your meditation and journalling exercises. If this stuff is important to you, don't just leave it to chance. Put it in the diary and make it a non-negotiable appointment for yourself. I would suggest you allow twenty minutes daily for the meditation and journalling prompt and an additional twenty minutes once a week for the illumination exercise. If you don't have twenty minutes, take ten. Make this work for you. Progress is progress and that is what we are shooting for.

An ideal week might look as follows:

- **Sunday:** Allow at least thirty minutes to complete the sentence stems, illumination exercise, a journalling prompt and the meditation of the week.
- **Monday to Saturday:** Take ten minutes to journal on one of the weekly prompts and ten minutes for your meditation.

SELF-COMPASSION

One caveat worth mentioning from the outset is the importance of bringing compassion and curiosity to all our mindfulness, journalling and meditation practices. Without compassion and kindness to ourselves any type of 'inner work' can bring about feelings of overwhelm or anxiety.

When we judge something, someone or ourselves we've boxed them off and cannot understand them. Rather than judgement, approach these exercises with an attitude of curiosity. In this curiosity we allow space for understanding, awareness and acceptance, which are the starting point of any change.

Thoughts of 'I shouldn't feel this way' are turned to 'I wonder why I feel this way?' Stories about 'being wrong about things I've done in my past' become gentle reflections of 'What can I learn from my past?' When we turn judgemental statements into curiosity-based questions we begin to gain a new understanding of ourselves. When we villainise or box off parts of ourselves or others we lose all capacity to understand and learn.

Think about a physical fitness plan. Our goal is to invest regularly in our physical practice to develop physical fitness and promote physical health. We might think about the programme in this book as our mental or cognitive fitness plan, a regular commitment to developing mental and emotional fitness with the hope of improving mental and emotional health. We will all experience health challenges, physical and mental, at certain points in our lives – no amount of gym, juice or journalling is going to make us invincible – but these small daily investments in ourselves will improve our resilience and our capacity to handle adversity and challenge while quickly finding perspective in difficult moments. These daily practices also highlight and identify areas in which we are caught in self-sabotaging patterns or unhealthy behaviours.

I got to work with thousands of people in my time in the fitness industry, and thousands more in recent years through my focus on emotional and mental wellness. The sheer number of people who have gone through seminars, courses and workshops have illuminated a key lesson for me, one that I see mirrored back in my own life. The clients who came to the gym with grandiose visions of completely transforming their bodies often became disillusioned and threw the towel in early. Similarly, the people who came to the workshops looking to 'transform' their lives and have a huge break-through also became frustrated and disillusioned. It was the clients who accepted where they were and focused on their first step who always saw results, built momentum and created sustainable change. If the picture in my head of where I should be, how I should look or how I should feel is a million miles from my current reality, I am effectively making myself wrong for where I am. Change begins with awareness, acceptance and compassion.

Wherever you are as you start this eight-week journey is exactly where you are supposed to be and you're doing great. It's often said that we can be our biggest critics in life. I am going to encourage you from here on out to focus on becoming your own biggest supporter.

AFFIRMATIONS AND COMMITMENT

'No matter how you feel, get up, dress up and show up'
REGINA BRETT

Brazilian jiu-jitsu is a great passion of mine. Like many martial arts it works on a 'grading' system; different-coloured belts signify your experience and level of skill. Traditionally, a martial artist wore the same belt for their whole career and thus the belt that started out white eventually turned black as it aged and was worn for decades. As martial arts entered the western world and became more commercial, a number of different-coloured belts were introduced to encourage participants to keep training and see their progress as they 'moved up the ranks'.

In Brazilian jiu-jitsu the path goes from white belt to blue, to purple, to brown and then black. This journey from white to black belt can take about ten years and even moving from one belt to another can take two years or more. To further mark a student's progress, little white stripes are added to your belt as your coach sees improvements in your skill set. Once you have four stripes on your belt you know you are close to being promoted to the next coloured belt.

So a new student will begin as a white belt and be given a 'stripe' as their first promotion after they have been training for a few months. Once they have received four stripes on their white belt they know they are coming close to promotion to blue belt. This is a great way of keeping people encouraged in the initial months when they can find themselves questioning their progress.

At my first jiu-jitsu gym we had a system that every time you trained you received a stamp in your own training booklet. After sixty sessions you were eligible for a promotion and thus your book-let showed your consistency and commitment to training. It would feel great to fill a booklet with sixty stamps, but the thing that really stood out for me when I looked back at a filled booklet was that I would not be able to tell you on which days I was motivated or which days I was tired. I would not be able to point out the days I was excited to go training versus the days I wanted to skip training. I would have no idea looking back whether I had felt I had performed well or poorly in each given session. All I would be able to see from the filled booklet was that I showed up.

There is a great confidence and trust that comes from consistently showing up for yourself, particularly on the days when you come up against resistance or feel like giving up. I know that if I only show up for training on the days I feel motivated to train, I might only complete a handful of great training sessions in the year. I know that if I show up four to five times a week, irrespective of how motivated I feel, the number of great sessions I will have will grow exponentially.

On page 313 you will see your own tracker for the next eight weeks. I hope it provides a useful visual representation of your own progress on this journey. Simply tick the box each time you complete the day's journalling and meditation exercises, and imagine the pride you will feel looking back eight weeks from now knowing you put this much energy, commitment and consistency into your own self-care and ticked all fifty-six boxes to represent fifty-six days of investing consistently in your mental and emotional wellness. If you miss a day, don't worry. Just carry on from where you were and continue to tick the box each time you complete the exercises in the book.

One more tool I'll share with you from my jiu-jitsu journey that will support you in going through this programme is the idea of having an affirmation that you can use to keep yourself on track when motivation fades. As much as I have grown to love Brazilian jiu-jitsu and as much as I can see how it adds to and supports all areas of my life, there are plenty of days when I'm tired after work and feel like sitting on the couch for the evening. There's a voice in my head that says it is more comfortable to just 'skip this one session and relax', but I always know I will feel better after training and, ironically, sitting on the couch for the evening will deplete my life energy more than getting to the gym. Knowing that a 'character' and story would inevitably emerge at some point and try to talk me out of going training, I came up with an affirmation that I say out loud or in my head – 'Get in the car.' I know getting from the couch to the car is the hardest bit and that once I am driving towards the gym I am already somewhat committed! When I notice stories emerging that encourage procrastination or skipping out on commitments I have previously made to myself, I interrupt those narratives with my affirmation, and 'Get in the car' reminds me of what I want in the bigger picture beyond the temporary desire for perceived comfort or pleasure.

As you go through this eight-week programme, you will likely, even with the best of intentions, come up against some form of resistance or a character telling you to skip your meditation or journalling today. Consider an affirmation you could use to get you on track. Some ideas might be:

'My inner work is a daily non-negotiable.'

'I give myself the space that I deserve.'

'I fill my own cup first.'

'When I take time for myself, everyone around me benefits.'

'I get better at what I practise and so I choose to practise "calm".'

Or you could pick something more direct:

'Do the work!'

'Put yourself first!'

'Get on the cushion!'

If you're new to meditation and journalling, during the first few days or weeks you may question your progress, so remember that these are *practices*. They are not something you are inherently good or bad at. Your only objective for the next eight weeks is to show up, give your full energy and attention to the twenty- to thirty-minute practice and then tick the box on the tracker to acknowledge your progress (see page 313).

PART TWO

Rewriting Our Stories

The Happiness Story

'Happiness cannot be pursued; it must ensue'
– Viktor Frankl

'The good life is a process, not a state of being.
It is a direction not a destination' – Carl Rogers

MEET THE CHARACTER – THE PESSIMIST

There is a character in all our minds called the Pessimist. The Pessimist is always looking to share a narrative of what's missing, what's lacking or what's wrong with our current experience of life. We could dismiss this character, villainise them and feel under attack from them as they seem to overtake our thoughts and rob us of our happiness and joy; or we could choose to come to understand them and appreciate what they are trying to do.

By understanding the Pessimist and being aware when it is them who is talking, we can decide to choose to respond in an appropriate way that points us back towards our potential. Choosing to shame ourselves for thinking 'negatively' or blame our survival-based thinking for our reactivity is denying and judging an important part of ourselves. Rather than judgement, we can meet the Pessimist with curiosity and see how understanding them further can support us on our journey.

It might seem that the Pessimist will stop at nothing to pull us off course, but in reality they are simply fulfilling their sole purpose, which is to keep us alive. The human brain is wired for survival, not for happiness, and when the Pessimist is speaking, their objective is to keep us safe, comfortable and alive another day.

In exploring how the Pessimist operates we will look at some of its key drivers and motivators:

- Negativity bias
- Hedonic adaptation
- Instant gratification
- Comparison

As we begin to see these patterns and drivers playing out in our own minds, we can recognise that we are allowing the Pessimist to take control and can instead choose to widen our perspective beyond the narrow viewpoint of this character.

'I'll Be Happy When ...'

A psychiatrist's chair wasn't where I thought I'd end up when I achieved all my goals, but I was struggling, crippled with feelings of anxiety and overwhelm, self-doubt and emptiness. I'd had all these feelings before, going back many years, but there had always been an external reason I could point to for my unhappiness.

In my early years I pointed to being bullied as a reason why I couldn't be happy and didn't fit in. Then when I did meet friends in secondary school there was always a voice in the back of my head who denied me happiness by telling me that eventually these friends would find out what I was really like and wouldn't stick around for long. To try to maintain the acceptance and approval of others in school, I looked at how they dressed and acted to figure out how I should show up and looked outside myself to fill the void and self-doubt I felt within. Maybe I wasn't happy because I didn't have brand name shoes like 'everyone else', or because I wasn't as popular as the 'cool kids'.

In college I numbed myself to my continued unhappiness by self-medicating with alcohol and nights out to mask my feelings of anxiety and unworthiness while chasing women to try to find an external validation that I couldn't seem to find within myself. After finishing college my next 'logical' step in the pursuit of happiness was to chase success, whatever that meant.

Fresh out of college, I moved to Dublin at twenty-two with aspirations of becoming a well-known fitness trainer, with a story in my head that if enough people came to like me surely it would translate to me liking myself. Fitness had been the one thing in life that had given me confidence, so it seemed the only logical career path for me at the time. I set out with the dream of someday owning a gym in the capital. In Dublin I spent two years trying to get a business off the ground, but to no avail. Adamant I wasn't going back home to Galway with my tail between my legs, I got full-time work in a clothes shop but pushed a false narrative on social media that things were going really well with my fitness business. My friends back in Galway saw me share photos of models I was training and assumed the reason I wasn't coming back to Galway at the weekends was because I was living the high life in Dublin. In reality I was training those models for free with the hope of getting some publicity. Never going back to Galway was my attempt to avoid reality and inevitable conversations with my family, who were worried about me and wanted me to move home and pursue a different path.

I was borrowing money from anyone I could to pay the rent and stay in Dublin, more concerned with looking like a success (despite my misery) than coming home a failure and facing reality. At my lowest point in Dublin I left the house I was living in on East Wall Road and walked around the city for hours, completely lost, overwhelmed and alone, nervous energy that I didn't know what to do with running through my body. After laps of the city I came to the docks and stared into the water, tears streaming down my face, convinced I had nothing left to offer the world. Late that night I rang my dad from the docks and broke down on the phone. He convinced me things would be okay, told me to hold on and said that he'd come to Dublin the very next day so that we could talk about where to go from there. Even then, despite how bad things had become, he still couldn't convince me to leave Dublin. The pursuit of my dream had turned into a nightmare, but my young ego and pride wouldn't let me give up.

A few months later I did give up, finally making the defeated journey back to Galway on Christmas Eve, feeling an overwhelming sense of shame at my inability to achieve the success that I was sure would bring me happiness. Unable to pay my own bus fare home, buy presents for my family or get something for my mum's birthday, which was on Christmas Day, this was a far cry from what I had planned when I'd left Galway two years earlier.

I got work in a pizza shop, moved back in with my parents and spent hours every day walking up and down the beach, searching for clarity and holding back the tears when I met friends of my parents who were excited to share life updates on their more successful children. Much of my shame stemmed from how much my parents had supported me throughout my life and how I felt I'd let them down. They'd fought hard to stop me dropping out of school at sixteen, they'd encouraged me to go to college and supported me financially and morally, eventually even helping me pursue a master's in exercise and nutrition science, something I'd never have thought possible only for them, due to my stories of not being academic or smart.

When I wasn't working in Fat Freddy's Pizzeria or walking the beaches I often found myself sitting in the local church, despite not being religious, praying to whatever god could help me find my way. I was completely lost.

A few months into working in the pizza shop I applied to go back to college to study physiotherapy. I'd always loved fitness but I wasn't sure there was an industry for it in Ireland at the time. My failure in Dublin had given me evidence of that. Physiotherapy would allow me to work in a similar capacity with people but have a better chance of 'finally' growing up and building a sustainable career. When I got accepted on that course it was like the light at the end of the tunnel and things were looking up for the first time in a long time. Just a week later I was sent back to the drawing board when I got an email from the university to say the course was being pushed back a year due to a lack of applicants. The deferral of the course felt like a kick in the teeth, but at least it would give me the chance to save some money for the following year and get a head start on some of the anatomy modules, which were completely foreign to me. In an effort to keep one foot in the fitness industry I decided to start teaching some fitness classes on Silverstrand beach in my home village of Barna. I printed five thousand flyers and dropped them everywhere, letting go of the lofty and unrealistic ambitions I'd had in Dublin and just teaching some classes for the sake of teaching some classes.

Those five thousand flyers brought me my first five clients, not a lot fewer than I'd had in my two years in Dublin combined, and to my surprise the classes grew quickly to the point that the goal of going back to study physiotherapy became a distant memory. Within three months up to a hundred people were training with me each week on the beach. Within a year I had written my first book and fulfilled my lifelong dream of opening my own gym. Interest from outside Galway prompted me to start putting my courses online and in a little over two years I went from being unable to pay rent to buying a new car and a house.

After the initial enjoyment and challenge of building a business I began to become scared of losing what I had worked for, and worked tirelessly on accumulating more. I liked myself when I was achieving and being praised, so the thought of losing that was a scary prospect. Every milestone achieved left me feeling happy in the moment but I'd soon fall back to my baseline of feeling something was missing. With my new-found success everything had changed in my life – everything but the voice in my head, which still seemed determined to defer my happiness.

The next four years I set and went after goals relentlessly with the story of 'I'll be happy when …' at the front of my mind, convinced that the happiness that had always eluded me was at the end of the next goal or achievement. I won entrepreneurial awards, delivered talks to large audiences and met some of my heroes. I continually pushed business and financial goals, travelled the world and got some work on TV and radio. The chase towards happiness was addictive because it never gave me what I wanted, only a quick fix that left me wanting more.

I wrote down what I wanted and made it happen, all in the pursuit of happiness. Some people told me they were inspired by my energy and zest for life, while wiser elders questioned what I was running from. These wise elders were people I looked up to in the wellness space and were adamant that if I did not slow down I would burn out. I naïvely convinced myself I was different and could maintain the ferocious pace of chasing goals, achievements and validation. I didn't want to admit that they were right and that I was running from something, but it felt like I was climbing met-aphorical mountains where rather than acquiring happiness at the top I'd instead be met with a view of one hundred more summits that might just have what I was looking for.

Alongside achieving the material rewards I'd pointed to in my unhappiness I also began to acquire the external attention and approval I thought I'd always wanted. To my surprise and disap-pointment my insecurities and self-doubt only seemed to get bigger as people looked to me as someone who was 'successful'. I didn't feel successful. I was getting exhausted and the anxiety of living in the future, always chasing the next achievement, was getting too much.

It was the first time in my life I didn't have anything I could point to as a reason for my sadness. I'd ticked all the boxes and achieved all the goals that were supposed to make me happy and it hadn't worked. Being miserable seemed a lot more understandable when I could point to a cause of my problems. Without something to blame I was at a loss as to where to go from there.

Here I was, sitting with a psychiatrist at twenty-eight, five years after the night at the docks in Dublin, my life looking completely different on paper, but despite all the achievements my internal reality still felt much the same. Although I didn't feel the same extreme darkness and hopelessness I'd felt those nights in Dublin, I did feel flat and empty.

Why couldn't I just be happy?

A Sense of Wounding or Worth?

I'd spent my whole life up to that point trying to change the external world to match the pictures in my head of what I needed in life to be happy. If the constant chasing for more and constant running from reality hadn't worked up to that point, what would make me think I could expect anything different from more of the same? The only common denominator in all my struggles up to that point had been me and my mind's chosen perspective. Changing my external world had become futile and so it became time to flip the script and change the internal lens I was seeing the world through.

Bronnie Ware, a palliative care nurse from Australia, spent years at the bedsides of people as they came towards the end of their lives. From some of her patients she heard stories of the joy that they had experienced from life, but in equal measure she heard many stories of regret. The final days of someone's life will no doubt bring about incredible perspective and although the subject is often avoided or brings about feelings of discomfort, really it is the great equaliser and probably the thing that can teach us the most about life. When we are knocking on death's door the masks fall away and the truth comes to the front. As the same regrets came up time and time again in the many different stories she heard, Bronnie saw a common thread and shared the lessons from these experiences in her book *The Top Five Regrets of the Dying*. The overarching theme in all five of the regrets outlined in the book centred on courage and trusting, not allowing fear or uncertainty to drive our decisions but having the courage to allow ourselves to be honest about how we can make the most of this one life we've been given. Among the five regrets shared by Bronnie was 'I wish I had let myself be happier'. What's interesting in the language used here is that people didn't say, 'I wish I'd been happier,' but 'I wish I had *let* myself be happier.'

I could look back on my own 28 years and share a similar regret. In retrospect every step of my life up to that point had been exactly as it was supposed to be and the suffering had come from me thinking it had to look different in order for me to be happy. I look back now with compassion to a 23-year-old old Pat sitting at the docks in Dublin, thinking, 'Why would you be so hard on yourself and even think about throwing in the towel?'

People have asked me since why I'd put such expectations and pressure on myself and I can see now with perspective that it was from a place of trying to fill an internal need with external accomplishments – an impossible task. I'd be willing to bet you'd have similar compassion for your younger self if you were to look back and see that you were only doing your best at the time. When it came to 'allowing myself to be happy' I could see that there had been countless magic moments that I had let pass me by because I stayed living in my head in the future or the past, thinking about how things were supposed to look rather than allowing myself to enjoy what was happening in reality. That denial of reality had held me back for years.

I suggest that it is our stories about how things have to look that stop us 'allowing ourselves to be happy'. Imagine two kids at Christmas, one with a list for Santa outlining the ten exact gifts they want, the other kid asking for a computer or a surprise. When the kid who wanted ten gifts 'only' gets eight of them, they are left feeling hard done by and that something is missing. The kid who asked for the computer or surprise, meanwhile, is thrilled with their surprise and even more excited if the surprise turns out to be the computer they'd asked for.

Think about this in the context of our own lives. How many conditions have we set up as to what needs to happen for us to allow happiness, and what has influenced these expectations? There are stories we've got running in the background about how our bodies need to look, how our partners need to be, how our boss needs to acknowledge us and how other people need to feel about us in order for us to be happy.

I'm not suggesting that we go through life aimlessly and without a picture of what we'd like, but instead that we loosen our grip on how things are 'supposed to look' and find appreciation for what is, in place of expectation of what should be. The greatest source of unhappiness in life is the gap between where we are in reality and where we think we 'should' be. The 'should' creates blame or shame, heavy feelings that stop us moving from where we are.

There's an interesting paradox: when we chase happiness we never seem to get there, but when we allow it seems to show up at random.

Maybe think of a time when you worked towards something that you were sure would bring happiness, only to be left disillusioned or disappointed at the end, versus a time when happiness just occurred in some random moment, interaction or experience.

Again, this points to expectation. I actually had plenty of happy moments throughout school and in my days of building my fitness community. Magic moments and experiences when I felt joy, presence and appreciation. Magic moments when I felt incredibly alive. It was only when I started judging where I was, comparing myself to others or obsessing over where I needed to get to that I would get stuck in my head and in negative thought loops.

If you're on or have been on social media maybe you can relate. All is well in the world, then we see something that puts us into comparison and expectation and we feel disconnected and like something is missing. There isn't anything missing in reality; the feeling of lack is always just based on a mental construct of how things 'should' look.

In thinking that happiness can only be found in reaching the next goal, we're constantly chasing the next goal and missing out on everything in between. When we consider the goals we have in life and the stories we have about what will make us happy, it is worth considering whether these stories are being driven by a sense of wounding or worth.

Goals driven by wounding are those driven by the idea that we are not enough and that there is something in the goal that will fill the void we feel within. Many of the goals I pursued in my own life stemmed from this place of feeling 'lack'. The problem with targets based on wounding is that you can attain the thing outside yourself, but there isn't ever an external solution to an internal problem. My own experience was that in chasing everything external in an effort to 'fix' the internal, my problems felt magnified.

Goals driven instead from a place of worth are things we are genuinely excited to pursue, not driven by ego and the head, but by intuition and the heart. By listening to our unique internal voice and compass and following a path true to ourselves, we go beyond the impossible task of 'fixing' ourselves from a wounded place and instead come to reconnect with ourselves in recognising that nothing is missing.

MEANINGFUL PURSUITS

In studying the incredible work of Austrian psychiatrist Viktor Frankl it is inspiring to know that of the more than thirty books he wrote and published it was the one that he planned to release anonymously that proved far and away the most successful of all of his work, selling over twelve million copies to date. His purpose in writing it was not for any external validation, notoriety or approval, but instead to go beyond himself and make an impact on the world with work that brought meaning to his life and struggles. This is a real-world example of Frankl's belief that the most important thing in life is meaning and that the happiness we are all seeking is an impossible target in itself; it is instead a by-product of this pursuit of meaning.

In that most successful book, *Man's Search for Meaning*, Frankl describes his time spent in Auschwitz and three other concentration camps. His background as a neurologist and psychiatrist and experience of enduring incredible suffering during the Holocaust formed the basis of logotherapy, the third Viennese school of psychotherapy.

In the first two schools of Viennese psychotherapy, Sigmund Freud had proposed the pleasure principle and Alfred Adler the power principle. The pleasure principle as outlined by Freud rests on the desire to fulfil our most basic wants and needs and find instant gratification, moving us towards pleasure and away from pain. The power principle proposed by Adler lay in the idea that we come from a place of feeling an inferiority complex and we should strive for superiority and domination of others. Frankl's logotherapy instead proposed that life involves suffering and its purpose is to find meaning in that suffering rather than getting caught up in solely seeking pleasure or power.

The three Viennese schools of psychotherapy have been compared to the developmental growth from child to mature adult. In this way of looking at things we could mirror the Freudian pleasure principle as being the guiding principle of a young child, their pursuit of happiness based on the desire to seek pleasure and avoid pain. The Alderian power principle then could then be seen as the guiding principle of the adolescent, eager to be seen, respected and loved with external validation and approval. Finally, Frankl's will to meaning is the guiding principle of a mature adult who sees the need for connection, growth and contribution beyond themselves and their own individual needs.

Mapping the three stages to my own experience, I could see that much of my twenties had been driven by these pursuits of pleasure, power, comfort and external validation, and it was only in the times when I sought meaning in my life that happiness seemed to show up consistently.

When we look around the modern world we see a huge amount of distraction pulling us away from ourselves and towards instant gratification, pleasure, comparison and external validation. Quick-fix efforts to find pleasure through things like social media, porn, gambling, fast food, alcohol and drugs pull us away from meaningful work, relationships and activities. Similarly, comparing ourselves to others and our desire to be accepted have us operating in a way that looks to power and external validation as a driving force in life.

In reminding ourselves that true happiness is the result and by-product of pursuing meaningful relationships and activities in life, we can come to bring increased awareness to the places in which we're relying on external validation or quick-fix efforts to always feel pleasure.

IT'S THE DIRECTION, NOT THE DESTINATION

If I start out on a journey towards achievement convinced that the happiness I'm seeking is at the top of that 'mountain', then I'm looking at a long climb of misery for a few transient moments of happiness. There are a few ways of climbing a mountain, just as there are a few ways we can approach goals in life.

The first is to set our sights on the summit and push hard to get to the top as quickly as possible, convinced that the happiness lies in the end result. Equally, we can set our sights on the summit but see it as being so far away that we don't ever get started.

The more rewarding approach, in my experience, is to first become clear on which mountain I am looking to climb and why. I am not only in it for the end result of reaching the summit but for the actual climb and journey, which will often be uncomfortable and challenging but will be worthwhile because I will know that I am moving in a direction that is true to myself and meaningful.

Going and climbing some real mountains helped mirror back to me how I'd been living my own life for so long. I took up mountaineering as a hobby at a time when work had taken over my life. The thought of travel, time to think and time away from technology, alongside a physical and mental challenge, appealed to my headspace at the time. Over eight international expeditions I've come to see that the team members who obsess over reaching the summit are the ones who let the experience pass them by, oftentimes losing sight of the process and falling sick or fatigued along the way, and never reaching the summit.

This pattern closely mirrored how I'd spent so much of my time: in a rush to get somewhere as fast as possible and missing out on much of the life happening between the 'I'll be happy when …' targets. At times I was in a rush to get to the next goal; at other times the goal was so far away I didn't even see the point in starting.

Of all the lessons I have learnt on my trips to the highest points of South America, Europe and Africa and trips to the beautiful mountains of the Himalayas and Andes, the understanding of embracing the journey has rung true time and time again and it is something that has shown up in every aspect of my life. 'Enjoy the journey' is a cliché, of course, but if you reflect back on any regrets from your own past or on times when you felt you didn't embrace or enjoy the moment, you'll recognise that the cliché carries weight.

My own process now on the mountains is always the same: look after the basics; know the desired outcome; stay in the present; and win the day.

I know there's never a guarantee of getting to the summit. In the same way, there's never a guarantee we'll achieve the goals we set out in our mind. Altitude sickness or a change of weather can mean I or the whole team have to turn around, but these things are outside my control. What is in my control is a commitment to staying in the present, embracing the journey and focusing on my daily process. Eat well even when my appetite is gone, stay hydrated, take it step by step, obsess over hand hygiene to avoid any tummy bugs on the mountain and relax as much as possible at camp in the evening with a hope of getting a few hours' sleep. That is the process.

When I arrive into camp in the evening I am not interested in counting how many days until we get home or talking about how tough the coming days are going to be. While others compare notes on what their next trip will be I'm knocking back water, knowing that the altitude will have me waking up dehydrated and lacking energy if I don't. While others discuss their confidence of summiting I'm looking for people who want to relax and play a game of cards now that our day's work is done. Imagining tomorrow or overthinking the days ahead is likely to take me away from my process – eat well, hydrate, take it step by step, look after hand hygiene and rest as much as possible.

I know that if I live in the process I am giving myself the best chance of reaching the summit and I'm making the most of every day, and if for some reason outside my control I don't get there I have made the best of the experience, grown as a person and done everything in my power to achieve the desired outcome while enjoying the journey. I also know that if I lose sight of the process and obsess on getting to the top, I am diminishing any chances of success and even if I do summit I won't have truly embraced the whole experience.

Ten years ago I approached my goals with the same tenacity as a mountaineer trying to win a race to the top of the hill. I achieved many of the things I set out to achieve but the experiences always passed me by. I actually ended up resenting goals for a while and just went with the flow, blaming the goals for my unhappiness.

In recent years I have found the sweet spot. Identify the goal, break down the process, do the work and then relax. This way of living ensures that even if I don't reach the goal I had hoped for I can find fulfilment, while an obsession on reaching a summit at all costs can sometimes bring 'success' without fulfilment, which in itself is the greatest failure.

The 'I'll be happy when …' myth has so many of us living life so focused on the next summit that we sometimes forget that our future is shaped by what we do today. Life is just a collection of days, but the obsession with getting somewhere fights with the reality that we are where we are and the only place change can happen is in the here and now. My goal now as I work towards meaningful challenges, much like my goal on the mountains, is to be clear on the right summit, look after the basics, stay in the present and win the day.

WHAT'S BLOCKING HAPPINESS?

Knowing some of the characteristics of our Pessimist character can quickly help us see where our attention has gone to what is missing, lacking or wrong in our lives and how we may be blocking happiness and appreciation of what is. By recognising these patterns, we can choose instead to come back to what is within our control and shift our attention to what we have in life, rather than what is missing. Stressful thoughts will always bring our attention to what is missing and out of our control.

Look out for the following four patterns of habitual ways in which the Pessimist operates.

Negativity Bias

The Pessimist in our mind is largely controlled by our negativity bias, a protective mechanism that recognises potential threats to our safety. In our caveman/cavewoman days it helped us identify physical threats; in the modern world our negativity bias is what overlooks the positive in our lives and finds what is lacking, missing or 'wrong' with our current experience of life.

I could dismiss the voice in my head that always sees my flaws as 'negative' or beat myself up for my inability to see the glass as half full – or I could recognise that this negativity bias is a hardwired programme which is outdated for the modern world but is really only there to keep me safe.

Initiate a conscious practice of gratitude. While negativity bias automatically takes our brain to what's missing, lacking or 'wrong', a conscious gratitude practice can help us balance our judgements and move from expectations of what 'should be' to appreciation for 'what is'. If you find your Pessimist character always looking at the worst-case scenario, consider challenging yourself each morning to write down three new things you are grateful for. You can get even more from this practice by adding why you are grateful for what you have listed. Simply add 'because'. Here's an example: *Today I am grateful* to live by the sea *because* I can walk on the beach and swim in the sea.

Hedonic Adaptation

Happiness is a part of a process, not a destination, and thus is always found in the present and not the future. Despite this my Pessimist character believes the 'I'll be happy when …' story and lives with the fantasy that someday everything will fall into place and things will be 'perfect' in life. In reality, irrespective of how much we achieve in life and how great we feel in the moment, we generally fall back to a baseline level of happiness. By recognising when our Pessimist character is living too far in the future we can remind ourselves to come back to the moment and find appreciation for our current experience rather than deferring happiness to the future.

Back in 2015 I met a guy called Dan Price at a networking event in Seattle. Dan had made world headlines when as CEO of his company, Gravity, he took a $1,000,000 pay cut and put himself and everyone working in his company on a minimum salary of $70,000 a year. The most interesting reflection Dan shared was that just twelve months later, after an initial boost in 'happiness' scores following the pay rises, all employees had fallen back to their baseline level of happiness. This is hedonic adaptation in action, where after a positive (or negative) event or experience and a subsequent increase in positive (or negative) feelings we tend to return to a base level of happiness.

Focus on the next step. We can fall into the trap of attaching end dates to our visions or believing the 'I'll be happy when …' stories. These rest on a fantasy that someday everything will fall into place and life will be easy and free from suffering. Knowing that hedonic adaptation brings us back to a baseline of happiness after all positive or negative experiences, we can instead focus our attention on our next step rather than obsessing on a faraway vision of happiness in the future.

Instant Gratification

The marshmallow test, a psychological test that correlates very closely with success in later life, shows the power of recognising our own pleasure-seeking tendencies and choosing to delay gratification. In that test children were told they could have a marshmallow now, or they could have two marshmallows if they were willing to wait two hours. Those who were willing to delay gratification and wait the two hours were found, decades later, to have lower divorce rates and higher salaries. This speaks to the importance of keeping our attention on the meaningful things we want in the long term and not being reactive to what we want in this moment.

Delayed rewards aren't as satisfying in the short term and so we have to have meaningful goals that help us override our reactive Pessimist. In the modern world we have an abundance of access to distraction, noise, entertainment and behaviours that provide instant comfort. Despite this, many report feeling a lack of purpose and fulfilment from life.

Remember what you're working towards. We lean into instant gratification when we become short-sighted and lose our vision of what we are working towards. By having a clear outline of some of the challenges we are currently looking to transcend (we'll do this at the end of this chapter), we can remind ourselves of our long-term meaningful pursuit when we feel the urge for short-term gratification.

Comparison

A number of years ago an aspiring fitness trainer attending one of my workshops asked for some advice on getting her gym off the ground. I asked her where she'd like to be twelve months from then and she said her goal was to have fifty paying clients each month. I then asked her how she'd feel if she got the fifty but another trainer opened up across the road and had a hundred. 'Disappointed,' she said. I think this speaks to our Pessimist character's constant need to compare ourselves to others and point out where we are falling short.

Without clarity about our own meaningful goals and ambitions we will find ourselves in a constant state of comparison. Even with a clear picture of what I would like to achieve, I must keep tabs on the Pessimist and ensure that I am only ever comparing myself to myself yesterday, and not to others who are walking a different path.

Be clear on what you're working towards. The clearer we are on what is meaningful and inspiring to us in life the less likely we are to find ourselves comparing ourselves to others. Without a meaningful vision for our future and understanding of what is truly important to us it is easy to look externally for how we 'should' be living.

Cultivating Happiness
(two-minute practice)

Shawn Anchor, a happiness researcher and author of the book *The Happiness Advantage*, shares a great written exercise for cultivating happiness. This exercise, like the gratitude practice shared earlier, encourages us to scan our environment for the positive and override our negativity bias.

The exercise involves taking two minutes each evening to journal about a positive experience you've had in the last twenty-four hours.

This type of exercise allows your brain to relive that positive experience and also increases the chances of you finding more positive experiences in your future. See if you can go beyond just the observation of **what** happened and also include **why** what happened is relevant and **how** it made you feel. This helps take the exercise from a cognitive practice to a more emotionally felt experience.

ALLOWING HAPPINESS

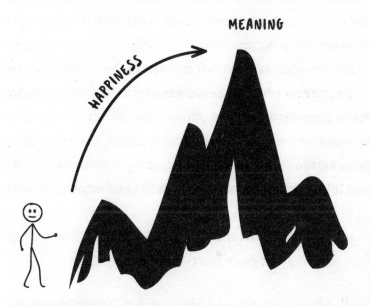

In theory it is easy to see that a life driven by the pursuit of instant gratification and external approval is not a long-term formula for happiness, but in a world filled with distraction and noise it is easy to fall into the pleasure and power traps, seeking instant gratification by taking the path of least resistance and falling victim to comparison.

By consciously taking time to step back, reflect and choose meaningful challenges to pursue in life, we give ourselves a road-map for finding meaning and growth with long-term happiness as a welcome by-product.

Without consciously choosing our challenges we are likely to be faced with less desirable challenges by life. When we do not seek meaningful challenges in life we create a vacuum that can be filled with addictions and discontentment. In my own experience, without some structure to provide discipline, I get caught in overthinking, overwhelm and addictive behaviours and patterns that leave me feeling flat and empty. When I give myself challenges to transcend I have a reason to focus on my own journey and not obsess over what everyone else is doing.

We can find clues to what brings happiness and meaning to our lives by continuously reflecting on what we are most proud of in life and during which times of our lives we felt happiest.

At the end of this chapter I will encourage you to identify three meaningful challenges that will promote personal growth and long-term fulfilment over short-term comfort and stagnation that leads to apathy and frustration. By reflecting on why our chosen challenges are so important to us we can again ensure they are coming from a place of worth and not a place of wounding.

Happiness – What to Remember

- The Pessimist character is constantly looking out for threats to keep you safe. The mind is wired for survival, not for happiness, so our 'negativity bias' is constantly on the lookout for what's lacking, missing, or 'wrong' in our lives. As our mind is always searching for potential threats to our safety and is always looking to seek comfort and instant gratification, we must have practices and awareness around how to find more appreciation, growth and meaningful challenge in our lives.

- Unhappiness is the result of unmet expectations. We all have pictures in our heads about what we need in order to be happy. When these pictures don't match our reality we often experience stress.

- Hedonic adaptation ensures that whatever we achieve in life or the difficulties we go through, we will generally return to a baseline level of happiness relatively quickly. Happiness lives in the journey and not at any given destination.

- Happiness is a by-product of the pursuit of meaning. Many of us make the mistake of searching for happiness in short-term pleasure or in the attainment of power over others. We find happiness through the growth associated with pursuit of meaningful challenges, through the contribution we offer in life and in the appreciation of what we have in our lives.

- The 'I'll be happy when …' story is an out-of-balance fantasy in which we see only the positives and overlook the other side of the coin. By recognising that irrespective of what we acquire or achieve there will still be challenges and drawbacks, we can bring our attention back to the journey and direction rather than deferring our happiness to any given destination.

- Practising gratitude and appreciation daily helps overcome expectations and feelings of lack. When I am experiencing stress I tend to focus on what is lacking and what is out of my control. Simple exercises for expanding this attention and finding appreciation and perspective can help balance our judgements and bring us back to feelings of presence and calm.

ARC EXERCISES

As we move into our first practical exercises of the book here in week one, I want to invite you to grab your journal and pen and explore the first of our weekly sentence stems and journalling prompts.

Begin by completing the following sentence stems in your journal:

- The thing that stops me from allowing happiness is …
- I am happiest when …
- Writing/saying that makes me feel …

- I would allow myself to feel happier by ...
- I am most grateful for ...
- To practise more appreciation I will ...
- One thing I can do today to allow more happiness is ...

Illumination Exercise:
Happiness – Meaningful Challenges

Happiness is a by-product of the pursuit of meaning, so our first illumination exercise is to bring awareness to some of the challenges we could look to embrace in our lives in the coming months.

These challenges will provide the healthy stress needed to develop and grow and through this growth we will experience the meaning, fulfilment and happiness we are all seeking. Remember that these challenges are more about who we become as opposed to what we achieve.

In this exercise we hope to move from interested to committed with some areas that we are ready to prioritise and some challenges we are ready to transcend. Of course most people want to change certain aspects of their lives, but commitment is a different level, a level at which we recognise that this change will not be easy, but it will be worthwhile. In commitment we go from the illusion of someday having a life of constant comfort without challenges to instead choosing to embrace healthy and meaningful challenges that inspire and energise us.

If you were to meet yourself six months from now, what are the three current challenges you are facing in your life that you would like to have overcome? Your answers to this question begin to point to some of the places meaning and growth can be found.

Perhaps you'd like to improve a challenging relationship, develop some healthy new practices or have completed six months of sobriety. All that matters is that these challenges are inspiring to you and will provide you the stimulus for growth. Rather than focusing only on the areas in which you feel strong, be open to exploring areas you may have neglected in the past.

Write out the three challenges you would like to pursue in the next six months and make these desired outcomes as tangible as possible. How would you know that you'd been successful? What 'key performance indicators' could you use to track your progress? For example, rather than saying, 'I want to get fit,' you could say, 'For the next six months I will go to the gym three times a week for forty-five minutes.' Rather than saying, 'I want to have become a better dad,' you might say, 'I will spend twenty minutes with my son every day, distraction-free, just talking and playing.'

Once you've narrowed the focus to three specific challenges you are ready to overcome, I'll ask you to 'brain dump' as many benefits as you can around each. For example, the primary benefit of training for a marathon over the next six months would be improving my fitness, but if I explore a little further and see how this will impact other areas of my life I am likely to make it more compelling. If I struggle to find a number of benefits, I may look to find an alternative challenge which may offer more meaning. Not only will the marathon training help me improve my fitness, it could also improve my confidence, give me headspace and 'me time', allow me the chance to catch up on some podcasts, prompt me to tidy up my diet a little and maybe drop a few pounds. It could also help with stress management, which might make me more present with my kids at home. By being more present with my kids I will feel less guilt and as a result I'll also be more present and productive in work. As I look to all the benefits I come to see that this is about a lot more than just getting fit. This is how I find leverage.

As the final part of this exercise I'm going to encourage you to write these three challenges on Post-it notes that you can stick on your mirror where you will see them each morning and night.

As we've said, growth is about the direction, not the destination. Each night, before going to bed, ask yourself a simple question: 'Did I move closer to or further away from my desired outcomes based on what I did today? If I moved closer, great. If I moved further, that's okay too. Refine the plan and move on. Tomorrow is another day.'

Journalling Prompts:
Happiness

1. Where in my life am I caught up in seeking instant gratification? What have these behaviours cost me in life up to this point? What will they cost me over the next three to five years if I continue?

2. In what moments in my life did I feel the most meaning? Reflecting on and learning from these moments, how can I bring about more meaning in my life?

3. What are the distractions, behaviours or habits that pull me away from being present in my work and relationships? How would life look if I removed some of these distractions and brought more presence to my day? What is the first small step I can take?

4. Write about some of your happiest days and memories from recent years. What can you learn from these reflections?

5. Take ten minutes to make a gratitude list. Share anything you are grateful for from your past or present including relationships, experiences, lessons, struggles or anything else that comes to mind. As well as writing what you are grateful for, include why

you are grateful, e.g. **I am grateful** for books **because** they allow me to learn from the experience of others.

6. Write a letter to your younger self with advice on how to live a happy life. Consider what you've written in the letter and how you could begin to apply some of your wisdom.

7. Take ten minutes to free write, beginning your sentence with 'I feel happiest when ...' Write anything that comes to mind.

Meditation of the Week:
Calming Exhale

Our first simple meditation this week is the calming exhale meditation. Set a timer for five to ten minutes and sit comfortably. Begin by bringing awareness to your breath, noticing how it feels as it comes in through your nostrils, following it as it comes into your body and then again following it as it leaves, with slightly warmer breath leaving the nostrils. After a few breaths you will begin to slowly extend the exhale, making it a little longer than the inhale. It is in this slower exhale that you will begin to notice your body and mind relax and settle. Notice how the quality of your breath affects the quality of your mind and how as your breath becomes slower and more relaxed, so does your mind.

WEEK TWO
The Success Story

MEET THE CHARACTER – THE PERFECTIONIST

The Perfectionist character in our mind is the one who has a very clear picture of what success should look like in different areas of our life. When our results don't match up to their expectations they are quick to point out our shortcomings or flaws. When we do meet our targets or expectations the Perfectionist tends to overlook our impressive results and instead focuses on how it could have been done better. The Perfectionist often keeps us stuck, afraid to try new things or step outside our comfort zone for fear of 'getting it wrong' or 'not being enough'. They look to keep us within the confines of what feels safe by prioritising certainty and routine over challenge and growth.

We recognised in the happiness story that it is in the pursuit of challenge and meaning that we find happiness and thus we must not allow the Perfectionist to talk us out of getting started or stop us recognising our progress en route to our goals.

The Perfectionist can often leave us in a state of anxiety, always feeling our worth comes from 'getting things right' with a debilitating fear that falling short will result in abandonment, rejection or ridicule.

The origins of this character often lie in childhood experiences in which we developed a story of not being enough based on an inaccurate interpretation of our experience. In our early years, when we believe the world revolves around us, we can take any sign of other people's perceived withdrawal of love as a signal of something we have done wrong. In response to the fear of being abandoned our Perfectionist character will develop defence mechanisms to help us avoid similar pain in the future. Perhaps the Perfectionist begins to tell us a story that we have to get things perfect to maintain the love and approval of others. Or perhaps the character decides that the best way of avoiding future pain is to stay in a comfort zone in which there is no risk of failure.

Of course, in any new pursuit there is a period when we go through a huge amount of failure before we become proficient. As children, learning to walk involved plenty of stumbles, learning to speak required nonsensical ramblings and mispronunciations, and developing a host of other skills we have acquired over time has required a similar journey of learning through imperfect action and experience.

With these early life skills – learning to walk, to talk and to navigate our way through the school system – we are supported by others and are rarely on the journey alone. As we grow older and look to step outside our comfort zone to try new things, we perhaps don't have the same reassurance and support as we embark on a path unique to ourselves and sometimes against the norm. For this reason we must ensure we communicate and work with the Perfectionist rather than allow it to take over. In recognising that true success in life is moving in the direction of things that are meaningful to us, we must recognise the voice of the Perfectionist and instead choose to lean into the discomfort of the 'messy middle', that uncertain territory we must walk through on our journey towards the success we dream of.

THE HIDDEN WINS

After an evening workshop in London I'm approached by a lady who's keen to do some one-to-one coaching. She says that she's stuck in a rut and never stays consistent with things. After a little back and forth she quickly skips over a mention of completing an Ironman triathlon earlier that year. An Ironman triathlon involves a 3.8 km swim, followed by 180 km on the bike and then a 44 km run (that's a full marathon distance). Alarm bells go off in my head as I see the disconnect between someone who says they never stay consistent but in the next sentence tells me they've completed an Ironman triathlon. It doesn't add up!

I ask her about the Ironman and it turns out she'd had a really difficult year. In the space of a few short months she'd lost her business and her home and gone through a divorce. At her lowest point she knew she needed a focus and so she signed up for this beast of a race. When I asked her about her background in endurance sport it turned out she'd never even done a 5 km run and here she was tackling her first Ironman triathlon in her early fifties! When I asked her how it had gone she told me she'd been really disappointed. I initially assumed that maybe the disappointment was because she had got injured in the lead-up to the race and hadn't been able to take part, or perhaps the race had been cancelled. The disappointment, it turned out, was because her goal had been to complete the Ironman in sixteen hours and it had taken her sixteen hours and fifteen minutes. My jaw nearly hit the floor. This woman, who had never even done a 5 km run, had completed a full distance Ironman. And she was beating herself up because it had taken her fifteen minutes longer than the sixteen-hour goal that she'd set.

Surprised though I was by her reaction, I understood it to some degree. We all do this to ourselves. We decide consciously or unconsciously what success and failure look like in our minds and then fight with life or with ourselves to make our external world mirror exactly how we think things 'should be'. Metaphorically speaking, we get a pimple on our face, and can't see our face any more, only the pimple! In other words, we achieve a great deal but allow the Perfectionist character to move our attention to where we fell short rather than acknowledging our progress.

I quickly went into coaching mode, asking questions with the hope of increasing the Iron Lady's awareness and perspective.

'Did you get fit training for this Ironman race?'

'Of course – the fittest I've ever been.'

'And what did it do for you mentally?'

'It pulled me out of the darkest days of my life.'

'Did you meet anyone new during the journey?'

'I met a group of ambitious people I wouldn't have otherwise met, some of whom I'll be friends with for life.'

'And where was the actual race? Did you get to visit somewhere new?'

'Yes, I got to visit Denmark for the first time.'

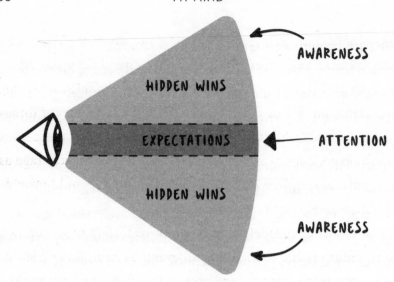

These questions uncovered what I call the 'hidden wins', the magic of life that lives outside our black-and-white stories about how things 'should be' in order for us to be happy or feel successful, the 'fifty shades of grey' if you will. Finding the hidden wins requires space, time and effort but the rewards can be transformative.

The importance of meaning, which we talked about in the last chapter, cannot be overstated. According to Viktor Frankl, meaning is generally found in three places:

1. **Creational values.** Creating something or completing a task.
2. **Experiential values.** Appreciating life, its people and its experiences, or fully experiencing something or loving someone.
3. **Attitudinal values.** The attitude we take towards our suffering or difficult moments.

Exploring the hidden wins associated with the disappointment this lady felt from her 'failed' triathlon attempt provided a means of exploring attitudinal values and extracting meaning from a past experience she had previously resented.

Going back to past experiences that we deemed failures and instead finding perspective and seeing our growth in those experiences can provide us with incredible insight and confidence to bring forward into our future endeavours. Holding resentment for things we have deemed failures rather than looking to extract the lessons from the experience can have the opposite effect and discourage us from putting ourselves into future challenges that could provide inspiration and growth on our journey.

Our tendency to label things good or bad, right or wrong, success or failure rather than seeing all events as neutral experiences that we can learn from contributes to this feeling of playing the lottery each day with how we'll feel. The idea of 'failure' really rests on the idea of something being finite, when in reality in most cases 'life goes on' and there are more opportunities, 'more fish in the sea', if we're willing to brush ourselves off and go again. If we can genuinely come to see failure not as something to fear or avoid, but as a fast track to success that provides feedback and insight, we will make big leaps in our growth and development. This will, of course, require an awareness of the Perfectionist character's efforts to keep us safe and certain as well as a willingness to instead embrace the uncertainty of stepping into new territories.

There might seem to be a contradiction in finding acceptance of, embracing, perhaps even seeking out failure, but when we understand that each experience provides us with valuable information we can choose to see our results as feedback, no longer in denial or afraid to look at the outcomes we had previously deemed failure.

The story of the woman and the Ironman triathlon ties in with the idea of black-and-white or all-or-nothing thinking (often referred to as 'splitting' in the psychology space). This cognitive distortion is a pattern of thought in which we polarise things and make quite extreme judgements of ourselves, other people or our experiences. The more extreme a judgement the more intense an emotion we might feel as a result.

We can direct this black-and-white thinking towards ourselves or others. Some examples of this can be seen in statements like:

- 'I can't stay consistent with anything.'
- 'I always procrastinate.'
- 'Nothing I ever do is good enough.'
- 'You never listen to me.'

This type of thinking shows up in a major way in our relationship to success and failure, with many of us leaving little margin for error in feeling accomplished in our efforts. 'Discounting the positive', another cognitive distortion, also frequently emerges around our relationship to success and failure. Here we overlook our progress and growth, perhaps being completely blind to it or choosing instead to label our progress as 'luck' or 'a fluke' while obsessing about our shortcomings.

Every January a large percentage of the population set themselves new year's resolutions and aim to make positive changes in their lives. We spend so much time looking outwards that we tend to set goals and targets based on what we see in others. Of course, we do not have a true understanding of anyone else's experience, but it can feel inspiring to 'model' people who have already achieved success in areas in which we would like to improve. When we look at the journeys of others their path looks like a straight line to success and we might assume that we should expect similar. On paper, the changes we are keen to make look straightforward and reasonable – save a percentage of our income, refrain from alcohol or sugar for a few weeks or find a regular exercise routine. We begin January all guns blazing, excited to make these positive changes. Perhaps after a Christmas of alcohol, sugar and inactivity we start January with a solid plan for daily workouts and a diet of wholefoods, health supplements and plenty of water.

Things go well for the first four weeks as we stick rigidly to the plan, then something happens. A friend comes to visit and we partake in a little too much wine. We sleep in and miss a workout. An injury throws us off track. In the blink of an eye a missed workout or deviation from the diet plan quickly blinds us to the progress we've made and shines light on another 'failure' in our efforts. Things seem to have just 'clicked' for those people we compare ourselves to. They don't ever fall off track. With our attention shifting from the daily workouts we have completed for the last month to the one workout we have missed, the story of 'always falling off the plan' triggers a cycle of disempowerment.

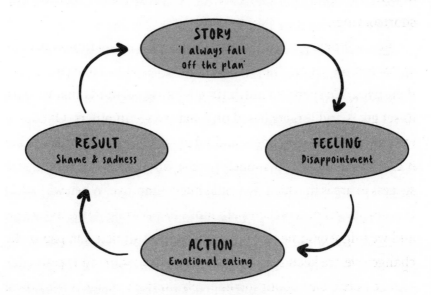

Coming back to the A/B/C/D exercise we looked at in the first chapter, we can catch our out-of-balance thinking and find perspective beyond our extreme judgements.

- **A (activating event):** I slept in and missed a workout.
- **B (belief):** I always fall off plan.
- **C (consequences):** I feel shame, guilt and frustration at myself for my lack of consistency. I feel sad and hopeless around creating positive sustainable change with my health.
- **D (dispute):** Prior to missing this workout I had trained consistently for the last month. I was making great progress, didn't miss a session and was really proud of the progress I was making – in fact my training partner acknowledged my consistency and commitment.

In this type of scenario, being aware of the story we are telling ourselves enables us to shift our attention back to the progress we have made rather than homing in on the slip-up. This could be as simple as changing the question from 'Why can't I ever stay on plan?' to 'What progress have I made in this area over the last four weeks?'

It is essential in our awareness of the way we talk to ourselves to understand the power of the questions we ask ourselves. Whatever question we ask will be answered by our unconscious, so to start getting better answers we must begin by asking better questions.

Our Perfectionist character, like a pushy parent, always sees the room for improvement and quickly skips over the evidence of progress. This constant focus on falling short can often discourage us from even trying, as our expectations just seem so hard to meet. When we do 'fall off the wagon' or have a dip in consistency, we can see it as a reason to give up rather than a part of the process that allows us to regroup and get back on track. I often reference a long car journey as a metaphor for our path to 'success'; if we take a wrong turn halfway through the journey we don't drive home and start again. Instead we will see where we took the wrong turn, reorient ourselves and get back on track.

The path to success in anything is never a straight line. I was reminded of this by a taxi driver I met in Dublin a number of years ago who shared with me his philosophy of life. When he asked what I did and I told him about my workshops he said he'd always dreamed of being a speaker. He then shared with me the message he would share if he were ever to stand on a stage: 'In my time driving the taxi I've met people from all over the world. Different backgrounds, hopes, dreams, fears and ambitions. The one thing that seems to be the same among all these people is their belief that success should be a straight line. They think that change and transition should be easy, that integrating new habits should be smooth sailing and that relationships should always be pleasant. I like to remind these people of the heart rate monitor that for as long as you are alive will go up and down and up and down. As soon as that line goes flat, you're dead! That is the nature of life and of success. It's nice to dream of a day where it's a straight line, but as long as you're alive it'll be filled with those ups and downs. We shouldn't see the struggles, the obstacles or challenges as a bad thing, but as a natural part of growth and development.'

SUCCESS METRICS

For many, the weighing scales serves as the success metric in their fitness journey. In my gym days clients would often leave a session beaming with confidence about the progress they were seeing in terms of improved strength and fitness, only to label all their efforts a failure when they got home that evening, weighed themselves and found that they hadn't reached their target weight for the week.

Much like the story of the sixteen-hour triathlon, my goal in coaching these clients was to take them from the isolated attention on where they had fallen short to finding the hidden wins that showed their progress and growth. A client who felt a failure for having plateaued with their weight loss quickly regained an empowered attitude when they reflected on the improvements they had seen to their sleep, energy levels, strength, fitness and mental health. When we attach our feelings of success to very specific outcomes we often blind ourselves to the progress we are making and allow our Perfectionist character to cling tightly to things having to look a certain way in order for us to feel successful.

Worse again, we sometimes attach our definition of success to things outside our control, such as other people's opinions of us. Basing our success on something beyond our control is giving up our power and rolling the dice with our chances of success, despite our best efforts. For this reason it is important that we ensure that whatever metrics we use to gauge our success are metrics that are measurable and controllable for us.

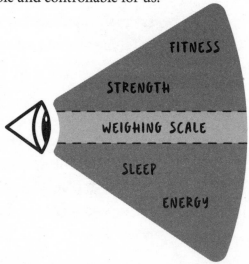

In moving away from an obsession with the destination and focusing instead on the journey, our feelings of success will be largely sparked by progress made in the direction of goals we have outlined that are meaningful to us. At the end of the Happiness chapter I asked you to outline three challenges you would like to overcome in the next six months to promote personal growth, meaning and fulfilment. Rather than seeing 'success' as the completion of these six-month targets, we can see success as any progress made in the direction of overcoming these three challenges.

With clarity about what we are looking to achieve we can reflect each day as to whether we moved in the direction of our vision or away from it. Movement towards our targets, no matter how small it is, can be deemed success, while moving away from the things we said were important can be labelled 'feedback' rather than failure. Much like having a destination in the GPS of our car and keeping our sights on that destination, knowing that even if we take some wrong turns along the way we can quickly get back on track, our six-month targets allow us to focus our attention on the pursuit of meaning.

With this in mind the importance of the word 'recommit' becomes evident. Commitment to change is an important step in creating something new, but in understanding that there will be inevitable slip-ups, challenges and wrong turns along the way, we can remind ourselves that recommitting will perhaps be even more important than the initial commitment.

A number of years ago I was working with a client who was tackling their alcohol dependency and looking to live a life of sobriety. One day he called to say, 'I've messed it all up and fallen off the wagon again.' He had quickly lost sight of the six months of sobriety he had just completed and had become fixated on what he deemed failure. I reminded him of the success he'd achieved over the past six months before the slip-up. We then explored the triggers and circumstances that had led to the relapse and figured out what we could do to learn from this incident and see it as an important part of his success journey and not a reason to throw in the towel. An injury had put him out of action in the gym, an activity that was one of the things replacing his excessive drinking. When he could no longer go to the gym he'd found himself at home feeling frustrated and battling the temptation of going back to alcohol.

After pausing, shining light on his previous progress, learning from the slip-up and reflecting on the lessons learnt, my client got back on the wagon and recommitted with a greater understanding and awareness of what might throw him off course in the future and strategies in place to keep him focused on his intention. I am happy to say he has stayed on his desired track since then.

Perhaps think of this story in the context of your own challenges that you've outlined for the next six months. It could serve as a reminder when any slip-ups, setbacks, obstacles or frustrations arise.

- Pause and check in on your progress to date.
- Reflect on what you've learnt from the slip-up. What triggers, people, thoughts or situations threw you off course and how might you handle these differently the next time?
- Brush yourself off and recommit, confident that you are more prepared than you've ever been.

Success and Feedback
(two-minute exercise)

As a very simple means of getting into a routine of embracing feedback through 'failure', you might consider the following exercise.

- Pick an area of life in which you are looking to make some changes.
- Write down the daily commitment or action you will take to support the change you are looking to make.
- At the end of each day write about why you did or didn't complete the action.

Remember, this is about feedback, so we are looking to learn every day, especially on the days when things don't go to plan.

Let's say that my intention is to drink two litres of water per day. On Monday evening I acknowledge that I 'succeeded' in achieving my goal and I briefly write down why I succeeded: 'I drank a litre of water first thing in the morning which made it easier.' Perhaps on Tuesday evening I acknowledge that I didn't reach my target. Rather than judge myself I see this as an opportunity to seek feedback. I ask the question, 'Why didn't I do it?' and see that 'I was out all day and forgot to bring water with me.'

Completing this type of exercise daily starts to help me find the 'winning process' as I start to shine light on what works versus what doesn't work, just sticking with facts and not getting caught up in feelings.

	AREA HEALTH	
	DAILY COMMITMENT DRINK 2 LITRES OF WATER	WHY DID/DIDN'T I DO IT?
1	✓	I DRANK A LITRE FIRST THING WHICH MADE IT EASIER
2	✗	I WAS OUT ALL DAY AND FORGOT TO BRING WATER

THE MESSY MIDDLE

The gap in life between our current reality and what we might like to achieve will lie either in our skill set or our mindset or both. As an example, if I have never run a marathon before and set my sights on this being my new personal goal, I will see that there is a gap both in my physical capacity to take on this challenge (skill set) and my mental belief as to whether or not I can do it (mindset).

I bridge this gap through my training and consistency of action over time. As I see new results through repetition I come to see myself and my capabilities in a new light. Of course, if I do not change my actions and develop the new skill set I am not providing myself with any evidence that allows for an 'upgrade' in mindset.

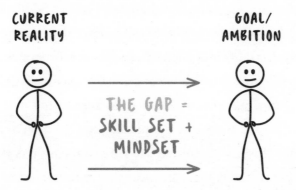

Our skill set will complement our mindset – as we practise a new skill we begin to slowly build a belief that it is something we can do. The challenge, however, lies in the 'messy middle', the days when the story in our head of 'not making any progress' or 'this is impossible' pulls us off course and leads me to abandon our goal. The Perfectionist character hates the messy middle and the uncertainty of learning or doing something new and not getting it right straight away.

In a world where Google provides answers to any question and we have easy access to an endless array of information on any imaginable topic, our modern-day challenge doesn't lie in an absence of information. Our greatest challenge is that we are 'drowning in information but thirsty for knowledge'. The greatest challenge in my own life has always been bridging the gap between knowing and doing. I can intellectually know what I need to eat to feel my best. I can read about how I need to structure my day to be most productive. I can become aware of how to communicate effectively in times of conflict to come to greater levels of connection – but applying this new information is so often where our greatest sticking point lies.

In setting our sights on the challenges we would like to pursue and transcend in life we begin this journey of developing new skill sets and mindsets. We will often shine light on an area that we would like to improve or develop and set out with a sense of uninformed optimism, knowing what we need to do and feeling ready to do it, blissfully unaware of the 'messy middle' that lies ahead. Failing to acknowledge this 'messy middle', when change isn't as straightforward as it looked on paper, often leads us to throw in the towel on our great intentions and retreat back to the comfort of our regular routines. By recognising that the path won't be clear and seeing how this uncertainty threatens and scares our Perfectionist character we can stay the course and walk bravely through this messy middle en route to the results we desire.

In setting our sights on pursuing something new and moving from 'knowing' to 'doing', it is useful to recognise and identify the four stages of competence:

- Unconsciously incompetent (Ignorance)
- Consciously incompetent (Awareness)
- Consciously competent (Learning)
- Unconsciously competent (Mastery)

The first stage, 'unconsciously incompetent', is where we are ignorant – we don't know what we don't know. In this stage we haven't yet seen a reason or need to learn and develop the new skill. Take driving. A child travels in the back seat of a car, doesn't have the desire or need to learn to drive, and thus is ignorant and blissfully unaware of what they don't know.

In the second stage of learning we reach awareness, where we are consciously incompetent. The child in the back seat has become a young adult who now sees a reason to learn to drive. At this stage we step out of ignorance and become aware of what we don't know. Here, our lack of knowledge may lead us to seek out further information and support in acquiring a new skill.

In the third stage, consciously competent, we come to the stage of learning. We are starting to piece together and learn how to demonstrate the skill. Perhaps after a few driving lessons we are becoming familiar with the process of driving. Though we are much more able than we were in stage two and we know how to use the skill, it still requires a lot of effort and concentration.

Finally, with enough practice we come to a point of being unconsciously competent. This is the stage of mastery; we have enough experience with this way of thinking or acting that we can do it without consciously thinking. We can drive to our desired location while holding a conversation, listening to a podcast or singing along to our favourite songs. In this stage the skill that once required effort and concentration is now so easy and effortless that we are no longer consciously aware of what we are doing.

The Perfectionist character hates the second stage in which we come to see just how little we know. It's overwhelming and feels uncertain and unsafe. This stage also triggers fear of not being good enough or of being judged. For this reason most people quit in this second stage and stay in a state of 'knowing' and not 'doing'. To try something new and seek to develop new skill sets, mindsets or habits is to go against our 'current identity' and challenge who we have believed ourselves to be. This of course is terrifying to our ego and thus when we reach the second stage of competence and see just how little we know and how much we have to learn, the Perfectionist can often panic and send us back to the comfort of our old routines and identity.

Though this second stage of competence is where we feel the most unsettled it is also the area in which we learn the most if we are willing to stay in the initial discomfort. We've got to be willing to fail a lot in order to learn and it is this second stage where we feel we are failing the most.

When we think about what true change looks like over time we might break it down into three stages:

- Intellectual understanding
- Emotional leverage
- An identity-level shift

The **intellectual understanding** associated with change is the easy part. Here we acquire more information and know what we need to do to create a new result in life. Perhaps we have encyclopaedias' worth of information on nutrition that we have accumulated over time and have a great sense of 'knowing', but have not yet moved to doing.

As we move from an intellectual understanding of the area to having some **emotional leverage**, we start to see a reason to move from knowing to doing, a reason to create change in our lives. This can often come from a point of inspiration or desperation. We might be inspired after seeing a friend transform their health and fitness and find the emotional leverage to pursue similar results in our own lives. Or perhaps we change our eating habits after the doctor tells us that our current behaviours are placing us on the fast track to sickness.

We could think of the intellectual understanding as the 'what' to do and the emotional leverage as the 'why' to do it.

When knowing meets doing and we practise our new skill consistently over time there comes a point at which we move to unconscious competence; our new skill changes from something we do to a part of who we are. By the time we have reached this **identity-level shift** we have come past the messy middle and created a new normal in our lives.

SURFING SUCCESS

After a few years of thinking about it I finally took a spin down to Lahinch in County Clare to give surfing a go. The day before I had told a friend that I was going away to surf for the weekend, to which they responded, 'Nice! One of my friends is a pro surfer too.' I didn't bother correcting them. This would be my first ever lesson and a far cry from anything even remotely professional.

When I arrived in Lahinch it seemed half of Ireland was there that day enjoying the good weather and ice creams on the prom. I headed to Ben's Surf Clinic and told them I had booked in for a group lesson. They said there were two groups about to head out and I could pick which group I wanted to join.

One group looked like a hen party, the other a ten-year-old's birthday party. I chose to join the hen party, then quickly changed my mind, retreated and became the oldest member of the birthday party. As I helped one of the kids carry a board twice the size of him down to the beach I felt someone grab my arm. I turned around to see a teacher from school who I hadn't seen in over ten years.

She told me how proud she had been to see me on the *Late Late* a few years before and how she'd told the students in school about me being her past student. Before she said goodbye she said, 'And now you're teaching kids to surf, I don't know where you find the time.' Again, I didn't fill her in on the reality of what was happening, allowing her to believe I was an instructor changing lives, not a thirty-two-year-old man who was about to spend two hours falling off a nine-foot board.

After a little instruction we headed out on the water and, as predicted, I spent two hours in the water with two minutes (at a stretch) standing up on the board. I fell, and I fell, and I fell, and I fell as I watched the rest of the birthday party quickly find their feet.

As the instructor blew his whistle and signalled that time was up I walked back to the surf shop, trying to hold the board in a way that might convince onlookers that I knew what I was doing. In retrospect the size of the board was probably enough of a giveaway to my lack of skills! I dropped back the board, had a quick shower and jumped in the car to go home to Galway smiling (and sunburnt) from ear to ear, fulfilled from a day of progress that was only possible by letting go of the illusion of perfection.

I had thought about surfing for years, but decided at twenty-five that I was probably a bit late getting started and should have got going at twenty. Five years later, at thirty, I looked back with similar thoughts – how much younger I was at twenty-five than I had realised at the time. When a friend reminded me, 'You'll never be as young as you are today,' I woke up to the reality that any thoughts of being too old, too young or too anything else is simply a comparison to someone else.

Driving home from Lahinch, an idea of a one-hundred-hour challenge popped into my head. What if I were to commit to one hundred hours of surfing over the next twelve months? What if I could let go of any expectations to make it look good, to reach a certain level or to achieve anything and instead just commit to clocking up one hundred hours in the water?

Surely I would improve?

So often the thing that throws us off course with our intentions is the disappointment of not meeting our expectations or of falling short. But what if there is no expectation aside from clocking up the hours and being present to the process?

Now, taking this one-hundred-hour challenge idea further, consider what you could give one hundred hours to over the next year – that's just two hours a week. Just imagine if, for the next five years, you picked one new skill or hobby and gave it one or two hours a week of practice, with no other expectation other than to give yourself that time.

What might be possible?

Maybe five years from now you'll be playing an instrument, speaking a new language and getting your blue belt in Brazilian jiu-jitsu. Or maybe you'll fall in love with whatever you pick on your first one-hundred-hour challenge and pursue that for the rest of your life.

As kids we are like sponges and learn at an incredible rate. Without expectations on ourselves as to how it looks, we embrace presence, curiosity and play and as a result quickly pick up new skills and hobbies without feeling it has to look a certain way or has to get us to a certain point. We do things to do things, not to constantly get somewhere. Sometimes as we grow older and we harden, much of what we do seems to have to serve a purpose beyond enjoying the experience. If you choose to commit to a one-hundred-hour challenge, remember to keep it playful and light. This isn't something you are doing for anyone else. It isn't something you *have* to do, it's something you get to do.

When we gauge our success in life by other people's results we become bitter, constantly measuring ourselves by things outside our control rather than choosing instead to only compete with who we were yesterday. Success is not just about progress; it's about staying committed to our own vision and not becoming distracted or seduced by 'more' for the sake of more.

SUCCESS THROUGH SIMPLICITY

The story of the businessman and fisherman reminds us that success is often a lot closer than we think and a lot simpler too. While on holiday with his family in Brazil a highly successful Irish businessman wakes up early and can't get back to sleep. He always struggles to switch off from work mode when he goes on holidays and so he goes for a walk on the local beach to burn off some energy while his family are still in bed. He sees a local fisherman arriving at the shore on a small rowing boat filled with fish he'd caught that morning. Impressed by the fisherman's haul, he asks him how long it had taken him to catch the fish. When the fisherman says it took just an hour the businessman is perplexed and asks why he doesn't go back out to try to catch more.

The fisherman says he has more than enough to feed his family.

'But what will you do for the rest of the day? It's not even eight a.m.!'

'Well,' replies the fisherman, 'I live a good life. I'll get home and have breakfast with my family and play with the kids. I might have a little nap in the afternoon and spend some time with my wife, then head to the village for a few beers with my friends. We usually get together for some games, play a little guitar and have a singalong.'

The businessman thinks the fisherman is naïve and innocent and decides he'll use his business experience to 'educate' him.

'Well, I have an MBA and think I might be able to help you. If you went back out and caught some more fish you'd soon be in a position to buy a second boat and get someone else working for you.'

'And why would I do that?' asked the fisherman.

'Well, in time, with two boats, it wouldn't be long before you'd be able to afford some bigger boats and from there, you'd be in a position to buy a factory where you could distribute your own seafood products and ship them all over the world.'

'And what then?'

'I have contacts in Ireland and the UK. I think in time you could open factories and headquarters over there too, sell products all over the world and make a fortune. You could eventually take the company to the stock market, sell your shares and retire rich.'

'But what then?'

'Well, then you could relax and live a beautiful life near the sea, fishing for fun, spending time with your family, enjoying the weather and good food and meeting with friends for some music and drinks in the evenings.'

'Isn't that what I'm already doing?'

Often in life our stories about what success needs to look like blind us to what's right in front of us and how close we are to the life we would like to be living. Because many of us have never created the space to consciously decide what success on our own terms would look like, we can easily fall into the standard way of seeing success based on our social conditioning. As such we chase certain targets that are rarely hit or provide little fulfilment when we do reach them.

While the businessman in this story continually chases success and struggles to enjoy the day-to-day, the fisherman allows himself to enjoy the present moment by prioritising meaningful work, activities and relationships and not becoming distracted by unnecessary noise or accumulation.

Back in 2012, when I was working in a pizza shop in Galway city
after my fitness business in Dublin failed, I became completely disillusioned with my position in life. In retrospect my time in Dublin
had been spent chasing other people's dreams. I had never taken the
time to outline what I really wanted myself. Like the businessman
in Brazil, I was operating under the paradigm that if I achieved the
financial wealth that so many seem to be chasing, 'someday', when
I was 'successful', I would be in a position to enjoy the fruits of my
labour. For that reason I deferred the things I really wanted to do in
life to 'someday' and never felt capable of enjoying my day-to-day life.

Everyone who reads this book will have different hopes, goals
and dreams for their lives; all our dreams point back to the feelings
that we want to experience in life. The goal of losing weight isn't
about an actual number on the scales, but the feeling of confidence
we associate with seeing that number. The thought of making mil-
lions isn't about the numbers on the bank statement, but about the
feelings of accomplishment or security we associate with those numbers. By recognising the feelings we look to create through our lofty
goals and ambitions, we can aim to bring about those feelings in our
day-to-day lives, rather than deferring them to 'someday'.

Back to the pizza shop. Around that time I sat down and completed a journalling prompt called the 'perfect day' exercise, which
I'd seen shared by a speaker called Frank Kern. My life at the time
was everything I didn't want it to be. I lacked purpose, play, fulfilment, connection and confidence. I saw little reason to get up in the
morning and felt life was passing me by. This 'perfect day' exercise
allowed me the chance to take my attention away from all that wasn't
working and instead create an image of what true success would
look like to me. Despite having spent years up to that point reading

personal development, self-help and goal-setting books it became evident to me in completing the exercise that all the goals I had set in the past were influenced by societal standards and not by what I actually wanted.

For twelve full pages I wrote in vivid detail what a perfect day would look like for me in twelve months' time, from the moment I woke up in the morning to the time I went to bed at night. There wasn't any talk about fancy cars, big bank balances or external validation. Instead I wrote about how I woke up with energy excited for the day ahead and went to bed proud of how I had spent the day. I wrote much about how I enjoyed my work, how I prioritised my health and wellbeing and how I was surrounded by great people who inspired me in life. The compelling vision I crafted inspired me – it seemed so much more attainable and accessible than anything I had written down as a goal in the past. A large part of the exercise also revolved around writing how I wanted to feel.

This perfect day exercise and the feelings I identified as most important to me provided a map that I began following. Life is, after all, just a collection of days. It is important that we seize the day and not be caught living for tomorrow.

Success – What to Remember

● Our Perfectionist character will always look to shine light on where we have fallen short or failed to meet their expectations. The Perfectionist's expectations are largely based on how we compare or measure ourselves against others. Black-and-white thinking leaves little room between our perception of 'success' and 'failure', so it is important that we track and measure progress and not perfection. By identifying our 'hidden wins' we can learn and grow through our experience even when we feel we have fallen short on our definition of 'success'.

● The gap between where we are and where we would like to be lies in our skill sets and mindsets. As we consistently practise new skills we come to see ourselves and our capabilities in a new light. The challenge lies in the 'messy middle' where our Perfectionist struggles with the cognitive dissonance between our actions and our beliefs. In these times we must override the judgements of the Perfectionist and persevere through the 'messy middle'.

● By committing to the process and having a number of metrics for measuring success we can protect our confidence and not be deterred as we go through the 'messy middle'.

● In a world where information has never been as easily accessible, an ounce of action is worth a ton of thinking or analysing that information. It is important to acknowledge where we are caught up in acquiring more information and staying living in our heads as a means of avoiding the discomfort of getting started and applying what we already know.

● Success is often closer than we think, not far off in the distance at the end of the next grandiose goal. Ultimately all our goals and visions of what success would look like tie back to a feeling we want to experience. By recognising this feeling and 'practising' the feeling every day we can make success a daily experience and not something reserved for the future.

ARC EXERCISES

Begin by completing the following sentence stems in your journal:

- Success is …
- Writing/saying that makes me feel …

- I would know I was successful if …
- My relationship to failure is …
- If I was willing to embrace failure I …
- The person whose judgement I fear the most is …
- I fear that person's judgement because …

Illumination Exercise:
Success – The Perfect Day

For this illumination exercise I suggest you complete the 'perfect day' journalling prompt that had a big impact on my own life when I completed it for the first time. It is an exercise I come back to regularly to reorient myself and check in with what I want beyond the social conditioning that sometimes pulls me off track and into comparison to others. Like the fisherman who is clear about the life he wants to live and keeps his life simple, this type of exercise allows us the clarity to simplify our own lives and ensure that we are not getting caught up in chasing other people's dreams at the cost of our own.

For this exercise, fast-forward twelve months in your mind's eye and get as clear as you can on what a 'perfect average day' would look like from your first waking moment in the morning to your last waking moment at night. We are looking at the perfect 'average' day as opposed to a one-off out-of-the-ordinary day of vacation or celebration. What might your 'average' day look like if you felt you were living congruently and in alignment with your own values? What would true success look like to you?

Here are some of the factors you might consider:

- How would you start your day?
- Where would you be living?

- What time do you wake up?
- Would you wake up alone or next to someone?
- What would you have for breakfast?
- What would your morning routine look like?
- What would you do for work?
- Who do you work with?
- What impact do you feel you are having through your work?
- Who would you spend time with?
- Who is in your 'inner circle' of family, friends and loved ones?
- What do you talk about with these people?
- How do you feel about the relationships in your lives?
- What do you do for fun?
- What do you do with your free time?
- Do you have any fun hobbies?
- What does the end of your day look like?
- How do you wind down in the evening?
- What time do you go to bed?
- How do you feel as the day ends?

Journalling Prompts:
Success

1. Explore the origins of your Perfectionist character. Where might this character have formed? What early experiences influenced how this character perceives success and failure? How is your Perfectionist character currently limiting or holding you back in life?

2. What is your relationship with failure? Where has your fear of failure helped you at times in your life? Where has this fear of

failure held you back? What would an improved relationship with failure look in your future?

3. How have you measured success in recent years? Exploring the metrics by which you have measured success, how much of your success was governed by the desire to be seen to be successful by others versus truly feeling successful without the need for external validation? How might you measure your success going forward?

4. When we hear about 'fear of success' or 'fear of failure' we are often really talking about a fear of judgement and being seen to have failed or succeeded. Whose judgements do you fear in life? How does the fear of judgement limit you? What might be possible for you if you could let go of the fear of judgement?

5. The messy middle is that part of a new relationship, goal, journey, hobby or job in which we begin to question ourselves and our abilities. How do you usually react when self-doubt, impostor syndrome, fear or overwhelm emerge? How might you respond in an empowering way when you meet this messy middle in future endeavours?

6. In thinking about an area in which you have struggled to find consistency and create lasting change, explore the thoughts, stories, emotions, people or triggers that have led you off the course of consistency. What can you learn from these past struggles that can support you in your future efforts?

7. Hidden wins: think of an event or relationship that you may have labelled a failure. Recognising our tendency to use black-and-white thinking, look to explore the grey area by finding the positives that came from this event that you had previously presented as or labelled a failure.

Meditation of the Week:
Box Breathing

This week we will be using 'the box breath' as our simple meditation practice each day, again setting a timer for five to ten minutes and committing to this short practice of focusing our attention and 'downregulating' the nervous system, sending the body and mind into a state of 'rest and digest'.

We call this the box breath (or square breathing) because we will be 'drawing' a box with our breath.

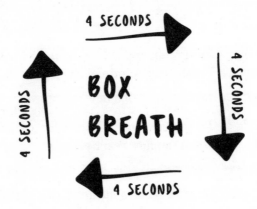

Place a hand on your belly and inhale through your nose for four seconds, bringing the breath low into the belly. Hold this inhale for four seconds before exhaling for a further four seconds. After your exhale hold for a further four seconds to complete your first 'box breath'. You will repeat this cadence of breathing for five to ten minutes, feeling yourself relax further with every breath.

If you find your mind wandering to the future or past or you notice any sensations in your body, simply bring your attention back to the count of the breath – inhale for four seconds, hold for four, exhale for four and hold for four.

The Confidence Story

'You have been criticising yourself for years and it hasn't worked. Try approving yourself and see what happens' – LOUISE HAY

'Those who always worry about what can go wrong might be well prepared against dangers but will never know how enjoyable life can be' – MIHALY CSIKSZENTMIHALYI

MEET THE CHARACTER – THE INNER CRITIC

Imagine how difficult it would be to navigate life with someone following you around looking over your shoulder and sharing a constant barrage of criticism and negative judgement. If such a person really were to follow us around we would quickly report them or perhaps turn to our Brazilian jiu-jitsu skills to put them in their place. Of course this character does exist for us all.

The Inner Critic, like all our characters, does have positive intent. Though their barrage of judgements might easily be labelled 'negative thinking', we might rephrase this as 'protective thinking' and then wonder what it is they are trying to protect us from. Our Inner Critic brings up defence mechanisms in the form of old stories, beliefs and thoughts which, though hugely outdated, feel as real and up to date as can be. Their hope is that by telling us fear-based stories about our limitations they can stop us stepping into the unknown and keep us within the safety of our comfort zones and routine.

Perhaps the Inner Critic remembers standing in front of the class and reading from a textbook only to be laughed at and ridiculed for stumbling over the words. Now, many years later, we have a belief that only 'confident' people can do public speaking or work presentations and that we 'don't have' that same confidence. While others seem to take this in their stride, we feel bogged down by the noisy barrage of critique from the Inner Critic. It might be twenty years on from the school incident but perhaps that is the last time we allowed ourselves to practise public speaking and thus that memory feels as real today as a grown adult as it did as a young child.

In listening to and believing the Inner Critic we become stuck in a cycle of non-action. This non-action yields no new results and thus our confidence remains stagnant or diminishes. Confidence is in large part a result of competence. We feel confident in the things we know we can do competently. In other words, we get better at the things that we practise.

Recognising that the Inner Critic is stuck in old memories and understanding, that we improve at what we practise and that we must be willing to start from where we are, we can begin to come to a new understanding about where confidence is found and how it is cultivated.

REDEFINING CONFIDENCE

I am coming towards the end of a short session I am delivering as a guest speaker at a wellness workshop with over four hundred people in attendance. After a thirty-minute talk on improving our relationship with ourselves, the floor is opened up for questions and a girl near the front row stands up to take the microphone. After telling me that she has no confidence she breaks down in tears and asks what she can do to build her self-belief and self-esteem. Perhaps in seeing me share from the stage I am someone she has labelled a 'confident' person.

Her perception or external view of me is, however, quite far removed from my own internal feelings and stories. In reality my own internal experience before going on stage to speak to a room full of people is often a strange cocktail of self-doubt and fear that slowly transmutes to acceptance, excitement and ease as I stay the course despite my initial discomfort. I have learnt and look to continually remind myself that feelings of self-doubt and fear are temporary and can be acknowledged but should not always be believed or acted upon.

Public speaking was without a doubt one of my biggest fears in life. I did not show up to school or college if there was ever a presentation to be given and it wasn't until I was twenty-five that I braved speaking in front of a group for ten minutes – albeit with a shaky voice and dangerously elevated heart rate. For a long time I assumed that, in the same way as some people seem to be naturally great public speakers or naturally good at learning languages, some were naturally confident individuals. I initially labelled myself someone who didn't have confidence, but this, like so many of the stories I had told myself for so long, was inaccurate.

If I had waited until I found what I thought confidence was before I set out on the public speaking journey, I would still be waiting. Our skewed ideas around what confidence 'should' look like can be the very thing that stops us getting started. The longer I wait for confidence to show up, the longer I live in my head. The longer I live in my head, the more airtime I give to my Inner Critic character who provides self-doubting commentary and a collection of stories and narratives about 'not being enough'.

In response to the lady's question around where she could find self-esteem and self-belief, I am quick to remind her that standing up, as she has, and speaking on a microphone in front of hundreds of people requires confidence and is something most people wouldn't be willing to do. Unbeknownst to herself, she has just demonstrated the very thing she feels is missing. Everyone else in the room sees confidence, but internally she identifies with the temporary feelings of fear and overwhelm that sometimes come up for her.

Much like the concepts of happiness and success, confidence is often mistaken for something that lives outside ourselves, some-where in the future, at the end of the next achievement or goal. In a world where so much of our attention is facing outwards, there is also the issue of comparison and the tendency to place others on pedestals and convince ourselves that confidence in life is something that comes naturally to or is reserved for a select few. Our tendency to compare our efforts or abilities to others' takes us away from our own journey and we become caught in a game that we cannot ever win. When I compare my results, efforts, qualities or abilities to others', I am always moving the goalposts on what I need to achieve in order for me to feel confident.

Imagine a child coming home from school and talking about the progress they'd made with their schoolwork that day, only for their parent to ask, 'Well, what are you going to do tomorrow?' without any acknowledgement of their progress; you might deem the parent quite harsh. Our Inner Critic operates in a similar way, always looking where we've fallen short or not done enough. Just as the child's confidence is built through acknowledgement of their own unique progress, we can build our own confidence by taking a step back from what everyone else is doing, acknowledging where we are on our own journey and then mapping, planning and seeing the small steps forward that help us find momentum and flow in life.

FINDING YOUR FLOW

Positive psychologist Mihaly Csikszentmihalyi's concept of 'flow' outlines the altered states of consciousness in which we become fully immersed in whatever activity we are doing at that moment. You will perhaps have heard of this state in the context of an athlete or performer being 'in the zone'. In these states of flow we often lose track of time, become oblivious to the outside world and lose our sense of self. In moments when we feel 'self-conscious' we have become very aware of ourselves as individuals and very caught up in the ego, and we experience noisy self-doubt. In moments of flow and losing our sense of self, we quieten the voices of the ego and particularly the Inner Critic as we become fully involved and focused on whatever we are doing in that moment, connected to life in the present moment. This presence is in contrast to the norm of being stuck in stories in our heads based on the future or the past. Needless to say, these 'flow states' are addictive and can provide a welcome break from distraction and overthinking!

We have all had these states at times without consciously looking

for them. Some find flow states through music or sport, others
through creative projects, art or work. They might even come in
the simple experience of being completely immersed in conversation
with a friend and feeling time and internal chatter disappear as we
become fully engaged in the present moment.

These peak states have been linked to increased satisfaction,
self-actualisation, creativity and fulfilment and may also provide
some clues as to where we might develop our confidence in given
areas. In recognising the moments in which we have found flow in
the past, we can look to reverse-engineer the process and allow for
more of it in our lives as a means of 'getting out of our own way',
lowering the volume of the Inner Critic and moving into growth
and uncertainty with confidence.

Csikszentmihalyi's 'flow state scale' gives us a means of understanding the times in which we are most likely to find flow and get
'into the zone'. Along the bottom axis of the chart is our level of skill
with a given task; the side axis shows the level of challenge involved
with that task.

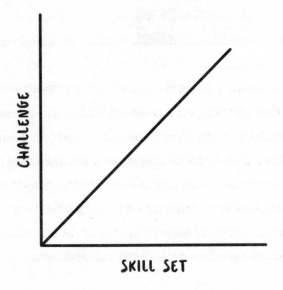

When we are completing tasks below our level of skill on a consistent basis we find ourselves falling into boredom and perhaps even apathy. Imagine completing the same physical workout for the next twelve months without any attempts to progress. Perhaps that workout provides some initial challenge to begin with, but as our skill set increases the challenge decreases and in time we fall into a rut disguised as a routine. Without growth or progression we wouldn't expect much in terms of increased confidence, and the lack of challenge in our lives leads to our Inner Critic getting plenty of air time and commentary on our lack of progress.

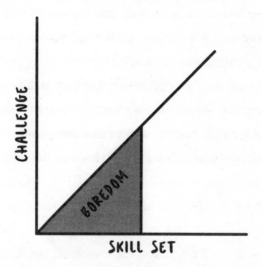

Perhaps wanting to 'shake things up', we commit to a change in our routine and take on a workout far beyond our current skill set. Coming back to the flow state scale, we see that when we find ourselves taking on tasks far above our current level of skill we fall into feelings of anxiety that generally lead to overwhelm and a retreat back to the boredom or burnout state. Again, the Inner Critic character is quick to remind us that we 'failed' in our efforts to create change and are better off back in our comfort zone.

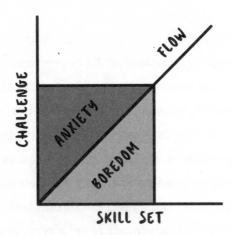

A little like the black-and-white thinking phenomenon in the last chapter, in efforts to find fulfilment and growth in life we sometimes jump to big changes and are left overwhelmed and in cycles of being 'off' and 'on' different wagons rather than in a consistent state of growth and progress. This cycle of being 'off' and 'on' the wagon heightens beliefs that we are inconsistent or cannot trust ourselves in our efforts. As a result our confidence is compromised.

In reflecting on times in our lives when we have felt most confident we will see times when we experienced growth and progress in a certain area. It might be something as simple as learning to tie your shoelaces as a child. The first time we try it seems near impossible, but with practice and competence we find confidence. Perhaps we forget that in areas in which we struggle with confidence, our challenge has simply been lack of practice.

Recognising that seeing progress and growth provides a great level of confidence, we can see how switching our approach and finding the 'sweet spot' of flow between boredom and anxiety might place us in a position of quieting the inner critic and finding consistent progress in our efforts, with confidence as the reward. At times in life, it can feel that we have got stuck at a certain level where our skill sets are no longer being forced to expand unless pushed to a level that feels overwhelming and frustratingly difficult!

When we think of our own lives and areas where we are feeling a little flat or empty, we might consider where we are spending time on the chart of comfort, panic and stretch. In comfort there is no requirement for growth, so we feel stagnant. In panic it's all just a little too much too soon and we're left overwhelmed and feeling 'less than'. When we find the sweet spot of the stretch zone, we're going a little beyond our current ability in a way that allows us to see progress and growth that yields confidence and fulfilment.

An ongoing commitment to life in this stretch zone of 'flow' in any area of life will yield almost unrecognisable results over a relatively short period of time. Much of what I learnt in my early days in the fitness industry translates across many areas in life. Among these lessons is 'progressive overload', the idea that the body adapts to whatever stimulus is placed upon it consistently over time. Again, much like our comfort and panic zones, we might see that no load or stimulus placed on the body will lead to no physical adaptation; a big jump in demands on the body will lead to injury. Thus, the secret is progressive overload, the stretch zone of adding a little more weight or a few more repetitions consistently over time, allowing the body to find a 'new normal'.

This principle of 'progressive overload' was demonstrated in the story of Milo of Croton, a sixth-century BC wrestler, who was a six-time Olympic champion. According to legend, Milo had trained as a young man by carrying a calf daily until it became full grown. Of course, the calf would have felt light on his shoulders those first few weeks, but as the calf grew, so did Milo's strength. There wasn't ever a huge leap in the calf's growth overnight, but over months and years, as the calf grew into a fully grown ox, Milo's muscles (skill set) were forced to strengthen to meet the increasing challenge. The lessons from Milo's story point to the importance of consistency and patience. We might consider where in our own lives we could add this little bit of progressive overload and how that might positively impact our confidence and results in the coming twelve months.

In the last chapter I mentioned the idea of the one-hundred-hour challenge in which you might commit two hours a week for the next year to some skill or area in which you would like to see improvements, growth and progress. I mentioned the idea of just committing to the one hundred hours and avoiding any expectations or comparison to others. Just showing up consistently and being in the process. Now, if we were to partner the hundred-hour challenge with the idea of living in the stretch zone I think you would be amazed at the progress you would see in any area of life and the confidence that would come with it.

We could pick a skill we want to improve at and live in a comfort zone for the one hundred hours, not making any progress or having any need to grow and develop, just looking to clock up the hours for the sake of saying we did our one hundred hours. (As I write that I have flashbacks of teachers telling us in school, 'You're here for the next hour, you might as well put in a bit of effort. You're not wasting my time, you're wasting your own!') Equally, I could get caught in comparisons and jump in at the deep end too quickly with a challenge far beyond my starting point. If we can be honest with ourselves about where our comfort zone lies and we can step to the edge and continually lean in, it is amazing the progress that can be seen in a relatively short period.

Think of your comfort zone as a circle. Imagine that every time you take a step out to the edge that circle expands slightly, and every time you 'refuse the inner calling' the circle retracts back in. The goal is not to jump out of our comfort zone, but to stretch that comfort zone consistently to the point that what once seemed impossible is now just another day!

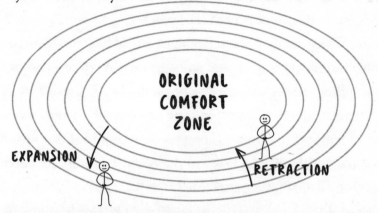

Collecting Confidence
(two-minute exercise)

Consider how we sometimes treat ourselves and how, despite accomplishing a great number of things in the day, our Inner Critic constantly expects more, without any acknowledgement of our progress.

As a simple means of developing our confidence we can begin looking backwards before looking forwards. In looking backwards we have the opportunity to 'collect confidence' and can quickly cultivate positive emotions by simply asking:

1. What progress did I make today?
2. Why and where is this progress relevant?
3. How can I build upon this progress tomorrow?

INTEGRITY AND CORE VALUES

Just as we develop confidence in our relationships with others through time, presence and curiosity, we come to know and trust ourselves only by taking time to listen, reflect and practise self-honesty and true self-care. As we slow down, reflect and create space for ourselves we gain clarity as to what is most inspiring and important to us in life.

We began this journey in the Happiness chapter where we looked at some of the meaningful challenges we would like to take on in the coming months. It is in recognising our own ambitions and needs and fulfilling those needs that we begin to develop greater levels of confidence and self-esteem. Ignoring or overlooking our needs in place of temporary comfort, acceptance or approval is a sure-fire recipe for self-doubt and leads to the real discomfort that comes from living a life that is out of integrity.

We can think of integrity as our thoughts, words and actions being in alignment. If I were to say that my friends and family were my main priority in life but my actions demonstrated otherwise, it could be said that I am out of integrity. Similarly, if I daydream all day every day about starting my own business but never take a step towards making that reality, I will feel a similar internal conflict and disconnect due to the discrepancy between my thoughts, words and actions.

Great emotional cost comes with being out of integrity; it is an internal battle that provides fuel for the Inner Critic who is quick to remind us of our shortcomings and lack of commitment to ourselves and our truth. Put most simply, our confidence results from listening to ourselves and consistently showing up for ourselves while aligning our thoughts, words and actions to live in integrity. We must catch ourselves falling into comparison and instead come back to listening and acting on our internal voice with a commitment to time spent in the stretch zone that brings a sense of growth and confidence.

A consistent commitment over time to showing up for myself results in what looks like a big jump in confidence. Suppressing my own needs or ignoring my inner voice for a prolonged period of time will manifest as a big jump in self-doubt. That is to say, confidence is a practice, not something that we inherently have or do not have. Like Milo carrying the calf consistently every day until it has grown into an ox, the small things we do or do not do daily are what feed either our sense of confidence or our Inner Critic.

My own quest for external approval and validation ended up putting my own insecurities under a large magnifying glass rather than eliminating them. We can't outrun ourselves or lie to ourselves about the life we wish to live. As the great Bob Marley once said, 'Don't gain the world and lose your soul, wisdom is better than silver or gold.' In this case we can think of wisdom as having good judgement and there is no better judgement than listening to and trusting yourself.

In order to develop confidence in ourselves we must develop a consistent practice of checking in on our needs and then taking action to support those needs. Our commitment to staying on our own path when it seems easier to seek short-term pleasure or external validation is where our confidence lives.

We've already outlined a few meaningful challenges that we would like to pursue in the coming months and seen that success is movement in the direction of that which is meaningful to us. We have said that even with precise clarity about some of the new ambitions we would like to pursue in life, we are met with the challenge of our strong addiction to our current identity.

Despite the best of intentions and clearest of plans we can often find ourselves tackling self-doubt, overwhelm or incessant chatter from the Inner Critic. In these moments our logical plans and thinking often go out of the window as our internal chatter and emotions take the wheel, seemingly intent on pulling us off course.

For many of us, our actions in life are governed largely by our feelings. When we feel motivated we take certain actions, when we feel flat we take others. Most of us are driven mainly by compulsive and impulsive behaviours, habits, feelings and expectations we've placed upon ourselves based on societal or familial conditioning. Many of these ways of acting are reactions rather than responses. We can think of reactions as being unconscious habits from our past and responses as being conscious choices for our future. When we live in a constant state of reaction we find ourselves caught in cycles, creating similar results in different scenarios. When we begin to respond instead, we start to rewrite our patterns and make way for new results.

An example of these reactions and responses might be seen in our relationship to conflict, something we'll talk about later in the book. Most of us have an unconscious response, a reaction that surfaces when we get defensive or feel threatened. A lack of awareness of how we react can leave us recreating the same cycles and patterns in different relationships. When we become clear on the future we are trying to create we shift from reaction to response, thinking not about survival and the thing we've always done, but about a new way of dealing with the same type of external challenge.

A huge percentage of our daily thoughts and actions are based on autopilot conditioning and patterns of the past as opposed to a clear vision and focus for the future. Making the shift to values-based decisions can help us stay connected to our future vision even when self-doubt and old narratives arise. Knowing and choosing to act on our core values is also a means of overriding the thoughts, stories or feelings that seem to want to pull us off course. To override our feelings is not to ignore, deny or repress them, but to act in spite of them. To go beyond our internal narrative or challenging thoughts is not to villainise those thoughts but to choose to see them as just thoughts and not something we have to believe or act on. Perhaps today I acknowledge that I am feeling a little apathetic and I recognise that the voice in my head is telling me to stay in bed for the day. Without making these thoughts and feelings 'wrong' or trying to push them away I can instead choose to take actions governed by my values and future vision and not my temporary feelings and internal narratives.

I recently invited my friend Brian Pennie for a guest training with one of my men's groups. After fifteen years of chronic heroin addiction Brian became clean and found a completely new lease of life. He's since gone on to pursue a PhD in neuroscience and wrote a brilliant book, *Bonus Time*, in which he shares the beautiful message that 'change is possible'. A question from the group about how Brian stayed consistent and overcame such a strong addiction opened the conversation into 'values-based decisions'. Brian talked about how reminding himself of his values provided a means of seeing past his temporary thoughts and feelings which might often try to pull him back to his past.

When we rely on certain feelings to show up on a given day in order for us to take action, we're always rolling the dice and will most likely fall into autopilot habits. We might have the best plan in the world, but when inevitable stress or fear emerges as we step into new territory, emotions can overtake logic and we can find ourselves stuck in old stories. A reliance on having to feel a certain way in order to take action can quickly hinder any confidence we do feel and leave us relying on hope as a strategy. When we instead begin to live in accordance with our values, we can find consistency and create lasting change.

Living in accordance with our values isn't always easy, of course; in fact, it's rarely easy. We are creatures of habit and seek comfort and familiarity above all else. However, knowing our values enables us to develop an internal compass that guides us in the direction of doing what creates meaning in our lives, not what creates short-term comfort for the sake of comfort.

Take the example of someone who goes to the gym when they feel motivated but skips it when the motivation isn't there. After the initial January motivation wears off, self-talk of 'I never stay consistent' or 'The results aren't coming quick enough' leads to feelings of frustration and disappointment, which in turn leads them to give up on their plans. This is an example of someone acting in line with their feelings or stories. If this same person were to identify that one of their values is 'consistency' or 'decisiveness' and they learnt to fall back on this value rather than falling back on a temporary feeling, it is likely they will actually create the feeling they were waiting for in the action they take.

Or there's the person who'd love to get up to sing karaoke but has a million horror stories in their head about how they'll be judged. Again, this person's behaviour is being influenced by their current self-image based on their past experiences of life. If that person identifies a value of 'adventure' in their life they'll perhaps be willing to see the karaoke opportunity as a chance to try something new and practise being 'adventurous' in spite of their nerves.

Values-based decisions allow us to act in a way that brings long-term meaning over short-term pleasure. It is in this long-term meaning that we find the happiness we are all seeking. These values can and will change over time. At the time of writing I'm reminding myself daily of the value I place upon courage, curiosity and compassion. There are times where I feel like judging myself or others, but I remind myself that I place a value on compassion and so I look to understand rather than judge. I value curiosity, so rather than beat myself up about not having achieved what I set out to achieve in the day I get curious and ask myself, 'What can I learn from this?' I get scared often, experience impostor syndrome and doubt my work, but I remind myself that I am courageous and willing to lean in to my edge and fail or learn publicly.

Many of our 'thoughts' are really just memories resurfacing, so we can find ourselves caught in patterns and cycles for years or decades, not recognising that it is our scared younger self who is showing up, not our current self. After being bullied at a young age I developed a belief that I didn't fit in, something I carried with me for years, decades even. I would meet friends or connect with people but in the back of my mind unconsciously believe that I was an outsider or that I could not trust people. I stepped into dozens of new environments but was always met with the same internal narratives of voices from my past who tried to keep me safe by keeping anyone I met at arm's length.

In recognising this pattern in my life I could see that it was something I would continually repeat until I chose to take back the pen and rewrite the script. In deciding that I wanted the next chapter of my life to be about connecting more deeply with people in my life and trusting them, I outlined 'connection', 'trust' and 'collaboration' as values that I would embrace and lean into. But because our conditioning is so strong, despite being very clear on my desire to connect more deeply with people, whenever I was invited to a party or event my old stories of fear, mistrust and isolation would surface. It was in these moments that I would fall back on my values of trust, collaboration and connection and act in accordance with those rather than the old outdated beliefs and stories. I see acting against these values as a sure-fire way of chipping away at my self-esteem and confidence and acting in line with these values as a means of developing greater levels of self-trust and self-esteem.

When you look at some of the challenges you outlined in the Happiness chapter or think of the bigger picture – what you'd like to do with your future – there are no doubt some outdated stories that will look to pull you back to your past and some old conditioning that will go against your new ambitions. This is where we'll look to pinpoint the values that will help us build confidence, self-esteem and new results in life.

At the end of this chapter we will complete an exercise in which I will help you identify some of the values which will serve as a moral internal compass to keep you on track towards a life that is true to your inner voice. Of course, as with any of these awareness-type exercises, knowing is not enough; we have to put our new insights into action and consistently put these values into practice for them to become our 'new normal'.

This can start with putting your three to five top values on your mirror and checking in with them every day, morning and night, as you brush your teeth. In the morning as an example – 'How can I bring my values of playfulness, adventure and decisiveness into my interactions and experiences today?' – and rounding off the day with a similar question – 'How did I demonstrate and live my values today?' These twice-daily reminders place the importance and significance of our values constantly at the front of our mind.

When we think of the word 'fulfilment' we can think of it as meaning 'to be filled from within'. In other words, fulfilment results from living a life of thoughts, words and actions that are true to our values. Picture an empty bucket that is filled with thoughts, words and actions, and when that bucket is full it represents fulfilment in your life. Fulfilment is the result of living an integral life of alignment based on your values. Now consider that that bucket may have some holes in it. Despite taking actions in line with your values and filling the bucket, there are perhaps other actions being taken that go against your values. These are the leaking points of the bucket!

Coming back to an earlier point, we can think of the thoughts, words and actions that fill the bucket as being aligned actions that build confidence and the thoughts, words or actions that go against our values as robbing us of confidence.

Confidence – What to Remember

- Confidence is a by-product of self-awareness, self-trust and self-acceptance. Our confidence in the relationship we have with another person is based largely on the fact that we know we can rely on them to show up when they said they would. Similarly, we build our own confidence by developing that self-trust in showing up consistently for the things that we know will benefit our health, wellbeing and happiness. As with any relationship, these commitments to self can start small and will build over time as we learn to trust and deepen the relationship.

- Our Inner Critic character narrates stories of being 'less than' or not being enough. Their 'negative thoughts', which can feel debilitating, are really just an outdated defence mechanism designed to keep us safe from feelings of judgement, ridicule or abandonment. The Inner Critic's volume tends to be turned up when given too much time to think about the area of concern. In recognising the Inner Critic's chatter as a defence mechanism we can allow it to have its say, but can question and challenge its outlook. One of the best ways to challenge the beliefs of the Inner Critic is through action, no matter how small, to develop our self-trust and confidence.

- Picture a child who is scared on the first day of school and requires encouragement from their parental figure to lean in to their fear and trust that it will turn out well. The child's fears, just like our own current fears, are simply stories being built about the future. Their lack of confidence stems from a lack of evidence or experience to find faith in. The parent's encouragement helps the child to lean into discomfort and reap the benefits of their new chapter and environment. We can think of ourselves as that young child in the moments when we struggle with confidence. When the Inner Critic's stories surface, we must gently remind ourselves that, like the child on their first day of school, it's never as bad as we think it's going to be! At times when we want to harness confidence we may fall back on reminders of times when we have acted in faith and reaped the rewards.

- We can often feel guilt or shame when we are out of integrity with our own core values. These feelings of being out of integrity or alignment create one of the biggest 'leakers' of confidence in our lives. If we think of confidence and fulfilment as the result of recognising and acting on our core values, those values can serve as an internal compass that helps us act in spite of stories of self-doubt or difficult feelings. Remember, our stories and feelings are temporary and short term, while our core values point to our more long-term desires.

- Our confidence is built through recognising the progress we are making in a given area of life. In order to develop further confidence we must lean into growth consistently and give ourselves the space to recognise our improvement. The concept of 'flow' reminds us that there is a sweet spot for growth in which the tasks we are completing lie just a little beyond our current skill set, forcing us to grow but not to a point that is overwhelming. Look to explore where in life you are in this stretch zone and where you may be stuck in a comfort zone or panic zone.

- Our certainty is found in the past, not the future. As such it is essential that we round out each day with reflection of what was done well and what we learnt from that day's experience. In the same way as children are encouraged in school through positive encouragement, which builds confidence, we must acknowledge our own progress and not get caught up in the black-and-white thinking of perfectionism.

ARC EXERCISES

Begin by completing the following sentence stems in your journal:

- I feel most confident when …
- More confidence would allow me to …
- Writing that makes me feel …
- I feel most in flow when …
- I would get into flow more if …
- Something that negatively affects my confidence is …
- I would feel more confident if …

Illumination Exercise:
Confidence – Your Core Values

For this illumination exercise, I want you to imagine you are at a celebratory event ten years from now. Maybe it's your birthday party or an event to celebrate a milestone or accomplishment in your life. You are surrounded by family, friends and people from your wider community. Everyone is in great spirits and you feel inspired and grateful to be surrounded by so many amazing people. It is exciting to think that all these people have come together to celebrate you.

After dinner someone from your family gets up to make a speech. In that speech they honour you and talk about the person that you've become and all that you've done over the last ten years. They share their appreciation for being related to you. They talk about how you've grown, how you've supported them, and they honour the person you've become. Everyone raises their glass and shares a toast to you as your family member finishes their speech.

Next, a close friend stands up to share their appreciation for you. They talk about what it's like to be your friend and they share some stories from the last ten years. Your heart is full as you hear their gratitude for you.

Then a colleague, or someone from the wider community, stands up and talks about the impact you've had beyond your immediate family and friends. You watch others in the room beaming with pride as they hear stories they may not have even been aware of about the impact you've had on your wider community.

Finally, it's your turn to stand up. You look around at the smiling faces and recognise how much love there is for you in the room. Your own speech gives you a chance to acknowledge what you're most grateful for in life and what you are most proud of. You share some of the highlights from the last ten years and really allow yourself to be seen and acknowledged for the work that you've done and the person you have become.

Now close your eyes and think about each of these four speeches. I'd like you to give yourself some time to write about what stands out to you the most from each speech. What did you hear from family, friends and other loved ones that filled you with pride? What are you most proud of and grateful for from the last ten years? What have you overcome and how have you grown? Write down anything that feels relevant and inspiring to you.

After giving yourself at least twenty minutes to write and really reflect on what's come up for you, I want you to look back over your notes and highlight any of the words, traits, accomplishments or themes that stand out. These highlights start to provide us with a map for our purposeful life driven by our values.

Finally, outline the three to five values or traits you most connect with. Waiting and spectating stop now. From this day forward, commit to living and embodying these values by asking, 'How can I live these traits today?'

Perhaps consider putting these values on a Post-it note and sticking it to your mirror, or use them as a screensaver on your phone or computer home screen.

Journalling Prompts:
Confidence

1. Get to know your Inner Critic character by exploring some of the stories they tell you. To identify these stories, look at an area of life in which you struggle and ask, 'What story do I tell myself around my struggles in this area?' Assuming the Inner Critic

has positive intent, what are they trying to protect you from by telling you these stories?

2. Make a list of at least twenty accomplishments from your life that you are really proud of. These might be related to health, relationships, career, finances, contribution or any other area that is important to you.

3. If you were to meet your ten-year-old self for a hot chocolate today, what would they be most proud of in terms of how you've grown, what you've accomplished and how you have lived your life up to this point?

4. Make a list of all of your positive traits, characteristics and strengths. If you struggle to think of more than a few, imagine stepping into a friend's shoes and writing the positive traits, characteristics and strengths that they see in you.

5. What would life look like twelve months from now if you made a commitment to acting in line with your core values every day and not being thrown off course by your Inner Critic?

6. Think of an area of life in which you could move from your comfort zone to your stretch zone. How might you challenge yourself in this area to encourage personal growth? If you were to continually live in this stretch zone, where might you end up twelve months now in that area of life?

7. A lot of confidence in life is a result of self-acceptance, which means accepting all parts of ourselves, not just the parts that we have labelled 'positive'. Write about some of the areas of life in which you have struggled to find self-acceptance and how you might bring more compassion and understanding to these parts of yourself.

Meditation of the Week:
Finding the Gap

This week our meditation focuses on 'finding the gap'. Again, I would encourage you to complete this practice daily and to set a timer for ten minutes.

Between our inhale and exhale there is a little natural gap or space, 'the space between'.

Last week, with the box breath, we consciously stayed in this space for four seconds after our inhale and four seconds after our exhale. This week, we will simply close our eyes and breathe naturally, in and out through the nose.

For a few breaths just follow the breath as it comes in through the nostrils and notice where it ends up in the body, then follow it back out as you exhale slightly warmer air through the nostrils. You do not need to change the breath in any way, only to follow it in and out of the body.

After a few breaths, once you feel settled, begin to notice the 'gap', that little space at the top of the inhale and bottom of the exhale where you are neither inhaling or exhaling. You won't be consciously pausing or trying to force this 'gap'; it is already there, so you are simply noticing it. Each time you notice or find that gap it becomes more familiar and, with practice, you will find yourself experiencing more and more stillness.

The Emotions Story

'So when you are listening to somebody, completely,
attentively, then you are listening not only to
the words, but also to the feeling of what is being
conveyed, to the whole of it, not part of it'
– JIDDU KRISHNAMURTI

'One ought to hold on to one's heart; for if one lets it
go, one soon loses control of the head too'
– FRIEDRICH NIETZSCHE

MEET THE CHARACTER – THE FIXER

We all form an understanding and collection of stories of what our emotions mean in our early years and we generally put our many emotions into the brackets of either good or bad, right or wrong. Our good emotions are those that are acceptable and approved of by others; the bad emotions are the ones we notice tend to make others feel uncomfortable or tend to lead to others withdrawing their love or approval.

Perhaps we notice that our anger, sadness, loneliness or depression are rarely welcomed and are negatively judged by others and thus we perhaps unconsciously decide to box them off and make them 'wrong'. As a result a character forms in our mind who is quick to notice when a 'bad' emotion arises and looks to get past the emotion as quickly as possible. I call this character the Fixer. The Fixer is a little bit like a friend who gets very uncomfortable when you tell them about something you're struggling with and goes straight to offering solutions before even listening long enough to understand what you are experiencing. Although the friend may think they are helping and supporting us, their approach can seem quite cold and detached and the lack of empathy and effort to understand us can leave us feeling disconnected, isolated, possibly even ashamed of what we have shared.

The Fixer character takes much the same approach internally, going straight to problem-solving before listening to, accepting and gaining an understanding of what the emotion is. As a result, we often find ourselves in destructive or addictive patterns in an effort to quickly escape the emotions we have made 'wrong'.

I'm bored, and the Fixer encourages me to pick up my phone and scroll. I try to sit and meditate for a few minutes, but when a feeling of sadness emerges the Fixer tells me to get up and carry on with my to-do list. I feel a little anger rising up in me and the Fixer says it's time for a bottle of wine. Though I may experience temporary relief in the moment as I escape the difficult emotion, acting on the requests of the Fixer deprives me of my chance to gain a better understanding of myself, my needs and my patterns. By quickly going to an external solution for an internal challenge I become further disconnected from myself.

Our closest intimate relationships with others are built not only on the good times of happiness and joy but also in the difficult moments when we provide or receive support through struggle and adversity. Our own intimate relationship with ourselves is similar. When we recognise that the Fixer is trying to run from discomfort like a fair-weather friend who only seems to be there when it suits them, we can instead choose to bring compassion and support to all parts of ourselves and our emotional experience. When we are aware that the Fixer is turning up, we can press pause and choose to consciously check in rather than unconsciously check out through destructive and disempowering addictive behaviours. This willingness to be with all of our emotions is the path of true self-love and self-acceptance.

EMOTIONAL AWARENESS

Simply put, my own story in younger years around difficult or 'negative' emotions was that they were 'bad' and got in the way. As a result, when feelings of loneliness, sadness or overwhelm emerged I did all I could to suppress, repress or deny them. Certain feelings just didn't seem acceptable, useful or something that 'successful' and 'happy' people dealt with. All the books and self-help gurus had told me to think positive, so when negative thoughts or feelings emerged I would make every effort to bypass or outrun them.

We can think of toxic positivity as the idea that we should always be 'positive' or take a positive outlook irrespective of how dire the situation might be. Ironically my efforts at positivity left me feeling worse about myself when I didn't feel positive all the time. As a result a bad hour would often turn into a bad day that bled into a bad week. While in reality these emotions were popping up as signposts to what I needed at the time to care for myself, I chose instead to deny them, leading to destructive patterns and addictive behaviours, which left me further disconnected from myself.

Without an understanding of and willingness to bring awareness to our emotions we can often feel that they run our lives. 'Positive' emotions tend to promote 'positive actions', while 'negative' emotions can seem to throw us completely off course.

Just as we have a tendency to go from awareness of our beliefs and stories to identifying with and believing our beliefs and stories, we also tend to go to identifying with our emotions rather than simply bringing awareness to them. If we have a physical injury such as a broken arm, we say, 'I have a broken arm', not 'I am a broken arm'. But when we experience feelings of anxiety we often say, 'I am anxious,' rather than 'I am experiencing some anxiety.' This identification can become overwhelming and make us feel as if we have been taken over by and are at the complete mercy of this temporary emotion. Instead of identifying with these emotions, we often look to disassociate from them completely and repress them, seeing them as *in* the way, not *on* the way.

If we go to the gym, pick up a small injury and decide to ignore it and continue training, we're at risk of doing ourselves long-term damage. The small injury in itself is our body telling us what we need – rest and recovery. If we listen to the body and give it the rest it needs we'll generally bounce back fairly quickly to full health. This example is easy and clear to understand in the context of a physical injury, but what if we took the same approach with our emotions?

If we recognise the intelligence, inner wisdom and huge amount of energy associated with our difficult emotions and understand that each emotion has a particular job and role to play, we can take a new approach to our relationship with the wide spectrum of emotions and allow ourselves to become more whole in the process. My new story around all difficult emotions is that they provide an invitation.

The invitation is to listen and connect back to myself, or to ignore and self-abandon.

As kids we are completely dependent on our primary caregivers to help us meet our needs. As adults it is our responsibility to become attuned to our own feelings and become our own carers. Denying our feelings is like a parent ignoring their child's cries for help or us listening to a friend who is struggling but choosing to ignore them and not offer any support. We need to give up on this denial or shaming of difficult emotions and see them as a healthy part of the human condition that, when listened to, can provide innate wisdom.

A temporary feeling of anxiety is perhaps our body's way of telling us that we've taken on too much work and need to slow down. Do we listen, become curious and ask what the emotion might be pointing to, or do we label it 'bad' and move to an addictive behaviour instead, in an effort to find temporary relief?

Feelings of anger, which we may have labelled as 'wrong' or 'bad', might just be a nudge to improve our boundaries, express ourselves honestly and tell people what is okay or not okay for us. Choosing to repress or deny that anger might make us feel that we're doing the right thing, but 'what we resist will persist' and that anger will most likely be directed towards ourselves for not expressing our needs, or come out as an explosion of toxic anger directed at the wrong person.

Every emotion serves a purpose and can be expressed in a mature and healthy way, but when they are denied or repressed these very same emotions can become toxic and unhealthy. A great deal of energy is required to hide our emotions from others and even from ourselves.

The analogy of the beachball is often used in the context of emotional regulation. If we're at the beach and we're experiencing difficult feelings of anxiety, worry and overwhelm –despite the sun shining and everything in the external world looking like it 'should' make for a relaxing day – we may make these emotions 'wrong' and decide to try and hide them. Imagine placing all these difficult emotions inside a beachball and heading out to the sea to try to sink it. As we push the ball under water, it pops back up to the surface. No matter how many times we try to make the beachball disappear, it stubbornly re-emerges from below the water. The more effort we make to push it down, the more energy it generates and the more forcefully it comes back to the surface. Realising that we can't sink the beachball, we might instead choose to come back to the beach and sit with the ball, looking for its valve before gently deflating it.

Mirroring this metaphor to our emotions, we might recognise that these efforts to hide, deny or bury our emotions require a huge amount of energy, and ultimately prove ineffective. If we instead sat for a few minutes with the emotion and looked for its 'valve' we could perhaps quickly move to self-care and reclaim the energy that was being used to try to keep it hidden.

Maybe consider the lightness you have felt after allowing yourself to cry after a period of built-up frustration, sadness or anger. Or consider how exhausted we can become after a time of trying to resist and outwork feelings of stress or overwhelm. There is a great deal of energy to be regained by removing the resistance and moving from repression to the healthy expression of our emotions.

'FINE' ISN'T A FEELING:
EMOTIONAL LITERACY

'How do you feel, Pat?'

'I feel good …' I quickly respond.

'Good isn't a feeling, it's a word.'

'Oh, you're right. I don't feel good, I feel fine.'

'Also not a feeling …'

I'm in New York for some work and staying with my friend Hallie Rose in Brooklyn for a week. Hallie is a yogi, a coach and a writer who's very much in tune with herself and her own feelings. I didn't know her that well prior to this trip but I'm coming to learn that she asks this question pretty frequently and she's not going to settle for answers like 'good', 'fine' or 'grand'. She wants feelings!

The day before leaving New York I tell Hallie I need to ask her a question.

'How do you feel?'

I'm half teasing and half trying to be funny, poking fun at how much difficulty I'd had with that question throughout the week, but the Irish sarcasm is lost in translation.

Hallie stops, takes a few breaths.

'Great question, Pat. At this moment I feel calm and grateful with a little bit of excitement.'

Heading home I wasn't quite sure what to make of the 'feelings piece' but I was a little perplexed as to how difficult it was to put words to my feelings beyond happy, sad, calm or anxious, and how uncomfortable it made me feel to try to check in with the present moment and not just blurt out a generic response of 'good' or 'fine' to the question 'How do you feel?' It wasn't until about six months later that the penny dropped and it started to make sense to me. Our fast-paced world so often pulls our attention to the external and the time spent internally seems to be largely in the head, thinking of the past or future and building stories based on memory or imagination. All this time in the head disconnects us from our emotional body and our 'intuition' or gut feelings take second place to the logical mind. My responses of feeling 'good', 'fine' or 'grand' might have been more accurately described as feeling 'numb'. When we try to shut down, repress or deny the emotions we have labelled 'wrong', we also shut down our ability to fully feel the emotions on the other side of the spectrum.

In the past I have at times labelled myself indecisive or a 'people-pleaser'. These types of label point to a lack of emotional awareness and an unwillingness to listen to our gut feelings; instead we try to keep everyone else happy while ignoring our own wants and needs. As a result we can come to experience resentment, anger, apathy and boredom.

When we consider how much emphasis is put on logic in the context of intelligence it isn't surprising that we generally find it easier to think than to feel. It wasn't until 1983 that Harvard professor Howard Gardner proposed that there were a number of other intelligences, including linguistic, spatial, musical and kinaesthetic. Gardner also identified interpersonal intelligence, which relates to how we sense other people's feelings and motives; and intrapersonal intelligence, which relates to understanding our own feelings, wants and needs.

It seemed in recent years I had become 'too busy' to feel and had lost contact with my own intrapersonal intelligence, choosing to live in and be run by my logical mind instead. At a time when I had achieved many of the things I was sure would make me happy in life, only to experience feelings of sadness and apathy, I judged those feelings and my logical mind pointed to all the reasons I shouldn't be sad, rather than recognising that the feelings were pointing to places I was out of integrity, caught up in people-pleasing tendencies and hiding behind social masks of 'success'.

Busyness and booze had been my ways of self-medicating when difficult feelings emerged.

CURIOSITY OVER JUDGEMENT

In December 2019 I decided to head to Thailand to complete a two-hundred-hour yoga teacher training course. On the first day we sat in a circle and introduced ourselves one by one, sharing a little background about our yoga experience. People mentioned having studied yoga for two years, three years, five years … then it was my turn. 'I've been to two yoga classes in my life. I didn't overly enjoy them but I keep hearing about the benefits of yoga so I thought I'd throw myself in the deep end and do the two-hundred-hour yoga teacher training. After doing two hundred hours of it in a month I should be able to make a call as to whether it's for me or not.'

I don't blame the others for looking at me like I was crazy, but I'm a naturally curious person and I like learning, so I thought it would be a great adventure. Two weeks in, we had to teach our first class to the other fourteen students on the course. I noticed Carla, one of the attendees, was quiet in the days leading up to her first class.

Like mine, her yoga experience was limited in comparison to the other attendees. She looked nervous and would frequently burst into tears and leave the room. The day before we all had to teach our first practice class I approached her after lunch and asked if she was doing okay.

'Please don't talk to me about it, I'll end up crying again.'

'Are you nervous about the class?'

She looked at me with tears in her eyes and nodded.

'And do you not think it's normal to be nervous? You've never taught a class before, and like me you're new to yoga. I think nervousness is a pretty reasonable response to having to stand up in front of a room of people and teach something you're new to.'

Her shoulders and face relaxed. 'I hadn't really thought about it that way.'

The stories we tell ourselves, as outlined throughout the book, have a bearing on how we feel. In this case perhaps Carla was telling herself a story of being an impostor or a fraud, or predicting what the others in the class would think of her. Then she was telling herself an additional story about her emotions and that she shouldn't be feeling anxious or worried because yogis are supposed to be calm.

I think most of us, at least from time to time, tell ourselves we 'shouldn't' be feeling a certain way and rather than acknowledge what is happening choose to deny or try to outrun it.

We'll sometimes go too quickly to the positive and invalidate our own emotions by saying, 'I can't complain, things could be a lot worse and I should be grateful for what I have.' We forget that validating our own emotional experience isn't taking away from anyone else's, and we can hold our difficult emotion alongside our gratitude for what we have and not have to choose one or the other.

An hour before teaching my own class one of the more experienced yogis gave me her two cents. 'I must say, Pat, you're remarkably confident about this for a man who can barely touch his toes.' My own 'confidence' and 'ease' around teaching a class as a complete novice wasn't based on a delusional idea that I'd be teaching a great class, but the recognition that I had no expectation of myself and thus didn't feel the tension of it having to look a certain way.

The story I was telling myself in that scenario was 'It's my first time ever teaching and so it'll be the best class I've ever taught!'

In reality I probably had feelings of nervousness and anxiousness, like Carla, but rather than make those feelings 'wrong' and adding resistance in trying to 'push the beachball under water' and deny my feelings, I instead allowed myself to feel nervous, which when given space morphed to a feeling of excitement. The word 'emotion' stands for 'energy in motion' and thus blocking off or trying to repress our emotions blocks a natural energy that, when allowed to, will run its course naturally.

I think so often the feelings we experience are perfectly normal, understandable and useful given the situations we find ourselves in, but we often villainise them. Rather than acknowledge and accept what's coming up for us and use it as feedback we desperately try to resist, sedate or suppress our feelings. When we place these conditions on how we are supposed to feel and villainise the feelings we have deemed unacceptable, we end up unconsciously placing these same conditions on the people around us and become overwhelmed when emotion surfaces in others. A willingness to allow our emotions to run their natural course and to be with them with compassion allows room for great insight, understanding and acceptance.

In logotherapy (the third school of Viennese psychotherapy) there is a technique called 'paradoxical intention'. An example of this might be seen in a therapist working with a client who is experiencing insomnia. Knowing that they are having trouble sleeping they begin to become anxious about falling asleep, and that anxiety in itself keeps them awake. In paradoxical intention, the therapist might encourage their client to go to bed and do their best to stay awake. When the goal is staying awake, the anxiety associated with trying to get to sleep disappears, the client relaxes and paradoxically they fall into a deep restful sleep.

Rather than acknowledge and accept that we feel a level of social anxiety around meeting new people, we try to hide our nerves and play it cool. What if we just told the new person we're meeting that we get nervous sometimes? Wouldn't that dissolve the heaviness of trying to hide our emotions and actually help us connect on a more human level?

ADDICTION

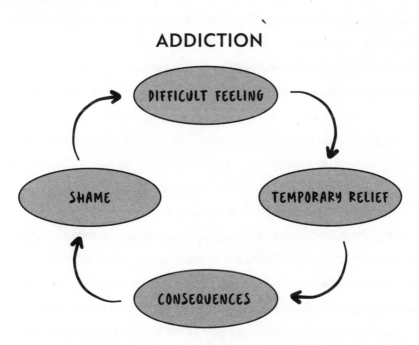

Addiction sort of rests on the idea that we 'should' feel good all the time. Some addictions are stigmatised and judged harshly by society; others are celebrated. Many will look judgementally at a drug addict on the street while putting someone who is a 'workaholic' on a pedestal. One of the most seemingly 'noble' addictions of all, helping people, will always win you approval, but when you look to save everyone else you often skip over your own wants and needs and in a way are trying to take approval from others rather than give from a full cup.

Addictions vary greatly but they are generally an attempt to escape the present moment. Why would we want to escape the present moment? Perhaps we are in pain, triggered by a thought or an uncomfortable feeling. So many of us have learnt that half the emotions or thoughts we experience are 'wrong' and thus we aren't comfortable sitting with them. Our need to judge everything takes away the curiosity about what our story or feeling might be there to tell us.

The cycle of addiction will look as follows:

- We experience some pain, discomfort or feeling that we want to escape.
- We turn to a distraction or behaviour to escape the feeling temporarily.
- After escaping temporarily we are later met with some form of consequence or hangover.
- These consequences bring about feelings of regret and shame and the cycle of addiction continues.

Take someone who's feeling lonely. The uncomfortable feeling surfaces along with the thought of 'I'm not supposed to feel lonely.' A quick attempt is made to escape the loneliness by reaching for a glass of wine, which turns into a bottle. This person wakes up the next day feeling the worse for wear along with having feelings of shame that continue a cycle of unconscious behaviours. Needless to say, nothing has been done to address the actual issue of loneliness.

Taking this example, it is easy to see as an outsider looking in that nothing is being done to actually address the root of the difficult feeling. Ignoring, denying, suppressing or sedating how we feel is like having a problem with the plumbing in your house but deciding that because you can't physically see the pipes you can pretend the problem isn't there. Ignore the hidden problem for long enough and suddenly cracks or leaks appear in the visible part of the house, in much the same way as the denial of our own feelings is manifested in our external actions and results.

Next, consider an even simpler example – someone who's feeling 'bored'. Again, the unconscious thought that 'boredom isn't good' leads them to reach for their phone and scroll their social media feeds. This is followed by a poor night's sleep, lower mood and more difficulty the next day, which may increase feelings of stress and overwhelm, and so they begin another addictive phone-scroll to numb those uncomfortable feelings. Again, masking boredom rather than acknowledging it feeds the cycle of ignoring our inner feedback system in favour of quick-fix remedies. In reality, boredom and stepping away from the constant stimulation of the modern world may well be the fastest path to developing a greater understanding of ourselves and a greater clarity around what we are looking to do in life.

Looking at the two examples above, we might ask what the purpose of boredom or loneliness is. All 'negative feelings' point to an unmet need. As humans we have an array of needs that are there to provide us with a level of security, safety and certainty. When these needs are absent we can often feel a little out of control. By bringing awareness to the pattern of always picking up their phone the bored person might recognise that the feeling that is leading to this behaviour is loneliness. When staying curious they might come to see that the loneliness is pointing to an unmet need for 'connection'. From there, they could think about how they could meet this need for connection in a more positive and empowering way than hours spent on social media. The unconscious effort to validate the need for connection via social media denies the opportunity to gain real connection, to get out and meet real people. The 'difficult' feeling of loneliness, then, is a gift in disguise pointing to the potential for more meaning in our lives, if we are willing to listen.

The boredom example will most likely look very obvious on paper, but our difficulty with 'emotional literacy' and naming our feelings proves the first stumbling block when it comes to recognising our unmet needs. If we can't put a name to and identify with our feelings due to so much time being spent in the intellectual mind, we will have a hard time helping ourselves tap into this wisdom.

SLOWING DOWN TO THE SPEED OF LIFE

Running a successful fitness business in my twenties brought its fair share of challenges. Though I really enjoyed the work, when I locked the doors to the gym on a Friday evening my mind would be racing after a busy week of teaching classes, running online programmes, travelling for workshops and being with the countless people who were walking through the gym doors over the course of the week.

As I mostly enjoyed the work, it didn't dawn on me that I might be experiencing some stress or overwhelm, so I'd often just assume that I was 'excited for the weekend'. Friday nights and, more often than not, Saturday nights were generally spent drinking too many pints of Guinness on Quay Street in Galway before demonstrating some of the worst dance moves ever seen in whatever nightclub would let us in. Considering how many nights out I had in my teens and twenties it's hard to believe how bad my dance moves have remained to this day!

Needless to say this routine of overworking Monday to Friday and then partying for the weekend wasn't sustainable and ultimately led to anxiety and panic attacks. At least part of this could be attributed to the shame of feeling out of integrity in promoting health during the week but overdoing it at the weekend. Looking back, it's much easier to find perspective and I can see now that alcohol-fuelled nights were an 'addictive' and impulsive response to feelings of stress, overwhelm, anxiety and even excitement.

Had I been able to identify and slow down long enough to be honest with myself about how I felt in the moment I'd perhaps have made better choices. My lack of awareness of how I really felt and my unwillingness to sit with difficult emotions led to the Fixer character in my mind forcing me to live at a million miles an hour in an exhausting effort to run towards feeling good all the time and away from ever feeling bad. The unwillingness to slow down meant the Fixer was given responsibility for trying to keep me feeling good in the moment. He encouraged busyness and booze as a means of self-medication.

All of our behaviours in life serve a purpose, even those addictive behaviours that seem counterproductive or self-destructive. In the case of my wild nights out a number of purposes were being served. They gave a social aspect to my life that was lacking in the rest of the week, when I effectively lived in my gym, where I worked. They also helped me slow my busy mind and escape my inner critic for a short while. Among other benefits the nights out were also my chance to be carefree and not be the boss. In the space of eighteen months I'd gone from having just five clients and no overheads on my local beach to having five members of staff, big overheads and hundreds of clients, and at times I wanted to switch off from being the responsible boss.

Now, having this awareness of what an 'addictive' or compulsive escape is giving us can allow us to instead choose a healthy response which fulfils our unmet needs in a conscious way. Of course, we often rely on willpower to create change and often shame ourselves for our impulsive behaviours, but by understanding why we do what we do we can encourage self-awareness and compassion.

To continue my story, when I took up Brazilian jiu-jitsu it gave me a social outlet outside my work, quietened my busy mind and gave me somewhere to go where I wasn't the boss and could just participate and then leave without having to worry about anything else. This ticked all the same boxes as the alcohol-fuelled nights out, but after a training session, rather than feeling more disconnected from myself I felt much more in tune with myself. I also took to breath-work and meditation, again a means of quieting the busy mind, and sea swimming, a place where I found a social outlet and community.

This is what I call 'the invitation'.

By acknowledging, recognising and accepting how we feel we can choose to respond in an empowering way that connects us back to ourselves. At the end of this chapter I'll encourage you to explore the needs you are trying to meet through addictive or disempowering behaviour and how you might meet those needs in a healthier and more empowering way.

EMOTIONAL CHECK-INS (A/B/C/D)

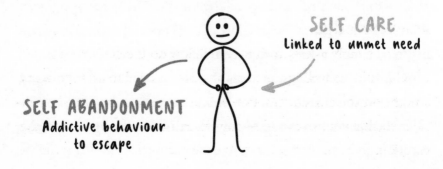

I've spoken of emotional literacy throughout this chapter and as a simple means of coming to a better understanding of the signs being shared by our emotional body throughout the day, I encourage a simple 'A/B/C/D' emotional check-in every evening, or better again a couple of times throughout the day. At the risk of confusing this with our A/B/C/D exercise from the first chapter we'll just call this one the **emotional check-in**.

Maybe you could set an alarm on your phone that goes off a few times a day this week as a reminder to ask yourself how you feel and identify what you need. Alternatively, if you frequently spend time on online conference calls, you could form a ritual of doing a quick check-in before logging in to each meeting. Or maybe do an emotional check-in every time you get into your car or put your key in the front door.

This emotional check-in is a chance to pause and listen and go from blindly 'doing' on autopilot to feeling and listening for feedback. Like any practice, it requires a little discipline, but this willingness to listen to ourselves is one of the greatest acts of self-care in the busy modern world. In my experience, overlooking or skipping these regular emotional check-ins can often lead to me unconsciously 'checking out' by looking outside myself for answers that lie within.

The A/B/C/D emotional check-in is as follows.

Acknowledge

Begin by simply asking the question 'How do I feel?'

Consult the feelings table on p179 if you need to and try to put a name on the current emotion you are experiencing. Maybe consider closing your eyes and seeing where in your body you feel the emotion.

Terms like 'heartache', 'gut feeling' and 'sick to my stomach' point to the physical nature of these emotions. With eyes closed, as you acknowledge your feeling you might reflect on the shape, size, colour, location and/or texture of the emotion.

Breathe

Silence the Fixer in your mind who wants to go straight to 'doing' and allow yourself to just be with the emotion.

You don't need to do anything with it, change it or fix it, just be with it like you'd be with a friend who's sharing something important with you. Your pattern may be to run away, but stay present and compassionate with some deep breaths.

Continue to breathe around the emotion and notice if it moves, morphs or changes in its shape, size, colour, location or texture. Perhaps it turns into a different emotion. Stay with it without judgement.

Check In

Being with the emotion, become curious and 'listen'. If this emotion was trying to tell you something, what would it be?

What unmet need might it be pointing to for you at this moment? Again, you might use the tables on the next pages as a reference to help you name your unmet need.

In the same way that we listen and create space for a friend to express themselves before trying to offer solutions, you are allowing the space to understand and act from a responsive place of understanding and not a place of reaction.

Decide

Once you feel you have listened to and become aware of the unmet need your emotion is pointing to, consider how you can honour yourself and take a step towards self-care.

Here's a little example of an emotional check-in:

- **Acknowledge:** At this moment I feel a sense of overwhelm. As I close my eyes I sense this 'feeling' between my gut and my heart. It feels like a dense murky energy and I sense it being a dark blue colour.
- **Breathe:** I allow myself to be with this sense and feeling of overwhelm, without trying to fix or change it. All I am doing here is breathing with and being present to the feeling, not judging, resisting or avoiding it.
- **Check in:** In 'listening' to this feeling of overwhelm I sense the unmet need for space and calm. It has been a busy start to the week and as I sit with this emotion I recognise I haven't given myself a full day off from work in two weeks.
- **Decide:** Recognising this need for calm and space I decide to allow myself to sit here in stillness for ten minutes for a short meditation. I also decide to take out my calendar after this meditation and block off a day in the diary where I will switch off completely from work.

The feelings and needs listed below are based on Marshall Rosenberg's work in his book *Nonviolent Communication*. While you don't need to limit yourself to the emotions and needs included here, they can provide a starting point in developing a greater level of emotional awareness and understanding.

NEEDS

Acknowledgement	Consideration	Justice
Adventure	Consistency	Nourishment
Attention	Contribution	Order
Authenticity	Creativity	Passion
Autonomy	Dependability	Peace
Awareness	Emotional Safety	Protection
Balance	Equality	Purpose
Belonging	Exercise	Reassurance
Calm	Expression (of self)	Recognition
Caring	Familiarity	Respect
Certainty	Friendship	Rest/Sleep
Challenge	Fun	Sexual expression
Choice	Gratitude	Simplicity
Clarity	Growth	Spontaneity
Comfort	Health	Stimulation
Community Companionship	Honesty	Touch
Compassion	Inclusion	Trust
Connection to others	Integrity	Understanding
Connection to self	Intimacy	Variety

FEELINGS

When Needs Are Met	When Needs Are Unmet
Affectionate	Agitated
Alive	Angry
Appreciative	Annoyed
Aroused	Anxious
Blissful	Apathetic
Calm	Ashamed
Compassionate	Confused
Content	Disappointed
Curious	Disconnected
Delighted	Discouraged
Ecstatic	Embarrassed
Empowered	Envious
Encouraged	Frustrated
Energetic	Furious
Enthusiastic	Grief
Fascinated	Guilty
Fulfilled	Helpless
Happy	Hopeless
Inspired	Irritated
Interested	Jealous
Involved	Lonely
Loving	Lost
Proud	Numb
Rejuvenated	Overwhelmed
Relaxed	Resentful
Rested	Restless
Tender	Sad
Trusting	Scared
Vibrant	Stressed
Warm	Tense
	Troubled
	Uncertain
	Unsettled
	Vulnerable
	Withdrawn

LISTENING TO OURSELVES

In addition to these daily emotional check-ins, consider making a regular practice of pausing before making decisions and listening to your innate wisdom and emotional body. Many of our decisions can be based on expectations and things we feel obliged to do as opposed to things we'd like to do. These people-pleasing tendencies can sometimes lead to resentment, feelings of self-abandonment and a subsequent drop in self-esteem.

Have you ever committed to meeting someone for a catch-up and been relieved when they cancelled? This is one example of a time when we made a decision based on obligation and perhaps didn't honour our own needs.

You can start with small simple decisions such as what you'd like to have for dinner or whether or not you feel like catching up with the friend who wants to grab coffee.

By listening to your gut, recognising what emotions arise for you and recognising your needs, you begin to tune back in to your intrapersonal intelligence. Over time your confidence and decisiveness will improve and you can bring the practice to bigger decisions, knowing that you are choosing from a place of self-care and not self-abandonment.

Emotions – What to Remember

- By moving away from the idea that emotions are 'good' or 'bad' we can acquire valuable feedback which often points to information in the subconscious. Emotional check-ins allow us to bring greater awareness to our lives and shine light on the dark.
- Every emotion is valid and has value. 'Fine' isn't a feeling, and an essential first step in understanding ourselves and our own

needs lies in developing a greater emotional literacy. We can begin to develop our ability to identify and name our feelings by simply checking in each evening and reflecting on what emotion or emotions were most present for us that day. Consider using the emotions wheel.

● Our more difficult feelings, which may have previously been labelled 'negative' or 'bad', can point to unmet needs. Each evening after identifying our primary emotions that day we can reflect on what those emotions are pointing to. If this emotion was trying to tell us something, what might it be saying?

● Difficult emotions are an invitation to honour our unmet needs and practise self-care. Denying these emotions will often lead to self-abandonment and destructive or disempowering behaviours. Addictions often stem from the desire to escape a difficult emotion rather than work with it.

● Judging or denying a feeling and turning to an addictive behaviour is like refusing to heal a small physical injury and doing greater damage in the long term. A key element of self-care is being willing to sit with all our feelings, not just the 'positive' ones.

● The Fixer is the character in our minds who wants to provide an instant solution and escape the emotion which we have judged. Much like supporting a friend, it is important that we listen and learn from our emotions before going straight into action.

ARC EXERCISES

Begin by completing the following sentence stems in your journal:

- What I learnt about emotions growing up was …
- When difficult emotions arise I …
- If I could be more accepting of all emotions I …

- The emotions that challenge me the most are …
- These emotions could teach me …
- Loving myself fully means …
- The first step I can take to be kinder to myself is …

Illumination Exercise:
Emotions – The Invitation

In this illumination exercise we'll dive into some of the patterns we've developed to help us cope with difficult emotions. As outlined in the 'invitation', our difficult emotions provide feedback which can point us towards ourselves and our needs or, when ignored, can lead to addictive behaviours and patterns. All behaviours provide some benefits, even when they seem to make no sense and go completely against what we say we want. Our aim with this exercise is to go from repression to expression.

For this exercise I'd like you to begin by identifying a habit or behaviour which you feel is having a negative impact on your life. This might be addictive tendencies towards things like alcohol, drugs, porn, work, gossip, social media or junk food. What is a behaviour that you feel is holding you back or leading to self-sabotage in your life?

Allowing yourself to be curious about what this behaviour is giving you, make a list of all of its benefits. Initially you may find it difficult to see how it is helping you, but you might see that it is a coping strategy for difficult or uncomfortable emotions. What other benefits do you see? Using alcohol as an example, I might say that its benefits include a social outlet in which I meet friends in the pub. I might also say it helps me manage stress, switch off from work and feel more confident.

Considering these benefits, try to get creative in terms of other ways in which you could meet your unmet needs and see similar benefits through a more empowering behaviour. Again using the example of alcohol, what are some other ways in which you could find a social outlet and manage your stress without the drawbacks of drinking too much? Perhaps it is starting a meditation practice, joining a social club or starting a new hobby.

Coming back to your current disempowering behaviour, write about where you will be three to five years from now if you don't make a change. What will this behaviour cost you in your life? Consider the impact it will have on your health, your relationships, your confidence, your mental health and any other areas that are important to you. We can often soften or justify certain behaviours to ourselves, but seeing the impact they will have over time can provide a wake-up call and the leverage to create change.

Finally, consider where you might be three to five years from now if you were to replace your current behaviour with one of your more empowering alternatives. How would this change impact your health, your relationships, your confidence, your mental health and other areas that are important to you?

Taking all the above into account, consider the first step you could take to replace your current behaviour. In my example, my first step might be to research local meditation classes or social groups that I could join.

Journalling Prompts:
Emotions

1. Write a compassionate letter to your Fixer, the character in your mind who looks to outrun or deny your emotions. Think about

where that character first came from. Explore some of the stories they tell you and recognise how they are trying to help you. What do you need them to understand?

2. In which areas of life do you frequently experience difficult emotions? If these emotions were talking to you what wisdom would they be sharing?

3. What are the emotions you would like to experience more in life? What are some practical things you could do to promote more of these emotions on a consistent basis?

4. If you had a friend struggling with some of the difficult emotions that you frequently experience, what would you look to share with them?

5. How could you show yourself more compassion when you are struggling with difficult emotions?

6. Write about the day-to-day activities, environments and people who bring a sense of calm and ease to your life. How can you bring more of these experiences into your life on a consistent basis?

7. With whom do you find yourself being a 'people-pleaser' who puts the needs of others ahead of your own? How does saying 'no' to yourself affect you? How could you begin to honour your own needs while also staying connected to those around you?

Meditation of the Week:
Slowing Down – Four and Eight

This week's simple meditation provides another opportunity to practise slowing down and creating stillness. Sit comfortably, with your back straight and your shoulders and face relaxed. Gently close your eyes and allow yourself to settle. Begin by bringing awareness to your breath as it is, without judgement.

What do you notice about your breath? Is it fast or slow? Short or long? How does the quality of your breath reflect the quality of your mind?

After this check-in, begin to lengthen your breath, breathing through the nose deep into the belly for the count of four. Extend your outward breath, making it twice as long as the inward breath, and feel your body and mind relax as you breathe out for a count of eight. Repeat this pattern for the duration of the meditation, filling your belly with each full inhale and letting go with each extended exhale.

If your mind wanders, that's okay. Don't push away thought, instead just bring your attention back to a four-second count as you breathe in and an eight-second count as you breathe out.

The Communication Story

'Once you can communicate with yourself, you'll be able to communicate outwardly with more clarity. The way in is the way out' – THÍCH NHẤT HẠNH

'Live your life as you see fit. That's not selfish. Selfish is to demand that others live their lives as you see fit' – ANTHONY DE MELLO

MEET THE CHARACTER – THE MIND READER

The Mind Reader is the character in our head who is constantly making judgements and assumptions about what other people are thinking, these judgements and assumptions often resulting in stress and worry. When a friend seems a little cold or detached, the Mind Reader builds a story and gives meaning to the other person's behaviour. Rather than allowing us to communicate with the other person externally, the Mind Reader keeps us in our head, building stories which are often far removed from reality.

I jokingly reference a clip from the reality TV show *Love Island* that I saw a few years back to demonstrate this character in action. (As I write that, my own internal Mind Reader is making assumptions about what you, the reader, will think of me watching clips from *Love Island*!) In the midst of a break-up, one of the girls on the show consults with her friends to rehearse what she is going to say to her ex, who is meanwhile planning the same conversation with his group of friends. As they consult with their peers, both are planning ahead, predicting the conversation that will unfold, based on memory and imagination – 'and when she says X I'll say Y, and if she says Y I'll say Z'. Unsurprisingly, when they come together to actually talk, the conversation doesn't go anything like they had predicted.

With so much of our lives spent in the future or the past creating stories based on memory and imagination and our internal characters doing everything they can to keep us safe within our current worldview, we often forget that everything that is happening outside ourselves is an assumption. We often listen to respond and put across our own view, rather than listening to understand – with the Mind Reader assuming they've got it all figured out already. The Mind Reader struggles to listen, assumes everyone has the same values and expectations from life and builds resentments as they fail to effectively communicate their wants, needs and frustrations.

Communication and relationships require going beyond how we have decided other people 'should' be and instead choosing to live in reality and be with what is.

COMMUNICATION STARTS WITH THE SELF

When we consider the impact our expectations and stories about how things 'should be' have on our experience of life it isn't surprising that relationships can be where we experience a large degree of stress and uncertainty. Our ego's intent to put across our own worldview can shut down the opportunity to learn, grow and connect openly and vulnerably with others. It is often the people closest to us who can trigger feelings of hurt, disappointment or sadness, which lead us to defensiveness and isolation. Like the golden Buddha covered in clay, we can struggle to show our true selves and instead find ourselves wearing masks and armour to protect ourselves from the vulnerability of being fully seen.

As with all other external experiences of life we can start by reminding ourselves that in our communication with others there are always two triggers: what happens; and the meaning that we give to what happens. As much of our worldview is shaped by our memories, simple breakdowns in communication can lead to disproportionate emotional responses within us as they trigger old emotional wounds.

Take an example of 'ghosting'. Someone feels devastated when they don't hear back from someone they have only been on one date with. The emotional response seems disproportionate to the given situation. It is the second trigger, the meaning that the person has unconsciously given to their situation, that is the source of their suffering. Perhaps memories of rejection, abandonment or hurt are triggered by this 'ghosting' experience, leading to this strong emotional response. When they label the experience as being rejected, the mind can quickly bring attention to moments from their past when they felt a similar experience of rejection.

By trying to come to each interaction with a 'beginner's mind' in which we let go of our judgements from the past, we are looking to be more present with the person in front of us and less in our heads, mindreading and making assumptions.

I have no doubt that my own experience of bullying had an impact on how I showed up for many years after – it still does, unless I stay connected to how I am communicating with myself in the moment. My Mind Reader character who remembers experiences of bullying will often assume others don't like me or I am not fitting in.

Perhaps a boy who is shamed for crying as a child finds it nearly impossible to express his emotions as an adult. Though he is now a grown man, the defence mechanism of shutting down emotion can be triggered in moments in which he feels vulnerable or scared. Being able to stay present and communicate these feelings internally or externally will allow him to feel safe and connected rather than resorting to self-preservation and shutting down communication and emotion.

Our communication with others begins with our communication with ourselves. Rather than play the blame game of 'You made me feel …', we can begin by checking in with our own internal narratives. This starts with an awareness around the meanings we are giving to what is happening, considering the origins of those meanings and then separating that from what is actually happening in the moment.

As a simple example, if I went to a job interview and got a call back saying the position had been given to someone else, I will instinctively give meaning to this experience largely based on my self-image and memories. Many in this type of scenario may label this as being 'rejected', making it about themselves and forgetting about the hundred other possible scenarios. A third party looking in without any vested emotional interest or triggering memories will most likely see the event as neutral, that someone else was better qualified, or had more experience. It is the negativity bias and memories of past 'rejections' that will often trigger the meanings we jump to.

A number of years ago, while out walking near my home in Barna, I saw an old friend I hadn't seen in ten years walking towards me. My last memories of this guy were from wild nights out in Galway ten years before where we did well to make it to 2 a.m. without being ejected from the nightclub by the bouncers. After catching up briefly I asked him what he'd been up to. He responded, 'You'll probably think this is crazy, but I've just got back from a ten-day silent retreat.'

I quickly snapped out of the memories from ten years before and assumptions of who was in front of me and recognised that I was in my head and not actually interacting with the person in front of me. 'The only thing I think is crazy about that is that I was only looking up ten-day silent retreats a few days ago myself!'

How often in our lives are we communicating with a picture in our head of who the person is rather than the actual person standing in front of us, particularly with the people closest to us? Perhaps in the early days of a romantic partnership or friendship we are curious and present, but with time our mind starts to make a collection of judgements and puts the people we know into certain boxes. Here lies our first challenge in communication – bringing ourselves back to the present moment, to the internal meanings we are giving to what is happening, and allowing ourselves to be with the person we are with as opposed to the picture in our head, based on memories or judgements, of who we are with.

EXPECTATIONS

Expectation is in my judgement the ultimate source of stress across all areas of life and it's undoubtedly a huge factor in relationships and communication. When your pictures of how things 'should' be don't fit my pictures of how they 'should' be, we can often fall into trying to change one another's way of seeing the world. We might instead consider widening our perspective by looking to understand the other and not become fixated with being understood first.

This idea of expectations in relationships is demonstrated well in the work of Gary Chapman, who is best known for his book *The Five Love Languages*. In that book Chapman talks about the different ways in which we show love. He noticed couples would so often be going strong but after the honeymoon period would drift apart and end up in conflict or feeling resentment towards one another. Though there are many ways in which love can be demonstrated, Chapman outlined five of the most common ways in which we show love:

- Gifts
- Physical touch
- Words of affirmation
- Quality time
- Acts of service

Couples who struggled, it seemed, didn't understand one another's love languages and assumed their partner 'should' have the same preferences as them. Imagine a husband liking gifts and thus assuming that'll be what his partner likes too. Unbeknownst to him his wife actually values quality time much more. Every week he comes home with gifts, and though his partner says, 'Thank you,' he feels unappreciated and like he's wasting his time. In his head he's thinking, 'I'm spending all this money and making all this effort and all I get in return is a half-assed thank you.' Meanwhile, she's thinking, 'This guy doesn't seem to want to spend any time with me and thinks buying me stuff is enough to cut it.' Each party becomes frustrated, upset and resentful towards the other.

It's natural that when we spend so much time in our own heads and are often caught up in busyness and survival mode, our vision tends to narrow. How often in life do we go into conversation more concerned with backing up our existing map of the world than seeing beyond it? It's worth considering how much of communication is governed by a need to back up what we already believe versus looking to understand the other person's viewpoint. Are we more concerned with fighting our subjective truth and staying small or in looking to learn from one another and expand our understanding?

Expectations go far beyond the 'love languages' and apply across all relationships, with each of us having a different set of values and expectations of how life should look. I once heard a mentor of mine tell a story of being approached by a woman whose son was having a hard time concentrating in school and had pretty much given up on academic study. Understandably worried and frustrated, the woman did all she could to change her son and make him understand how important his studies were, but to no avail. He had been labelled as having 'attention' issues and his teachers had told his mother that he wouldn't sit still and was disruptive in class. When my mentor sat with the boy and asked him about his interests, he was intrigued to hear that although he seemingly couldn't sit still in class he would happily sit in front of his computer for five to six hours every night. It turned out he was playing flight simulator games, which tied into his dream in life of becoming a pilot.

After gaining an understanding of the boy's passions, dreams and values the mentor was able to communicate with him from a place of understanding his worldview and not trying to change it. He reminded the boy that prerequisites for going to aviation school included good results from his academic studies and that it was essential to make some changes to the way he was approaching his schooling if he were to pursue his dream. Very quickly the boy developed a new focus and his behaviour shifted dramatically as he recognised that school was an essential step in moving towards something he valued so much.

As a side note, we can take the same approach in communicating with and motivating ourselves to do things we struggle to stay consistent with by understanding our own values and drivers. If we really struggle to stay consistent with exercise, but socialising is a value we hold very highly, we might consider linking the two together and joining a gym that encourages a big social element as part of its culture. This way we go from 'forcing' ourselves to get fit to making it something that supports what excites us in life – socialising.

Knowing that our parents, kids, friends, colleagues, employees and employers all hold different values, we can perhaps begin to communicate in a way that supports what it is that they want from life and not fall into the trap of assuming that everyone needs to hold the same values and expectations as us for us to be happy. Put simply, we might try to separate what is being said from why it is being said – two very different things.

A young adult who wants to travel the world and who labels their parents 'negative' or 'critical' for not supporting them isn't seeing that while they may value freedom and adventure, their parents value security and stability. If the young adult could recognise that their parents' 'critical' nature is really just a means of trying to keep them from disappointment in life, this simple perspective could drastically change their communication with one another.

Our minds' tendency to deviate to black-and-white thinking has been highly magnified by social media in recent years. Websites and media outlets seeking to garner attention in a distracted age share clickbait and polarised viewpoints. Partner this with the algorithms that give us more and more of the type of content we've already expressed interest in and you'll see that social media is looking to force us into having a one-sided view of the world. As a result of this we can often assume that when someone doesn't agree with our every action or ambition they are being 'negative' or critical. This often leads to judgement towards them or second-guessing ourselves in an effort to have everyone agree with us. There's an incredible freedom in not having to be right about everything and being open to learning. There is a lightness, too, in allowing other people to be who they are and removing the expectations we have as to who they should be.

We often feel judged when others take a different standpoint or question our way of doing things in the world – though we make the same judgements about others, denying them the chance to be supported in living a life true to their wants, needs and values, instead expecting them to match up to the pictures in our heads about how they 'should' be.

I commonly see a pattern when people message me to tell me how much 'self-help' work they've done and how frustrating it is to be surrounded by negative people. Again, the 'negative people' statement is a judgement based on someone having a different worldview and is projecting our own negativity onto someone else rather than recognising that there are areas of own lives in which we are 'negative' or critical and other areas in which we are positive and optimistic.

Talk to me about accounting, politics or most TV shows and you'll think I'm a 'negative' person. Talk to me about Brazilian jiu-jitsu, meditation or psychology and you'll probably think the opposite. For years I placed expectations on the closest people in my own life and blamed them for the stress that was really just a case of the outside world and the people in it not bending to meet my narrow picture of how they should be.

The next time you experience stress with someone in your life, pause and ask, 'What is the story I am telling myself about how this person "should" be?' It is this 'should' that is so often the source of our stress, trying to play god and change something that is outside our control.

EMPATHY AND UNDERSTANDING

In the last chapter we began to look at the simple idea of becoming more emotionally aware and linking our more difficult emotions to unmet needs. This process of moving from self-abandonment to self-care can be hugely empowering in gaining a greater understanding of ourselves and our ability to take and implement feedback based on our emotions. We can also take this type of practice into our communication and relationship with others.

In creating the time to 'listen to' our own internal emotions we allow space to respond in a healthy way rather than allow the Fixer to go straight into impulsive action. Similarly, when we create the space to understand others rather than make assumptions based on the Mind Reader, we allow for greater understanding of the other person's emotions, wants and needs.

I have had to, and continue to, work on listening to understand rather than listening to respond. Too often, my struggles to be present and my ego's desire to back up my worldview make me jump straight in with my own experience when someone shares something with me, before allowing them the space to be understood. In the past I have been quick to respond to stories shared by friends with my own outlook or experience, before digging deeper into understanding their perspective and reality. It wasn't until I got feedback from someone about my poor listening skills that I recognised the need to improve! This type of feedback isn't always easy to hear, of course, but it can be an opportunity to learn and grow, as opposed to an attack on our character. I'll share an exercise at the end of this chapter for anyone willing to go and ask those close to them for feedback on their blind spots!

Steven Covey's classic book *The 7 Habits of Highly Effective People* includes the habit of 'Seeking first to understand, then to be understood'. Covey strongly encouraged a change from 'autobiographically' listening to empathetic listening. In autobiographically listening we tend to respond in four ways:

1. We **evaluate**, either agreeing or disagreeing based on our own worldview.
2. We **probe**, asking questions again from our own perspective and not the perspective of the speaker.
3. We **advise**, giving advice based on our own perception and experience.
4. We **interpret**, trying to figure out people's motives based on our own motives and behaviour.

Conversely, empathetic listening provides a means of understanding the other person's perspective and connecting with the part of ourselves that has felt what they are feeling.

It provides a means for deepening connection, allowing vulnerability and getting out of the assumptions of the Mind Reader, who's quick to try to evaluate, interpret, probe or advise.

Theresa Wiseman, a nursing scholar from the UK, outlined four attributes of empathetic listening:

- **Take the other person's perspective:** Here we are looking to step away from our own perspective and simply listen, stepping into the other person's shoes and cognitively understanding their worldview. We can come back to our perspective later, but first we need to listen fully.
- **Stay out of judgement:** In looking to understand the other person's view we are looking to stay out of judgement or needing to analyse, fix, minimise or interrogate their experience.
- **Recognise their emotions:** In order to connect vulnerably with someone else we must first connect with ourselves. Here we are looking within ourselves to see if we can identify the emotion the other person might be experiencing.
- **Communicate our understanding:** Communicating to the other person our understanding of what they are thinking, feeling or experiencing.

We can communicate our empathy through mirroring, in which we put words to the other person's feelings, needs, thoughts, values, wants or experience. In mirroring back what we are hearing we are ensuring that the other person feels understood and we are not stuck in our own perspective and 'autobiographically' listening.

Mirroring can be broken down into four parts:

1. Listen carefully and attentively.
2. Imagine their perspective and feelings.

3. Stay out of judgement.

4. Paraphrase their feelings and problems.

This type of communication might seem awkward or difficult at first, or maybe it comes completely naturally to you, but the practice of mirroring and listening from a place of trying to understand and not just be understood is a practice that quickly improves connection and communication.

Consider consciously going into your next three conversations with a view to practising empathetic listening. Notice the judgements and assumptions that come up for you and where you feel the need to put across your point. Instead, look to go beyond these judgements and stay curious, asking questions and allowing the other person the space to feel more understood than they have in a long time.

COMMUNICATION AT SEA LEVEL

In February of 2018 I headed for Mendoza to attempt to climb Aconcagua, the highest mountain in the world outside the Himalayas. Mountaineering was one of the new hobbies I took up in my late twenties as a means of living more in the moment and learning to enjoy the journey. By this point I'd been to Nepal and Peru and had climbed to the highest points in Africa (Kilimanjaro) and Europe (Elbrus).

Aconcagua in Argentina, the highest mountain in South America, was the next logical step in many people's mountaineering adventures. For a guy who had had such a hard time enjoying the journey in my younger years, twenty-one days on a mountain to spend fifteen minutes on the summit at 6,969 metres above sea level was a good means of learning to take it day by day and not wish my life away always trying to get to the end point.

In our team meeting at the hotel before leaving for the mountain, our American guide, Max, went through the plans for the next three weeks in great detail. A mixture of jet lag and excitement had us all struggling to focus. We just wanted to kick back and enjoy a few local beers and a famous Mendozan steak. A few times over the course of Max's hour-long brief he had to snap us to attention before reminding us, 'It's essential that we get this stuff right here. When we go up that mountain it's going to get colder and less comfortable. We're going to have less food, less water and there's going to be less oxygen in the air. You're going to have a hard time sleeping and some of the days are going to be gruelling. We've got to be clear right now on exactly what we're doing and how we're approaching this. I need to hear about any concerns or questions here, these aren't things we want to be stressing about at altitude'.

Fast-forward three weeks to summit night. We leave at 1 a.m. and start from camp four at 6,500 metres. It's only 400 metres to the top but it'll take hours, and with fifty per cent less oxygen in the air, strong winds and bitter cold, everything is difficult.

Myself and Niels, a twenty-two-year-old Dutch team member, are in high spirits, laughing and joking as we take our first break two hours in. Suddenly Niels collapses, falling back on his backpack and struggling to stay conscious. In the blink of an eye he's gone from high spirits to suffering the effects of cerebral oedema, a swelling of the brain due to the altitude. Max is quick to act and knows exactly what to do. Niels receives a steroid shot and is quickly pulled down to camp four by a local guide. Helicopter rescues don't go above 5,500 metres and the only cure for altitude sickness is to get down quickly.

We carry on, a little shaken from the experience, and in the end Dylan, an American soldier, and I end up reaching the summit with

Max early the next morning. Throughout the night I'm thinking of Niels and wondering how he's recovering. I also think back to the meeting three weeks before at the hotel where Max outlined every little detail including what would happen if someone experienced this type of sickness. He was right – that wasn't something we could leave to chance and figure out once things got bad; it was a conversation that needed to happen at sea level before stress and pressure built.

Dylan, Max and I arrived back hours later to be greeted by the rest of the team, who'd had to turn around for different reasons. Niels appeared from his tent with a cup of tea, a hug and a smile, I think still a little unaware of how dangerous his collapse had been but looking like he was getting back to his energetic self.

How often in life do we fail to communicate at sea level and end up 'at altitude' or in a storm where we say things we regret or end up fighting over something that isn't the real issue?

The discomfort or difficulty with honestly expressing ourselves leads to us burying what needs to be said, building resentment, living in our own heads and catastrophising rather than addressing the concern head on.

Similarly, at times when we sense something is a little 'off' in someone else's communication with us we are left frustrated and perhaps anxious, not knowing where we stand or what unspoken expectations are going unmet. In shutting down further our Mind Reader character can build resentment and stories around the meaning of this lack of communication.

We can choose short-term discomfort by communicating at sea level or long-term pain in letting things turn into a pressure cooker. We can take our frustrations towards others and map those frustrations back towards feelings and unmet needs, allowing us to communicate our feelings and needs rather than communicate with words of criticism stemming from frustration.

While our initial reaction to our partner coming home from the shops having forgotten to buy the one thing we asked them to buy might be 'You never listen to me,' if we check in with our feelings and unmet needs we can own what is ours and stay specific to the frustrating situation. Rather than making sweeping generalisations such as 'You always', 'You never', 'You made me feel …', we can address the situation at sea level without criticising the other person's character or putting them on the defensive. 'I felt sad this evening when I noticed you had forgotten to buy the thing I asked you to buy.' This statement, staying specific to the given situation and owning our own feelings, evokes a very different reaction from 'You never listen to me!'

The Gottman Institute, a relational health establishment that I've done some study with, promotes the idea of the 'twenty-minute conversation'. It's exactly what it says on the tin, a chance to come together and talk to your partner for twenty minutes every day without any distraction. It's a chance to reflect on what's going on in one another's lives and to share any micro stresses or challenges that, if left unspoken, might turn to resentment and stressful conversations or arguments 'at altitude'.

This might be a space in which you choose to practice the empathetic listening we've talked about while staying connected to how you are communicating with yourself internally. It is also a chance to notice frustrations or criticisms and look to map them to feelings and unmet needs.

Of course, a ritual like the twenty-minute conversation does not have to apply to just intimate relationships. This type of ritual could become something done in any type of personal or professional relationship, again as a means of working on communicating honestly and openly and not falling into brushing uncomfortable topics or discussions under the mat.

CONTEXT

Just as we spend so much time in our heads building stories and assumptions about what others might be thinking, so do those around us, and it can be easy to forget that others cannot read our minds and figure out what we want, need or expect. While our Mind Reader character might assume that our struggles and challenges 'should' be obvious to those around us without having to be explicitly stated, without context, our behaviours, reactions and responses can seem to make no sense to others. By sharing context we can let others know how they can best love and support us. Setting context allows those with whom we are interacting to see things from our perspective and check some of the assumptions their own Mind Reader character may be making based on their worldview.

Imagine being in a restaurant and the waiting staff running around you but ignoring your attempts to place an order. After a few minutes you would quickly grow frustrated and possibly leave. If, instead, when you arrived a member of staff had given context by telling you, 'It'll be about a twenty-minute wait before we can be with you,' you'd have a complete perception and understand that they were busy but would be with you soon.

As another example, if we are juggling a lot of challenges in our personal life and finding it difficult to be social and outgoing at work, we might let our colleagues know that we are feeling a little overwhelmed at the moment and just need a little space.

This type of context setting helps combat the cognitive distortion of 'personalisation', the tendency to make everything someone else does or says about ourselves. In our example of being social at work, 'personalisation' may lead to colleagues deciding they have said or done something that has led to you withdrawing your interest in engagement. Without context for your change in mood they can be left mindreading and potentially making unfair judgements.

This type of exercise can be useful at home too, of course, particularly in relationships with those who have an 'anxious attachment' and have a hard time feeling secure in relationships. By setting context in times in which you need a little space or are experiencing stress or worry, you are 'communicating at sea level' and helping them overcome judgements and assumptions that will only hurt you both.

Communication – What to Remember

- Communication with others begins with communication with ourselves. Having an understanding of our own emotions, stories and needs allows us to clearly communicate in an open and transparent way. We can easily fall into old memories and become reactive rather than responsive unless we stay present to the way we are interpreting what is happening in the moment.
- Most stresses in relationships or in communication are a result of expectation, where the other person is not showing up the way we think they 'should'. We all have a different set of values and often make the mistake of expecting others to hold the same value system as we do. Rather than trying to change others, we can try to view the world through their eyes and find greater perspective.

- Instead of listening to respond, listening to understand allows us to overcome the assumptions and judgements that are often our source of stress and step into the other person's shoes and perspective rather than always fighting for our own.
- Avoiding difficult or uncomfortable conversations can often bring feelings of resentment or expectation. Because everything that happens outside of ourselves is an assumption, communicating these assumptions is of key importance. By communicating 'at sea level' we have the important conversations before they become urgent.
- In much the same way as we can match our own difficult feelings to unmet needs, we can match our frustrations towards others to needs and communicate our needs rather than meet them with criticism.
- The Mind Reader character in our heads is often communicating with a past memory of the person and not the person in front of them. Look to override the Mind Reader's tendencies by coming to your conversations with a beginner's mind.

ARC EXERCISES

Begin by completing the following sentence stems in your journal:

- My biggest struggle with communication is …
- Leaning into this struggle will allow me to …
- Writing that makes me feel …
- Becoming a more empathetic listener would …
- I hold unfair expectations towards …
- I would be more accepting of this person if …
- I could bring 10% more of my authentic self to my relationships by …

Illumination Exercise:
Relationships – Seek Feedback

For this exercise I am going to encourage you to reach out to three people you trust and value to get a feel for how they see you show up in life. So often how we think we are seen is vastly different from the outsider's perspective or viewpoint.

It is important that this is framed correctly, with the people you choose understanding that in their honest feedback they are providing you with a gift. There will be little to no value beyond a quick fix for the ego in giving this to someone who's going to tell you that you're perfect! Equally, this isn't about someone tearing you down.

This exercise is useful for both the person giving and the person receiving the feedback.

The person giving the feedback is getting the chance to communicate honestly and openly about where they see your strengths and weaknesses. In a way, you are giving them a chance to communicate 'at sea level' and share any little assumptions or resentments they may be holding. The person receiving the feedback is getting the chance to practise receiving both praise and criticism while staying balanced and non-reactive.

Generally this exercise will bring up at least a few pleasant surprises and blind spots that you'd overlooked. Of course, it can also bring up a little discomfort or tension, which is a chance to bring curiosity to why being seen that way is difficult or uncomfortable for you. Remember, we all see the world through a different lens and the person giving the feedback is giving you their perspective. It is up to you what to choose to do with that feedback. The feedback itself is neutral. The judgement that you give it is what makes it 'positive' or 'negative'.

This is a fun and enlightening exercise and so don't be surprised if the person giving feedback becomes curious and asks you to return the favour.

It is important, of course, to receive whatever is presented to you as a gift and not an attack on who you are. Remember, you are not being 'called out' but 'called forward' by people who care about you and perhaps see a potential you can't yet see. If they were to tell you that they see you out of integrity in certain areas, your ego may feel attacked; from a different perspective you can see this as them recognising your greater potential which you have forgotten.

That doesn't mean that you'll agree with everything that's said; it just means that you're open to hearing some different viewpoints and then reflecting on how they sit with you.

Think of a time when your initial reaction in the heat of an argument was to fight back from a place of defensiveness, and you later came to see that there was perhaps truth in what the other person shared that made you feel uncomfortable in the moment.

The suggested questions are as follows, but you may choose to alter them or add some more. You could email the person these questions if it feels too much to ask them face to face.

1. What would you see as my greatest strengths?
2. Where do you see me struggle or fall short?
3. What do you appreciate the most about me?
4. How could I show up better for you?
5. Where do you see me out of integrity, saying I want one thing but doing the opposite?
6. What is the number one thing that you see holding me back in life?

After receiving the feedback from your three acquaintances, take some time to reflect and journal on what's come up. Are there any commonalities or similar threads in how people see you? Is there anything in terms of strengths and weaknesses that surprises you? Why might people see you in the way they've outlined? Is there a small action or change you'd like to make based on the feedback you've received?

Hopefully this exercise provides you with some interesting insights and food for thought. It's one that's worth revisiting every six months or so.

Journalling Prompts:
Relationships

1. Write a compassionate letter to the Mind Reader character in your head who struggles with communication and jumps to assumptions and expectations. How can you come to better understand one another?

2. What is the one relationship you would most like to improve in your life? What would you like that relationship to look like six months from now? What will be required to move towards this six-month vision?

3. Is there anyone in life you need to forgive? Consider their position and worldview and how that impacted on how they hurt you. Write a letter of forgiveness to this person.

4. Pick an important person in your life and spend ten minutes writing about what you appreciate about them.

5. Consider a recent challenge you have had in a relationship or in communication. What was your expectation about how things 'should' have looked? Stepping into the other person's shoes, what would their perception be of how things should have

been? Finally, consider what an impartial third party would have
thought about the interaction.

6. How could you show up more authentically in your relationships? What parts of yourself do you hide? What has that cost
   you in the past? What could you and the people in your life stand
   to gain by welcoming all parts of yourself?

7. Where have you been hurt in relationships in the past and what
   do you need to heal? What empowering lessons have you learnt?

Meditation of the Week:
Loving Kindness Meditation

This week's short meditation is a loving kindness meditation in
which we will direct loving attention to ourselves and then outwards
to the world, expanding our sphere of loving awareness.

Begin by sitting comfortably and allow yourself to settle. Picture
yourself from an outside perspective and send some loving attention
towards yourself by repeating the phrases 'May I be happy. May I
be healthy. May I be free from pain. May I live my life with ease.'

Next, bring someone you love to your mind and direct that same
loving attention towards them with the phrases 'May you be happy.
May you be healthy. May you be free from pain. May you live your
life with ease.'

Now bring your attention to a neutral acquaintance, someone
you know but do not have a deep relationship with. Repeat the
phrases again as you picture that person. 'May you be happy. May
you be healthy. May you be free from pain. May you live your life
with ease.'

Now picture someone with whom you have had some difficulty.
See this person clearly and direct your loving attention towards

them. 'May you be happy. May you be healthy. May you be free from pain. May you live your life with ease.'

Finally, expand your attention from people you know to all living beings everywhere and direct your loving attention outwards with the same phrases. 'May you be happy. May you be healthy. May you be free from pain. May you live your life with ease.'

The Conflict Story

*'Every criticism, judgement, diagnosis, and expression
of anger is the tragic expression of an unmet need'*
– MARSHALL ROSENBERG

'We're all just walking each other home' – RAM DASS

MEET THE CHARACTER – THE PROTECTOR

The Protector is the internal character in our mind who pops up to defend us in moments when we feel criticised, particularly by those closest to us. The Protector, like all the other characters we've met so far, comes from a place of being reactionary rather than responsive.

From the Protector's standpoint, any sign of conflict is an attack on the ego and a call to defend.

As young children we rely completely on the acceptance of and attachment to parental figures and others who keep us safe. It is scary to feel love or approval temporarily withdrawn and thus the Protector character is formed.

Fearing vulnerability and communicating our feelings and unmet needs, the Protector defends the heart by communicating from the head. In earlier years this Protector character learnt some patterns that they continue to play out to this day. The shortcoming of their patterns, however, is that the armour they wear to keep us safe is the same armour that keeps us from the deeper levels of intimacy and connection that we crave.

OUR CONFLICT STORIES

Our stories of what conflict means and how it should be handled are often formed in our earliest years. The patterns we created as kids to keep ourselves safe often go on to play out in our adult lives when we feel the threat of judgement, ridicule or abandonment. By bringing a greater awareness to how we view and approach conflict, we can come from a place of presence rather than a place of unconscious patterns.

Coming back to an earlier analogy of the foot on the accelerator or foot on the brake, we can remind ourselves that when the nervous system is in its sympathetic state, we can begin to feel out of control and reactive rather than responsive to what is happening in the moment. In heated or tense moments with people who challenge or confront us, it very much feels like the accelerator is pushed hard, emotions are amplified and we quickly feel emotionally flooded as our body skips into 'fight or flight' mode. We move from awareness to attention, with our focus moving to an internal story of being under threat and needing to defend ourselves and keep ourselves 'safe' at all costs. From this space of fight or flight we go to autopilot and old emotional wounds, stories or memories surface, alongside old reactions in the form of defence mechanisms. Our desire to defend ourselves can overtake our ability to communicate effectively in a way that turns conflict to connection. Have you ever had the experience of looking back on an argument after calming down and thinking, 'I might have been … completely in the wrong!'? Or maybe we were only partially wrong but unfortunately reacted in that moment in a way that has caused more hurt and disconnection in the long term.

In the heat of the moment we give our attention to a story of how we are right and the other person is wrong. In the heat of 'battle' our goal is to defend. We close off, and connection and understanding shut down. With space and perspective, our goal is to understand and to be understood, and so we might say that in our efforts to improve our conflict resolution we are hoping to move from a state of judgement to curiosity, and from hardening through our defensiveness to softening into vulnerability and connection.

When we do what is easy in the short term we often deprive ourselves of moving towards what we truly want, so it's important that we recognise that responding well and growing through conflict is a healthy and important part of finding meaning and deeper connection with ourselves and others. Surface-level conversation designed to have the other person like us at all costs, or an unwillingness to have uncomfortable or difficult conversations when needed, can prevent us reaching the intimacy or meaning that we crave in our relationships. As a result, we get stuck in our heads, mindreading and living in a world of assumptions and confusion about what's going on in the other person's head.

When conflict does occur we often find ourselves acting out in anger or resentment that masks a sadness and a desire to be understood and feel connected. Rather than praying for relationships that are devoid of conflict or disagreement it would be advisable to instead learn to embrace the idea of conflict resolution in a way in which we can find deeper levels of connection and understanding with the people in our lives.

PLAYING OUT PATTERNS

From here on we'll look at exploring the relationship we have with conflict with our romantic partner or previous romantic partners. If we often felt abandoned, let down or hurt in some way by the people who were closest to us in our younger years, it's usually the people closest to us in our later years who make us feel most vulnerable and triggered.

Though we'll talk a lot about romantic relationships in the coming pages, many of these principles and the general idea of slowing things down, observing our patterns and choosing a new response will remain the same.

We tend to expect things in our relationships that we saw in the relationships of our parental figures growing up. As we've said throughout the book, we'll have built unconscious stories and a 'blueprint' about how love 'should look', about how love 'should' be demonstrated and about how happy partners 'should act' with one another in good times and bad. When something comes up in our existing relationship that challenges this blueprint we've made, we can feel scared and unconsciously resort to defence mechanisms, more eager to protect our worldview than to deal with the uncertainty of creating something new.

In addition, we'll often look to fulfil the things we felt were missing in our younger years – our 'voids'. When these expectations or desires are challenged or go missing in our adult lives it can trigger old emotional stories or wounds that result in us falling into defensive states which might have kept us safe at one point, but are no longer serving us.

We will use a hypothetical example of these expectations, voids and desires to demonstrate how old 'blueprints' of unconscious beliefs might trigger an argument that seems to go from a small issue to World War III in the blink of an eye.

Jess grew up in a stable and encouraging household where she was given everything she ever needed. She never had to worry about money or security. She never saw her parents argue or raise their voices to one another. There were a lot of expectations placed on her as to 'who she needed to be' to be loved by her parents. Though she was grateful for the life she'd been given she felt she wasn't able to live adventurously and lacked the freedom she would have liked. Now in her adult life she values freedom and adventure and her understanding of the world through her blueprint is that when a couple are in love things go smoothly and there aren't ever any rows!

Jess's partner, John, grew up in a household where there was a huge amount of freedom and few, if any, rules. He frequently saw his parents argue and disagree about things. Shouting matches were commonplace, but it always seemed to work out in the end and they'd kiss and make up. Despite the love shown to him by his parents, having seven children they struggled to offer him as much attention as he would have liked and often failed to follow through on promises they'd make to him.

Now in his adult life he sees arguments and disagreements as an obvious part of a romantic relationship, and governed by his 'childhood void' and the structure and consistency he felt was lacking in his youth, he desires some structure and someone who sticks to their word.

Jess comes home forty-five minutes late from a night out and John criticises her for not letting him know she'd be late. She sees his criticism as an attack on her freedom and she becomes defensive. John feels hurt that she hasn't stuck to her word but criticises her rather than communicating what he's feeling and experiencing. 'You never get home at the time you say you'll be home.' Jess is unsure how to handle conflict and so she shuts down emotionally and stonewalls.

John, who needs to feel some reassurance and an explanation of why she didn't stick to her word, becomes more heated and upset by her unwillingness to take ownership of the fact she was late home (not sticking to her word). He sees her emotional check-out as a sign that she doesn't care about him and his mind goes into overdrive thinking of all the other evidence he can conjure up of occasions when she hasn't cared.

Behind the criticism and defence mechanisms are the emotional woundings and unmet needs. Jess feels her need for freedom is being threatened. John feels his need for security is being ignored. Generally, in disagreements with those closest to us, 'the thing is not the thing' and when we consider that ninety-five per cent of our thoughts will be the same as or very similar to yesterday's, when we get heated we dive back into old stories about abandonment or not being good enough or whatever it might be.

Again, as we've talked about throughout the book, there are two triggers – what happens and the meaning we give to what happens. Jess has attached to John calling her out the meaning of her freedom being taken. John has attached to Jess showing up later than she said she would the meaning of not being able to rely on her.

With a sense of curiosity, grab your journal and take a few minutes to consider the expectations and voids based on your own

childhood experience. Think about the unconscious stories you tell
and reactions you have when these feel withdrawn or under threat.

Expectations and voids:

1. What have I come to 'expect' in a relationship based on what
    I saw growing up?
2. What story do I tell myself about how the other person is treat-
    ing me when these expectations are threatened or aren't met?
3. The one thing I needed or wanted the most as a child that I
    didn't receive was …
4. In which areas of my life do I seek to fill this unmet need
    or void now?
5. What story do I tell myself when someone or something
    threatens this void or unmet need?

Perhaps in recognising some of your voids, expectations and
reactions you can begin to see how often in adult relationships it
isn't the mature, healthy adult version of ourselves who shows up
but instead the scared 'inner child' who fears abandonment and
rejection.

Just as we've got our automatic thoughts and stories, we've got
automatic reactions in terms of how we show up in conflict that is
deemed a threat by our body and mind.

As we've mentioned, when we're 'triggered' we become flooded
and slip into fight or flight response, going to our default setting
and moving from the logical mind to the primitive brain which
prioritises survival and acts on emotion. The prefrontal cortex, the
part of our brain responsible for problem-solving, shuts off and we
struggle to interpret or make sense of what the other person is saying.

In these emotionally flooded states, alongside fight or flight, we
can also add freeze or fawn as ways in which we typically respond.

- **Fight:** As a fighter you may feel yourself always putting blame on the other and being the attacker in moments of conflict. You get very emotional around your feelings and thoughts. The general thought process of the fighter is 'I am right and you are wrong.'
- **Flight:** You run away from moments of conflict because of the discomfort you feel around them. You may leave or walk out, and avoid the conversations that make you feel uncomfortable.
- **Freeze:** You may disassociate or numb out, withdrawing and going silent. You don't listen or talk and thus don't learn anything, meaning that nothing becomes resolved.
- **Fawn:** You always appease the other person, find it hard to say what you really think or feel, put other people's needs above your own and apologise for everything. For this reason you get caught in surface-level engagement that doesn't resolve anything meaningful.

Taking some of the examples of frustrations you currently experience or have experienced in a relationship, consider what the unmet emotional need was in each example. Following on from this, consider how you reacted to this emotional need being ignored or neglected and then consider the earliest memory in your past of this emotional need being neglected or ignored.

Here's an example of an 'outdated pattern' resurfacing in the present day:

Frustration:
Partner was bossy and always called the shots.
Unmet emotional need and story I tell myself:
The unmet need is the need to be heard.

The story I tell myself is 'What I want to do doesn't matter to her.'

How do/did I react?

I froze by 'stonewalling' and shutting down, withdrawing emotionally.

Earliest memories of this need not being validated:

When I was a kid my siblings were always louder and so they got what they wanted. I often felt unappreciated and unseen.

How did I react as a kid?

I shut down emotionally and went to my room.

I would encourage you to grab pen and paper and explore five frustrations you currently have or have had in your current or past relationships, before checking in with the needs, reactions and origins of these 'emotional wounds'.

HEARING BEYOND CRITICISM

We've talked a lot about recognising our unmet needs and becoming aware of and responding to them before going to autopilot reactions. We should also consider that criticisms directed at us are also a poor expression of the other person's unmet needs.

We can take this into consideration the next time we feel criticised and encourage the other person to share their unmet need. If they are unwilling or unable to recognise and understand their needs we will have to get curious and creative, do some mindreading and try to figure out what might be going on behind their words. For example:

Criticism:

'You're always working and even when you're not, you're completely disconnected.'

Unmet need:

I'm imagining they need to feel loved and respected, and that they are a priority in my life.

What might they really be trying to say beyond the criticism?

I want to spend more time with you and want to feel like I'm a priority in your life.

Looking at this type of exercise allows me to come to understand my emotional needs in a relationship, allowing me to express them going forward rather than getting caught up in criticism or blame. It is said that we form many of our emotional wounds in relationships in our early years and so it is in relationships that these wounds will typically resurface.

WE LIVE AND WE LEARN ...

Back in 2017 I undertook some training with the Gottman Institute to better understand 'relationship health'. The institute has completed over forty years of research working with over three thousand couples. If you'd told twenty-four-year-old Pat, whose only concern was getting people to do push-ups and eat broccoli, that a few years later he'd be doing a couples therapy certification he'd have laughed at you!

Based on their extensive research, John Gottman and his wife, Julie, had outlined three key components to a long-lasting and healthy relationship. They might seem obvious, but sometimes it's easy to forget the obvious stuff and get distracted by shiny lights.

Their three key components are:

- Building friendship and intimacy
- Shared meaning
- Conflict resolution

Building friendship and intimacy relates to the understanding that, like anything in life, there isn't ever a 'finish line' when it comes to a healthy relationship. In much the same way as physical, mental and emotional health require consistent commitments and practices, so too does the health of a relationship.

Failing to invest regularly in our mental fitness will lead to a feeling that we're putting out fires with regard to our mental wellness as stresses build and reach boiling point. Similarly, a lack of investment in our closest relationships can cultivate resentment and unfair unmet expectations. We constantly make investments of energy in the important relationships in our life and we don't take them for granted. If this healthy base isn't there, when difficulties come up we shouldn't be surprised when we crumble. Of course, this isn't always easy. Life gets busy, we are juggling commitments, and our struggles to communicate feelings of stress or overwhelm leave us feeling isolated and disconnected. It is easy to fall into ruts disguised as routines or to label and box off our loved ones, thinking that we know them inside out, but the consistent investment in a relationship is a key aspect in gaining depth, meaning and intimacy.

It is also easy to convince ourselves that the countless hours we spend at work are for our family and loved ones, but our time and presence are the greatest currency we have available to us. Right now, you might consider how you spend your one hundred and sixty-eight hours of the week. How many of those hours are spent with the people you say are a priority? And when you are with them, are you really with them? This is certainly an area in which I have had to improve.

Some things you might consider to consistently build this friendship and intimacy:

- A weekly date night with your partner.
- A little time spent daily giving each of your kids some of your undivided attention.
- Twenty minutes every day with a loved one to talk without distraction.
- A rule of removing phones from the kitchen and/or bedroom.

Alongside building friendship, the Gottmans' suggestion of focusing on the shared meaning aspect of a healthy relationship centres on the creativity of evolution as a couple; two people coming together and creating a life together that is completely unique and unlike any other relationship out there. The Gottmans suggest that couples find shared meaning through goals, rituals and roles. How much of the one hundred and sixty-eight hours of the week do we spend sitting down, with no distractions, just talking and getting to know one another, maintaining the playfulness and curiosity that the relationship began with?

Even when we focus on our 'relationship base' through deliberate practices of building friendship, intimacy and shared meaning, it is inevitable that at times we will experience challenges in our communication, and conflict may arise. Just as we have developed unconscious beliefs and habits in all areas of life that we are often blissfully unaware of, we will also have developed autopilot reactions and patterns that show up for us, usually unconsciously, in our relationships, particularly in times of tension or conflict.

The Gottman Institute outlined four common defence mechanisms that they have found to be among the most destructive behaviours in relationships. We might call them the four horsemen. In unhealthy conflict these are four places we will tend to go, because as habitual behaviours we feel these patterns will keep us safe. Again, these patterns are often seen or formed in childhood and play out when we listen to our internal Protector character and get into stressed and reactive states.

1. Criticism

Here, when we feel threatened or under attack our response is to verbally criticise the other person. This attack isn't about offering them useful or well-thought-out feedback on a specific event or situation; it's a critique of the core of their character. Criticism can make the other person feel rejected or hurt, often resulting in both parties falling into other aspects of the four horsemen.

2. Contempt

More hostile than criticism, contempt is about belittling or trying to bring the other person down. This can be sarcastic, mocking or disrespectful. The Gottmans have noted that contempt is the single biggest predictor of divorce – but it's important to note that it can be turned around.

3. Defensiveness

Defensiveness is a means of deflecting away from the criticism or point that's being brought up by 'playing the victim'. As well as victimising themselves the defensive person will often turn the blame around on their partner. Defensiveness doesn't work as a means of managing conflict because responsibility isn't taken.

4. Stonewalling

This involves shutting down or withdrawing. People who stonewall will emotionally check out as they struggle to communicate rationally when they feel 'flooded' and so instead opt to tune out.

Consider some of these more constructive responses when you notice one or more of the four horsemen surfacing as your Protector character appears.

Criticism

Speak in language that takes ownership of your own feelings and experience. Rather than saying, 'You made me feel …', use 'I' statements and specific examples of the other person's behaviours, rather than criticising their character.

For example, instead of 'You only think about yourself' you might consider something like 'I felt sad when you made plans for the weekend and didn't ask me what I would like to do.'

Contempt

In contempt our negativity and confirmation biases place our attention on all the other person's flaws. A more constructive response when we are experiencing feelings of contempt is to draw our attention to their positive traits. You might even consider making a list that you can refer back to when you feel yourself falling into resentment.

Defensiveness

Avoid justifying or defending your position and instead take ownership of anything you need to own directly related to the other person's criticism. Acknowledging their perspective and feelings does not negate your own, but it is important that they feel heard and understand that you can see their perspective.

Stonewalling

If you find it difficult to communicate with your partner as you become emotionally flooded, communicate to them that you need a little space to process and collect your thoughts. Rather than making them feel rejected, allow them to understand that you just need to check in with and take care of yourself before continuing the conversation.

IN THE HEAT OF BATTLE

So what now? We've brought some awareness to our patterns, seen how we might take criticisms or frustrations and link them to unmet needs and we've maybe begun to make some sense of the expectations or desires that provide a blueprint for how things 'should' look in our closest relationships.

All these exercises have allowed us to slow down and gain perspective, but of course finding this type of perspective is not as easy when we are in the eye of the storm. We become flooded, emotional and reactive, rather than grounded and responsive. For that reason our first port of call in the heat of any argument or disagreement needs to be to **slow things down**.

Breath

Allow the breath to down-regulate your nervous system. Look to breathe in through the nose for three seconds and slow down the exhale to a count of six, sending a signal to the body and mind that everything is okay.

Repeat a couple of these breaths and imagine you are slowing down a car that's getting out of control, so that you can take back ownership of the steering wheel, and begin steering things in the right direction.

Reflective Listening

Continue to slow things down by allowing the other person to speak and not reacting to criticisms being thrown at you or feeling the need to defend your position. Perhaps you can imagine what their unmet need might be behind the criticism they are giving you.

Look to become curious rather than judgemental about how they feel and why they feel that way. Let go of your own viewpoint for a minute and just listen. If you notice any of the four horsemen creeping up, and defending yourself becomes more tempting than understanding the other person, recognise that this is an old and outdated pattern that doesn't work. Continue to breathe and listen.

Once they have said what they need to say, mirror back what you have heard. 'Can I just reflect back what I've heard you say, just to make sure we are on the same understanding?'

So often what is heard is very different from what was said, so we need to make sure that they feel you understand their viewpoint – it doesn't mean you have to agree with it. After reflecting back what they've shared you might ask, 'Is there anything I've left out or anything you'd like to add?'

Ownership

Once the person has said their piece and you have confirmed with them through reflecting back what they've said that you understand their position, you might choose to take ownership of certain elements of it. For example, you might begin by saying, 'I can see how you felt I was a bit disconnected and not making much effort and I'm sorry for that.'

This shows that you are seeing things from their side and trying to connect with and understand their viewpoint. Ownership is about 'owning it' without the need for justifications or stories behind why you did what you did.

Share How You Feel

When we argue we tend to operate from the ego and speak from the head. We often criticise and condemn using language that either negates the other person's position or defends ours. We should try to be present and notice any feelings or stories that are coming up for us as we go through these experiences of slowing things down. 'Right now I feel sad and a little guilty. You are one of the closest people in my life and knowing how upset we both are over this hurts me.'

By slowing down we allow ourselves to find perspective and go beyond our polarised thinking of right or wrong, good or bad. We allow ourselves to gain balance and understanding. This is a practice; it's not something that's going to be easy or look perfect!

During my two-hundred-hour yoga teacher training we were constantly reminded to 'breathe and soften' despite the discomfort we were experiencing in many of the poses. Perhaps the next time you get into conflict, you'll remember that mantra of 'breathe and soften', knowing that letting go of the tension and rigidity of how the other person 'should' be showing up will make room for a new level of openness and understanding.

Conflict – What to Remember

● Conflict, handled well, can lead to greater levels of truth, love and connection. In much the same way as challenge is an essential part of personal growth and any idea of growth without discomfort is a one-sided fantasy, this same discomfort must be welcomed in a relationship as we seek to grow together.

- The Protector is the character that shows up in reactive ways when our expectations or voids are unmet. Seeing the Protector emerge is our invitation to breathe and encourage the mature adult, not the scared inner child, to communicate.

- The first port of call is to slow the car down. In moments of conflict we go into a state of fight or flight and our body and mind go into survival reactions and autopilot. As a result we can often close off, put up our armour or fight to protect our perspective. By slowing things down, breathing through the discomfort and looking to reflect back what we hear, we can find perspective and allow the space to connect through conflict.

- We need to hear beyond the criticism and listen out for the unmet need. Just as understanding our own needs allows us to make healthy and empowering choices in life, understanding the emotional needs behind the words of criticism from another can help us to communicate from the heart and not from the head.

- By understanding our default conflict pattern we can choose to respond differently in the future. Old reactions will appear, but our increased awareness and willingness to slow the breath and 'soften' allow us to choose a new more constructive response.

ARC EXERCISES

Begin by completing the following sentence stems in your journal:

- What I learnt about conflict growing up was …
- Writing that makes me feel …
- My most common frustration in relationships is …
- The unmet need behind that frustration is …
- My earliest memory around that need going unmet is …
- Ways in which I could meet that unmet need are …
- By learning to better handle conflict I will …

Illumination Exercise:
Conflict – Dark and Gold Shadows

In this illumination exercise I'm asking you to list three people you admire greatly and three people you judge harshly. For each person you've listed, outline the trait or action that inspires or upsets you. In this list you are seeing your greatest potential for self-acceptance and compassion.

Now, alongside each of the traits listed, I'm going to challenge you to list three ways in which you demonstrate, have demonstrated or could potentially demonstrate that very same trait. As an example, if you've listed 'creative' as a trait that you greatly admire, look for three ways in which you have, do or could demonstrate creativity in your own life. If you've listed 'ignorance' as a trait you dislike, look for three ways in which you have, are or could be demonstrating ignorance in your own life.

This type of exercise can be difficult at first as the ego doesn't want to acknowledge unlikable traits, but stay with it. Recognise that by shining light on this darkness you are reclaiming your admirable qualities. If you're struggling to acknowledge where you demonstrate a trait, you might consider how you demonstrate the given trait towards yourself, towards the person you're judging or towards others. For example, if you've picked bullying as something you detest in others, you might not see examples of times you have bullied others, but there have probably been times when you have bullied yourself.

If you've chosen to list an action rather than a trait, you might struggle to find a direct example of where you demonstrate that action. For example, if you've said you detest people who cheat on their partners and you cannot find any time you have cheated on your partners, consider the energy behind the action and explore that instead. You might say that the energy behind cheating is betrayal, and then you can explore where you have betrayed yourself or others.

To finish the exercise, reflect on what you have learnt about yourself and what areas of the shadow you have brought light to.

This type of written exercise begins to help us find perspective. Over time the challenge is to find perspective in the moments in which you are triggered, recognising the trait or action that is making you uncomfortable and seeing it as a part of you.

As a final note, there is a difference between being informed and being disturbed. Moments in which someone's behaviour or actions inform us are moments when we might not agree but we don't become emotionally invested. Moments in which we are disturbed are the moments in which we have an emotional response, moments in which we are being given shadow material to work with.

Journalling Prompts:
Conflict

1. Write a compassionate letter to your Protector character acknowledging them for the efforts they have made to keep you safe and communicating with them how you'd like them to show up from now on.

2. Remembering three specific arguments you've had, tune in to the story you were telling yourself in those moments. What was the 'second' trigger, the meaning you were giving to what was happening? With space and perspective, can you find any alternative meanings you could have given to those situations?

3. Remembering three specific arguments, reflect on what your unmet needs were and what feelings you experienced in those

arguments. How can you communicate your feelings and needs more effectively in future conflict?

4. Consider a time in which you experienced conflict in a relationship. Behind the criticisms directed towards you, what might the other person's unmet needs have been? Behind any criticisms you directed towards the other person, what were some of your own unmet needs? What can you learn from that experience?

5. Write about some examples of times in which you've been 'emotionally flooded'. How did you react and what patterns did you find yourself going to?

6. Which of the four horsemen do you find yourself going to most frequently? What is this costing you in your relationships? How could you show up in a more constructive way?

7. What are the lifestyle factors, habits and activities that allow you to feel less reactive and more responsive in life? How can these contribute to your ability to respond when you experience emotional flooding?

Meditation of the Week:
Being with Discomfort

Back in 2017 I was lucky enough to spend a week with Wim Hof, the 'Iceman', near his home in Poland. Wim has become well known for the Wim Hof Method, which promotes using ice baths alongside a breathing technique which includes deep breaths followed by breath retention. His nickname comes from his incredible ability to be in freezing cold temperatures wearing nothing but shorts.

We won't be going to freezing cold temperatures this week, but for our 'meditation' of the week I am going to channel your inner Iceman or Icewoman and encourage you to become comfortable in the uncomfortable by taking a cold shower daily.

This is a meditation in that our reaction when the cold water hits our skin may be to jump out of the shower or turn the dial to warm. Rather than *reacting*, I encourage you to *respond* by noticing how, as you slow your breath and extend your exhale, your body and mind begin to settle and become comfortable in the uncomfortable.

If cold showers are new for you, start on warm, switch to thirty seconds on cold and then finish on warm. If you are more experienced, start on warm and finish with thirty to sixty seconds of cold, and if you want more of a challenge try a two-minute shower with cold water throughout.

The Fear Story

'The cave you fear to enter holds the treasure you seek'
– Joseph Campbell

MEET THE CHARACTER – THE SCARED CHILD

As grown adults who have made it to this point in our life, grown tremendously and no doubt been through many challenges and adversities, a lot of our current fears can often seem irrational and difficult to understand. Why is it that we can speak for hours to a friend without a worry in the world but the thought of standing in front of a room full of people and introducing ourselves or sharing a few words is terrifying? Why does uncertainty in a relationship or career leave us feeling helpless or overwhelmed? Why is it that asking someone out on a date can trigger immense feelings of insecurity and self-doubt?

Our Scared Child character surfaces in moments of fear and craves comfort, security and safety. They vividly remember moments in which we felt abandoned, rejected, helpless or hurt. So the thought of leaning into the unknown or falling short of the expectations we have of ourselves can leave us feeling safer staying in our comfort zone and doing the same things in the hope of staying secure and free from discomfort.

By recognising the memories of this Scared Child character, acknowledging them and finding perspective beyond the initial judgements we have put on these memories, we can begin to dissolve some of the fears that hold us back in life and instead choose to embrace the uncertainty that is a given in life, rather than trying to avoid it and feeling overwhelmed when it appears.

FEAR OF JUDGEMENT AND REJECTION

Conversations around fear may immediately make us think of spiders, small spaces, snakes, needles, or heights, but these are not the primary fears that warrant our care or attention. It is not these fears that really debilitate and hold us back in life. The fear that holds us back the most, consumes our vital energy and limits our possibilities is the fear of judgement or rejection from others.

This fear of judgement can be painted in different ways – the fear of failure, the fear of success, the fear of putting ourselves out there, the fear of public speaking … In reality, all of these point back to the concern around what other people will think of us and whether we will be able to attain or maintain the approval and acceptance of others. Our fear of failure is really the result of thinking, 'What will other people think if I don't achieve what I set out to achieve?' The fear of success is 'What will other people think if I choose to allow myself to be and show more of who I want to be?'

As we've said throughout this book, when a story or thought of fear emerges and we begin to identify with it, the primitive part of our brain becomes activated, going straight to survival mode and to emotionally charged decisions rather than decisions based on logic and what we truly want. We might have great intentions of achieving or changing something in our life, but when our mind goes to imaginative stories or memories of rejection or judgement and we believe those thoughts and stories, we can find ourselves paralysed or stuck, knowing exactly what we want to do, but being consumed by fear that stops us in our tracks. The fear of rejection, judgement or ridicule can feel like death to the ego, that collection of ideas we have built about who we are and how we fit in the world.

A number of years ago I spoke with a friend who works as a men's dating coach in London. He works with men from all types of background who are eager to overcome fears around rejection when approaching women they are attracted to. The sheer power of fear around rejection was highlighted to me when he told me about a man he was coaching who'd just come back from serving time in the army in a war-torn region and carried more fear around going up to a woman and saying hello than he had in putting his life on the line in a real life-or-death situation. This might seem bizarre, but it does remind us of the sheer power the stories in our heads based on memory and imagination can have on us. This man's fear of rejection, a mental construct, had more of an impact on him than the actual physical threat of being injured or killed in war.

I suggest that our fears are a projection of memories in which we feel things didn't go as they 'should' have. As such, when we find ourselves experiencing the fear of rejection or abandonment as adults, it is our Scared Child character who is experiencing the fear based on a memory of a time when we felt rejected or critically judged in our past.

In our lifetime we have had countless thoughts, but there are probably a handful of memories that really stand out. These are typically the more emotionally charged memories that we labelled either 'really good' or 'really bad' experiences or memories. When we have a polarised perception of a past memory and see it as 'bad' without having any balance or perspective, we will try to avoid any possibility of something similar happening in the future. If, however, we can find balance in our memories and look for the 'gold in the muck', the charge associated with our future fear will begin to dissipate and dissolve. We will feel more capable and trusting of leaning into our fears in the future and not trying to avoid them.

When thinking of our own fears in life, particularly those around rejection, ridicule or judgement, we should consider the earliest memories that triggered similar feelings. These early memories are where our Scared Child character is stuck. Perhaps the soldier terrified of saying hello to a woman he is attracted to is subconsciously reliving an experience of being ridiculed as a young man when he professed his love for a classmate who wasn't interested in him. Labelling that memory as a negative experience protects him by signalling danger and fear at the prospect of experiencing that type of pain again. As we've explored throughout the book, our judgements take us from awareness to attention and narrow our attention to just one side of the coin. Looking back at his 'negative' memory of the past, the soldier can seek out the positives from that experience that currently live in the dark.

With time we often come to find perspective naturally. A break-up that was incredibly difficult at the time makes perfect sense ten years later when we are walking down the aisle with the person we've decided to marry, something that never would have happened had we not experienced that painful time in our life. With pen and paper, and actively choosing to search for the gold in the muck, we can gain perspective much quicker and remove much of the unnecessary suffering that comes from holding resentment for the past.

Consider where and with whom the fear of judgement shows up for you the most in life. Thinking of this fear and recognising the Scared Child, see if you can tap into the origins of this fear. Is there a specific memory that stands out, one that you deemed a 'negative' experience which you don't ever want to experience again? Now, looking back at this memory, see if you can widen your perspective and balance the judgement. Was there anything positive that came from the experience? Were you supported by others during that time? Did you learn anything that was helpful going forward? Did you come to understand yourself better or develop certain strengths and resilience that came about as a result of this challenging time?

Spend some time searching for the gold in the muck and recognise that as you begin to balance the judgement of that situation, you come to acknowledge your ability to handle future challenges and adversities that will inevitably arise in life.

LOOKING OVER THE FEAR WALL

In moments of fear we go from awareness of all possible scenarios and outcomes to attention on what we believe will inevitably go wrong. We put on a pair of blinkers, lose all perspective and can only see the worst-case scenarios based on stories being built in our imagination. The thought of having an amazing conversation with someone we are attracted to disappears and is overridden by the story of them rejecting us. The thought of impacting the lives of an audience by sharing our story on stage is replaced with the horror story of standing on that stage and drawing a complete blank about what to say. An initial burst of inspiration to try to speak a few words of a language we've been learning is replaced by the fear of the native speaker judging or ridiculing our efforts.

I used an exercise called the 'fear wall' as a means of pushing past my resistance to public speaking. I continue to use this exercise frequently to help find perspective and leverage in leaning into the fears that are holding me back in life. If we think of our fears as a wall that is standing in our way and the size of the wall is relevant to the size of our fear, we can begin to think about our reason for trying to climb the wall. If we are solely fixated on the wall (the fear) and don't see anything worthwhile on the other side of it, it makes much more sense to stay comfortable where we are. If, however, we can begin to see some benefits and reasons to go beyond the wall, everything starts to change.

Taking the common fear of judgement or rejection, we can go from looking *at* the fear to looking *beyond* the fear and at what we stand to gain by overcoming it. Perhaps, on reflection, we see that leaning into our fear of judgement will enable us to connect more honestly with ourselves and others, will perhaps enable us to meet a loving partner, will help us to be more confident in job interviews and will enable us to pursue work and hobbies that are really mean-ingful to us and go beyond what we feel others expect of us. This reflection has taken us from attention on the worst-case scenario to a greater awareness of the possible positive impact. This is the type of leverage that we need as a reminder to embrace uncertainty, trusting life and ourselves.

Taking this a step further, we can begin to think about what we stand to lose or miss out on in life if we choose to be controlled by our fear of rejection. We're less likely to connect authentically with the people we love and to form new genuine relationships and friendships. We're likely to stay in a comfort zone at work that will lead to lack of fulfilment and passion for life. The longer we avoid the fear the more likely it is that it will consume us and rob us of our energy and potential for personal growth and acceptance in life. This further reflection allows us to see that although this unwillingness to lean into our fear might look like an effort to keep us safe, it is severely limiting our potential and possibilities in life.

Painting these two pictures of what we stand to gain and lose as a result of tackling or avoiding our fear starts to give us perspec-tive and leverage which we can remind ourselves of when fearful thoughts emerge and challenge us.

Exercise:
Looking Beyond Your Fear Wall

In moments of fear we become obsessed and fixated on what is going to go wrong and we lose sight of what is possible on the other side of that fear. Imagining our fear as a wall, we want to consider what lies on the other side of the wall that makes the climb worthwhile.

Take some time to explore the following prompts and develop leverage to support you in taking courageous steps forward:

1. What is the number one fear you feel is holding you back in life? Looking back in time, what is your earliest memory of experiencing that type of fear?
2. How has this fear impacted or held you back in the past? How is it affecting your day-to-day life in the present?
3. What do you stand to gain in life if you choose to climb the fear wall? What lies on the other side? If you were to lean into this fear, what positive impact would it have across all areas of your life over the next three to five years?
4. If you continue to avoid this fear, what will you miss out on in life? How will staying where you are negatively impact you or hold you back across the different areas of life over the next three to five years?
5. What is the first step you can take to move yourself into action and begin climbing the wall? How can you communicate with your Scared Child character to make them feel safe as you lean into your discomfort?

RE-PARENTING AND SUPPORTING OURSELVES

Fear is often the result of jumping ten steps ahead of where we are and having excessive goals or ambitions based on comparison rather than seeking progress over perfection. We look to others to figure out what success should look like and see going from where we are now to where we'd like to be as one giant leap rather than a number of shorter steps. Our minds spend so much time in the future that we find ourselves predicting what will happen ten steps ahead of where we are rather than focusing on our starting point in the here and now.

It's in taking that first step and living in the stretch zone, which we talked about earlier, that we build the confidence to take the second step, but so many of us stay rooted in the fearful stories in our heads, which feed on time, rather than moving to action, where we can find evidence of our progress and potential. Like standing on a diving board, the longer we wait in life the scarier things get and the quieter our inner voice of courage becomes as it is drowned out by the overthinking mind. If we simply concern ourselves with crossing each bridge as we come to it, we can develop momentum and become comfortable with greater levels of uncertainty.

The first day of school is a big moment in many parents' lives as they wave goodbye to their infant and send them off into the world to 'fend for themselves'. You'll often hear a parent say, 'I think I was more scared and emotional than them,' as their child quickly meets friends and settles into their new routine. Other kids cling desperately to their parents and beg them not to leave, emotional, crying and completely overwhelmed by this new experience. In these moments the parent supports, encourages and reassures the child that it'll all be okay. Generally, in a relatively short time the child comes to see that the reality of the situation is nothing like the fearful stories they had built in their head and school becomes something they are excited for.

When we step out into the world as fully grown adults who don't have that parental figure holding our hand and encouraging us every step of the way, we can feel like the child clinging to our parents and begging them not to make us leave our comfort zone. It's important in these moments that we check in with our Scared Child character and communicate with them, first seeing why they are scared, then acknowledging their fears and reminding them that as an adult you are here to look after them.

You might encourage a nervous child by reminding them of scary things they've overcome in the past or of things they do for fun now that were once foreign; we can remind ourselves and collect confidence from our past by recognising the challenges and adversity we have already overcome in life. In the same way, it is important that the Scared Child knows that even if things don't go to plan and their fear comes to be realised, you will be there to comfort and protect them.

When the thought surfaces of leaving a job that is no longer providing fulfilment, the Scared Child character might protest, insisting on staying where we are comfortable but uninspired. In communicating with them and seeing that they are overwhelmed at the thought of having to go to a new environment, meet new people and take a gamble on whether or not we'll fit in, we can start to understand the child's fears and hesitations. We might put them at ease by reminding them it doesn't need to be a clean jump from one job to another, it might start with maintaining the current job and looking into upskilling in the evenings, before taking the next step when it appears.

Listening to the Scared Child character doesn't mean letting them make your decisions and drive the car. It simply means listening, acknowledging, reassuring and supporting that part of ourselves that is experiencing overwhelm.

JUSTIN BIEBER, STOIC PHILOSOPHY
AND A BEACH PARTY IN THAILAND

After two weeks in Bangkok and Phuket, my girlfriend at the time and I landed on the beautiful Thai island of Koh Tao. The place looked like a postcard, idyllic and everything we had anticipated Thailand would be. After dropping our luggage and grabbing some local seafood we headed down to a nearby beach where we could hear music and see fire dancers performing near the water.

The second we arrived at the beach my girlfriend was straight out on the dance floor enjoying the music and encouraging me to do the same. I told her I'd run to the bathroom and join her when I got back. When I did get back she'd met a girl from the UK who seemed to enjoy dancing as much as she did. Relieved, I headed for the bar, grabbed a beer and proceeded to repeat this cycle of going between the bar and bathroom for the next hour in my best efforts to avoid getting out on the dance floor. I'd always had resistance around dancing – to my mind it wasn't something Irishmen did sober, so I decided at least a few beers were needed first!

As I was getting another round at the bar I met the boyfriend of the girl from the UK. It turned out he had a similar story around Englishmen's ability to dance sober. We planted ourselves at the bar and promised our girlfriends we'd join them after the next drink. This went on another while, with our only trips to the dance floor being a quick delivery of cocktails to the girls before retreating to safety of the bar.

Suddenly, without warning the music came to a grinding halt and the DJ left the booth. All the signs were pointing to the night being over and I felt a sinking feeling that I had missed my chance to get on the dance floor to let loose and have some fun with my girlfriend. I'd let my completely irrational fears and insecurities around dancing rule me and now the night was over. How was it I had only felt ready when the music finally stopped?

My mind works in a funny way and I immediately thought of the DJ being like the god we meet at the end of our lives who says, 'Okay, time's up, hope you made the most of it.'

Will I have the same thought then? Will I say, 'Don't tell me life is over now, I finally feel over my self-doubt, fear and insecurities and I'm ready to start living'? We all know our time will come, but in many ways we live as if we're immortal, deferring the things we want to do to 'someday' and allowing our fears to keep us small.

Two thousand years ago the Stoic philosopher Seneca wrote, 'You live as if you were destined to live for ever, no thought of your frailty ever enters your head, of how much time has already gone by you take no heed. You squander time as if you drew from a full and abundant supply, though all the while that day which you bestow on some person or thing is perhaps your last.'

Suddenly in the midst of my contemplation about fear, insecurities, self-doubt and the shortness of life I heard Justin Bieber blaring over the speakers. A second chance at the dance floor with no room for overthinking or self-doubt!

The Stoics shared a philosophy of *memento mori*, a Latin phrase that means 'remember you must die'. Reminding ourselves of death and the shortness of life isn't a morbid exercise, but one that provides perspective and appreciation for the time we've been given. When I think about advice I'd give to my younger self it centres largely on being kinder to myself, allowing myself to take chances, having the courage to be true to myself and not wear masks based on seeking the approval of others. I think so often the advice we'd offer our younger selves is the very advice we could benefit the most from now.

Similarly it can be useful to stare death in the face and acknowledge that some day your day will come and you can either look back with regret over fears that held you back or appreciation for how you allowed yourself to be with uncertainty, trusting that you are capable of responding to and being with whatever happens.

Just as my comrade and I at the bar in Thailand encouraged one another to stay within our comfort zones, far removed from the dance floor, often those closest to us can give us a false illusion of safety in discouraging us from leaning into new challenges or possibilities. If one of us had gone out dancing, the other might well have followed. As we begin to bravely expand our comfort zone, we allow those around us to feel they can do the same.

A year after the beach party in Thailand I found myself on a dance floor of a different kind in Austin, Texas. Ecstatic dance is a form of dance where you let yourself go completely and look to merge with the music as it goes almost through a journey or story. It's quite a sight from the outside as people let go of their inhibitions and connect fully with themselves and their emotions. The rules are: no alcohol, no drugs, no cameras and no judgement. Getting out on this dance floor among a hundred and fifty people at 10 a.m. was a far cry from sitting on the sidelines downing drinks at 10 p.m. the year before, but in facing our fears we take back the energy associated with avoiding them. I was struck by something the facilitator said as he introduced the session.

'We've all developed patterns in the way we move. As little boys or little girls we began shutting down certain movements or gestures because they were shamed or criticised. As a result we've become quite rigid in our way of movement.'

As an Irishman whose hips hadn't moved in a number of years I could attest to this and it of course mirrors the limitations we have on ourselves through the stories we've told ourselves for years and the parts of ourselves we've shut down because of shame or criticism.

The facilitator told us to move our bodies in ways we hadn't in a long time and to break the patterns that had been set on autopilot. Before the music began he reminded us that 'Between you hearing the music and you moving your body there is a space. We're trying to get rid of that space and become one with the music.'

Now that might sound like some hippie jargon to the sceptic but what I heard was that the longer we live in our heads overthinking life, the more scared we get. If we can cut down that space between being inspired to do something and going and doing it, we give ourselves a much greater chance at quieting fear.

Someday the music is going to stop, so make sure you get out dancing and don't watch from the sidelines!

Fear – What to Remember

- Our fears are often projections of past resentments. Our prediction-making mind takes difficult memories and projects them into the future in an effort to keep us safe. Thus, oftentimes the fears that surface for us in the present are a result of meanings we have given to our past experiences. By going back and looking at the past from different angles we can begin to dissolve the emotional charge associated with these future fears.

- Action is the antidote to fear. Remember the diving board? The longer we wait, the scarier it gets, fear feeds on time and our mind turns to horror stories about what it believes will inevitably go wrong. Take a step, no matter how small, to lean into our fear and not away from it, to get us out of thinking and into action.

● In a world where so much of our attention is directed outward it is impossible not to find ourselves slipping into comparison with others. As such we sometimes have huge expectations on ourselves on what growth and change 'should' look like. Much of our fear in life can come from trying to run before we can walk. Start with the smallest step, acknowledge that step and collect the confidence from that little bit of progress.

● Fear takes us from awareness of all potential outcomes to attention on what we believe will inevitably go wrong. It doesn't make sense for us to lean into our fears unless we bring awareness to what we stand to gain by tackling our fear and lose by keeping it. You can use the fear wall exercise at the end of this chapter as a means of developing leverage and a strong positive emotional charge around making a change and tackling your fear.

● Our fears rob us of a tremendous amount of energy and limit our possibilities and potential in life. In running towards rather than from our fears we claim back that energy and can direct it into what is most meaningful to us in life.

● It is often our Scared Child character who surfaces in moments of fear. By acknowledging and communicating with this character we can self-soothe and help ourselves feel safe and taken care of rather than berating ourselves for 'lack of courage'. Remember, when we look after the child we can show up as the adult.

ARC EXERCISES

Begin by completing the following sentence stems in your journal:

- The fear that holds me back the most is ...
- Writing that makes me feel ...
- If my fear could speak it would say ...
- In response I would say ...

- Overcoming this fear would allow me to …
- I would tell a friend experiencing this fear to …
- I can better support my inner child by …

Illumination Exercise:
Fear – A Meeting between
Your Older and Younger Self

Imagine meeting your younger self, back at a time in your life in which you felt anything was possible. Close your eyes and picture yourself sitting down with that younger version of you and listening to the advice that they would offer you.

Don't try to 'think' of what they would tell you, instead just take some deep breaths with eyes closed, picturing your younger self sitting in front of you and listening to their wisdom. There might be a tendency to dismiss their advice as naïve, but instead sit with them as though they are a guru with incredible insight and perspective on how to approach life.

Once you have listened deeply, open your eyes and write down the advice they gave you. After taking this time to write out all of their advice, circle or highlight the one message they shared with you that stands out the most at this point in your life.

Now, press fast-forward and imagine meeting a much older version of yourself as you come towards the end of your life. Sitting with this wise elder, again listen deeply to what they have to share with you. Maybe you want to ask them specific questions that are pertinent to where you are in life right now, or maybe you're happy to just listen to the advice they are eager to share with you. Either way, 'listen' to your intuition and natural response rather than intellectually thinking of what they would say.

Write out their advice and again highlight or circle the line that stands out for you the most. Looking now at the advice shared by both your younger and older selves, what is it you most want to focus on or action at this point in your life? What can you do before going to bed tonight to set the wheels in motion towards putting this advice into immediate practice?

Journalling Prompts:
Fear

1. Write about what you would do in life and how your life would feel different if you didn't have any fear around judgement from others.

2. Looking at your greatest fear, consider what the worst thing that could happen around leaning into this fear would be. How would you respond if the worst-case scenario were to happen?

3. Write a compassionate letter to your Scared Child character acknowledging their fears and offering them support, guidance and comfort.

4. Write about how fear feels in your body. What physical sensations do you have?

5. Write about some things that were once scary to you that are now easy. What made you want to tackle these fears and why did you go about doing that? How can you use this wisdom going forward?

6. Imagine you have been given an hour-long session with the world's best coach who is known for helping people quickly get past their fears. Write about the advice they give you in the session.

7. If today was your last day on earth, what fears would you regret? How would you have lived differently?

Meditation of the Week:
Shake it Out!

We are switching up this week's meditation and going with ecstatic dance. I will be encouraging you to dance or shake it out!

This isn't performative; it's not about being a 'good dancer' or having 'rhythm'. It is an opportunity to express yourself through your body and shake out any stress or tension you may be holding.

In much the same way as we go to autopilot thoughts, stories and beliefs in our minds, we tend to be very limited and 'shut down' in how we move our bodies. This week, take at least ten minutes daily to move in ways you haven't moved in a long time.

Allow yourself to be free in your expression. You can do this with the light off if it is more comfortable for you. This doesn't have to be pretty; in fact you can use this time to shake out any anger, frustration or other difficult emotions you may be holding.

When we experience stressful situations in life not only is there a cognitive reaction but also a somatic reaction in which we 'feel' it in our body. Imagine how you might tense up in your body on receiving harsh words of criticism from a loved one. This tension can often be stored over time, leaving us feeling heavy and sick.

We see animals in the wild 'shake' off their stress and tension after getting to safety and away from a predator. In the stressful event there is a release of stress and adrenaline which floods the body and once the stressful event is over the animal will have what looks like a 'seizure' as they get rid of the tension and stress being physically held in the body.

Your daily ecstatic dance this week provides the chance to do something similar. Get out of your head and into your body and if you have more than ten minutes give yourself that time.

The Purpose Story

'It's a terrible thing, I think, in life to wait until you're ready. I have this feeling now that actually no one is ever ready to do anything. There is almost no such thing as ready. There is only now. And you may as well do it now. Generally speaking, now is as good a time as any' – HUGH LAURIE

'Don't be seduced into thinking that that which does not make a profit is without value' – ARTHUR MILLER

MEET THE CHARACTER – THE SPECTATOR

The Spectator character in our head seems more interested in watching life than in experiencing it. They put people on pedestals and take more of an interest in other people's lives than in our own. They encourage us to spend our lives on screens watching what others are doing rather than being excited about what we could offer the world. They point the finger at what's wrong with the world and don't see the three fingers pointing back. The Spectator also overlooks our own magic and beauty when they point to those who inspire us, again missing the three fingers pointing back to ourselves. The Spectator is always looking outwards and seems to refuse to look within. This character's favourite day of the week is 'someday', with hopes, dreams, ambitions and purpose pushed into the future and procrastination fuelled by distraction prioritised today. From the time we get up in the morning to the time we go to bed at night, the Spectator nudges us to be distracted by what's going on externally and makes us feel like an extra in the movie of our own life, rather than the director or main character. Their efforts to keep us safe from the judgement of putting ourselves out there and living a life true to ourselves leaves us struggling to find meaning and purpose as life feels like it's passing us by.

Of all the characters it is perhaps the Spectator who is subject to the most conditioning from the external world always vying for our attention with distraction and noise. Knowing that life goes by fast, it is essential that we bring awareness to the patterns of our Spectator and take back the pen to write our own script for a meaningful and well-lived life.

WHERE IS PURPOSE FOUND?

'Spirituality' can be sometimes seen as a 'fluffy' word by those who are caught up in the chase for more material success in life, though in my judgement the absence of the 'spiritual' is what prevents so many of us finding the depth and meaning in life that we are seeking. I have heard Russell Brand say that 'there isn't ever a material solution for a spiritual problem'. I can relate, based on my experience in achieving many things that I was sure would make me happy, only to be left questioning, 'Is this all there is?'

Despite the comforts we have in the modern world relative to previous generations, the technological advances and the increasing choices we have in what to pursue in life, we are seeing increasing rates of mental health challenges, loneliness and disconnection from ourselves and from one another. The decline of faith and confidence in organised religion in the West in recent years has left a void for many people, who feel isolated and lost in life. In living a life governed by purpose we wake up to a new way of being in the world beyond the automatic behaviours and habits we have lived in up to this point.

Spirituality, to me, relates to finding meaning in life beyond the pursuit of the boxes we've been told we have to tick in order to be happy. Our world is filled with distraction, noise and efforts to pull our attention away from ourselves. As a result, the pursuit is often a fast-paced effort to acquire external things that we're being sold to try and fill internal voids. We can often look outside ourselves and become disillusioned with the state of what's going on 'out there'. The media, celebrities and politicians provide the perfect distraction from going within and seeing how we could impact on and make a difference to the world. Making a positive difference in the world might seem like a grandiose notion, but is our responsibility and opportunity. How we approach life ripples out to those closest to us and has a knock-on effect far greater than we might ever realise.

In my teens and early twenties I read every business and personal development book I could get my hands on, obsessed with the idea of becoming 'successful'. Ironically, I was so caught up in trying to improve my life that I rarely felt I was actually living. Many of the books and gurus suggested writing down your life purpose and gave examples such as 'In my lifetime I will positively impact ten million people through my work,' or 'In my lifetime I will end world hunger.' These life purpose statements were intended to make you 'think big' and give you direction and meaning in life, but they seemed so far removed from where I was that they did little more than discourage me and leave me putting the gurus on pedestals far above people 'like me'.

The Spectator character in my mind would try to convince me that I was too small to make an impact and that I should instead watch from the sidelines. Much like happiness and confidence, I put purpose outside myself, far away into the distance, always out of reach and reserved for other people. My internal story of what purpose 'should' look like and the grandiose visions I saw based on the people I looked up to always seemed to stop me getting started.

Many of my own podcast listeners or seminar attendees over the years have come with questions around purpose in one form or another. It seems that, much like the 'I'll be happy when ...' story, many of us believe that our purpose lives somewhere far off in the distance or that somebody else has the answers to what we should be doing. Our mind, wanting to box things off as black-and-white, will convince us that someday our purpose will show up out of the blue and everything will fall into place or, on the flipside, that we won't ever find purpose. Much of this comes down to comparison. When we see other people's highlight reels shared on social media, we can feel confused or frustrated by our own difficult feelings or internal dialogue. Other people seem to know what they are doing and have this game of life figured out.

One of the questions I'm asked most often is 'What was the turning point? How did you find out what you wanted to do?' For years I have told the story of turning up to Silverstrand beach in 2012 and being greeted by my first five clients. Between 2012 and 2017 those five clients grew to over twenty thousand clients from all over the world training with me in my gym in Galway or through my online programmes. The story I've told less frequently is what prompted those five people to take a leap of faith and join me on the beach.

While I was working in the pizzeria and trying to figure out what I was going to do with my life I spent months in a depression, completely lost and seeing no light at the end of the tunnel. My dad did all he could to help me lift the fog, resorting to a little tough love, telling me, 'Part of the problem is how much time you're living in your own head, thinking about your own problems and nothing or no one else. If you got out there and helped people in some capacity you'd soon feel less miserable.' It was hard to fathom how I could help anyone else when I couldn't even seem to help myself, but I took his advice on board and posted on social media to let friends know I was offering free custom training and nutrition programmes if anyone was interested. Between split shifts in the pizza restaurant I began meeting people for coffee and sharing these free plans and for those short meetings I felt for the first time in a long time that I was of some value and was making a difference.

Twelve weeks after meeting one of the first people who'd requested a plan I received an email with his progress pictures and a note to say, 'Thank you so much for your help. I'm down two stone already. If these photos are of any use to you please free to share them.' It was when I shared this man's progress pictures that I got those initial five clients to the beach. The rest, as they say, is history.

Purpose starts from where we are today, not from where we think we are supposed to be or where we think we need to be in order to find more meaning in our lives or in the impact we have on others.

We have got to do what we can with what we know and trust that, as we take steps forward, the next steps will appear. Fear, uncertainty and a lack of clarity will often be a result of jumping too far ahead, rather than acting from where we are standing. Fear always lives in the future; purpose is always available to us in the here and now.

We sometimes feel trapped by our position in life, constrained by the practicality and reality of commitments to family or to paying the bills. Comparison to others without any understanding of their unique journey or internal experience can lead us to think, 'It's okay for them.' In this justification we not only discredit their journeys but also do ourselves a disservice in fighting for our limitations rather than fighting for what we want. To become the hero of our own story or the king or queen of our own kingdom we've got to begin listening to ourselves and acting on what we hear. I often remind people that if you are working in a job in which you are discontent and have dreams of starting your own business, the dream doesn't start the day you make your first sale or the day you register your new business, it starts the day you show up to your current job knowing why you're there and what you are working towards.

We all have gifts and opportunities in life that are waiting to be used. When we ignore the gifts we have been given and choose to focus on what is missing, we will later be punished with the pain of regret. When we instead choose to use the gifts we've been given, we are rewarded with more as new doors and opportunities are opened to us. Sometimes using the gift and leaning into uncertainty is scary, but we are always rewarded with new understandings, lessons and opportunities if we are willing to start where we are, with what we have and a trust that the bigger plan will unfold over time.

THE HERO'S JOURNEY AND
SHARING YOUR MEDICINE

The famous American life coach Tony Robbins has been quoted as saying, 'Success without fulfilment is the ultimate failure.' This quote speaks to the people who have achieved the material objectives or outcomes they thought would make them happy only to be left feeling empty and unfulfilled. According to human needs psychology, for us to feel true fulfilment we must fulfil the two spiritual needs of growth and contribution. So many of the people I've met who appear to have purpose-filled lives have found a means of fulfilling the spiritual needs for growth and contribution by taking the struggles they have experienced and using those struggles as a way of helping others going through similar situations. We might feel like cursing the challenges or difficult experiences we have encountered in life, but it is these adversities that carry with them the seeds of our growth and transformation. Without challenge or struggle we would most likely move through life unconsciously and 'asleep', never realising our purpose and potential. Our greatest challenges in life wake us up to new ways of seeing and approaching the world and present us with the opportunity to awaken.

We can either see our challenges as happening *to* us and feel like victims of our circumstances, or we can see them as happening *for* us. When we choose to see our difficulties as opportunities for growth and transformation we change from victims to creators of our reality. Getting through these challenges is what enables us to connect on a deeper level with ourselves and with those around us, creating a sense of expansion in our world. Denying or avoiding these challenges can lead to a feeling of our world contracting and becoming limiting and small.

Across all times and in all cultures there have been heroes who inspire and awaken something within us. So what is it that makes a hero? Mythologist Joseph Campbell shared the idea of the 'mono-myth', or hero's journey, which he saw as a recurring theme across countless stories shared all over the world. I would be willing to bet that you will recognise this story arc of the hero's journey in the books, films or stories that have inspired or captivated you in your own life. We are inspired by people to whom we can relate on some level and thus we see a part of ourselves and our potential in the people we are influenced by. In recognising the arc of the hero's journey you will most likely also see your own position on the journey and how this arc has played out in your past.

You wouldn't be drawn to watch a film or read a novel in which the protagonist's journey is a straight line from A to B, with the main character experiencing a clean-cut transformation devoid of adversity. Instead we are drawn to the characters whose stories are filled with challenge, adversity, obstacles and struggle. In their struggles and vulnerabilities we recognise our own, and in their growth, journey and transformation we see our potential mirrored back to us. The hero's journey is one of deep inner transformation, in which the hero leaves the comfort zone of their current perceived reality and steps into the unknown, meeting new parts of themselves as they leave their ordinary life. After going through the journey the hero returns to their old ordinary world with 'medicine for the tribe' in the form of wisdom and experience to share with their people. The hero's journey is a journey of self-discovery, purpose and living a fully realised life.

As much of our life is spent looking outwards, we can sometimes forget that we are projecting our own internal narratives and expe-rience onto the external world. But we should take time to stop and ask ourselves, 'What would full ownership and personal leadership in my own life look like? What might the next stage of my hero's journey be?'

I know that in my own experience, looking outward with judgement towards people in power that I deem to be poor leaders, indecisive or untrustworthy provides an easy means of looking away from myself – and the areas in which I show poor leadership, am indecisive and untrustworthy.

While projecting my frustrations onto others might temporarily allow me to escape the discomfort of looking at my own shortcomings, it also takes away my power, my potential for growth and for 'being the change I would like to see in the world'. In essence, it distracts me and denies me my own 'hero's journey'.

Similarly, when I look at my 'heroes' and place other people on pedestals, I am often seeing the potential in someone else that I may currently find difficult to see in myself. For many of us it is as uncomfortable to see our own brilliance as it is to see our shortcomings, and so the Spectator character appears and pulls us away from our own potential.

When we begin to see those people and situations that upset or inspire us as holding a mirror up to us, we can begin to find clues to the areas we must pursue to walk our own hero's journey and find the purpose that comes with it.

WHAT'S WORTH STRUGGLING FOR?

In viewing the world as a mirror, we can begin to see gaps between how we are living and how we long to live. These gaps point to the hero's journey, a potential path of deep inner transformation in which we lean into adversity and emerge transformed. Perhaps at a time in life when someone is feeling a little flat and bored, they notice how inspired they are by their favourite musicians and see this as an invitation to embrace their own creativity and pick up an instrument for the first time. Or maybe someone else becomes so frustrated with a societal problem that they commit to stepping up and being the person who creates change. Both individuals have committed to living rather than spectating.

There is an energy and enthusiasm that comes as we step into these new inspiring places, but there is also the reality of the struggle and work that will be required. Much like the 'I'll be happy when ...' story, where there is an out-of-balance fantasy of a life without discomfort, some think that finding our purpose results in everything falling into place and becoming smooth sailing. It is important that we recognise that suffering and discomfort are inevitable in life and the choice we have to make is what we are willing to struggle for.

If we choose to avoid the short-term discomfort of physical training of some kind we will have lower energy levels and even serious irreversible illness in the long term. If we choose to avoid the short-term discomfort of telling our partner about something that is upsetting us, we perhaps run the risk of feeling the long-term discomfort of resentment, frustration or anger.

By choosing our struggles and leaning into them we find meaning in our lives. Avoiding struggle leads to greater struggle over time. Similar to the exercise we outlined at the end of the Happiness chapter, we see that choosing some of our challenges and creating more discipline and structure in our lives lessens the need for chaos, unconscious patterns and reactionary behaviours.

If we avoid the discomfort of acting on our inner voice and pursuing things that are meaningful for us, deferring them until some future time, we will suffer the discomfort of feeling out of integrity alongside the perhaps irreversible discomfort of regret later in life. There are always two sides to every coin, to every decision and to every outcome.

We are all juggling many commitments all the time, and pursuing purpose isn't about flipping our lives upside down, but instead about looking to figure out how we can invest more of the one hundred and sixty-eight hours a week in the things we love, even if we start with just one hour a week for ourselves.

A number of years ago, I hosted a three-day retreat in Galway called 'Camp Reconnect'. It was a chance to disconnect from technology and reconnect with life. We had an amazing group of attendees and a schedule of surprise activities including African drumming, a kickboxing session, a silent disco and an art class. Four weeks later I received an email from a man whose wife had attended. He had noticed a remarkable difference in her mood, energy and excitement about life. The one change she had made following the retreat, he told me, had made her a better partner, mother and daughter, and she just seemed much happier in herself. What was that one change? It was very simple. We had had a salsa class. This lady had loved salsa years ago but had stopped doing it when she became a mum and her life became busier. Salsa was the one change she'd made in her life and it had changed everything.

Much of the energy we sometimes feel is lacking in life is a result of not plugging in to the activities and people that make us come alive; we get bogged down in the 'should dos'.

And so the question becomes, 'What am I willing to struggle for?'

We sometimes look at professional athletes, musicians and actors and think we'd love to do what they do, again with an out-of-balance fantasy. We see the fruits of their labour but have a complete lack of awareness around the realities of the sacrifices that are made to be where they are in life. Perhaps I would love to make the money a professional football player makes, but I would not love the fifteen years of daily discipline, sacrifice and struggle that it took to get them to where they are. Though there will have been plenty of struggle in their own journey, they aren't pursuing something that they feel they 'should' be doing; it instead feels like something they 'must' do. There might be pain associated with doing the thing, there is perhaps more pain associated with not doing the thing!

The Hindu text the Bhagavad Gita reminds us, 'You have the right to work, but never to the fruit of work. You should never engage in action for the sake of reward, nor should you long for inaction.' In the context of purpose I feel this is the reality. We cannot have expectation or obsession over the result of our efforts; we must instead be completely committed to the process – not because it is something we feel we 'should' do but because it's something we 'must' do, because we feel called from within. Perhaps our must-do calling is to paint or to write or to run. Maybe it is to bring communities together, or support those who are struggling. Maybe it is to stand on stage and share our story or to start the business we have always dreamed of starting.

If we come back to an analogy we used earlier in the book, of our goals being like mountains we are looking to climb, we can remind ourselves that all mountains will provide challenges and obstacles, and thus it is important that we're climbing the right mountains and making sense of the challenges and struggles rather than climbing other people's mountains and going through all that suffering for a feeling of emptiness at the top. The struggle in pursuing things in life that are meaningful for us might involve having less disposable income for a period of time, having less sleep, spending time outside our comfort zone or enduring criticism and judgement from people close to us who don't understand our path.

Being honest about what we are willing to struggle for and recognising what is worth struggling for ensures that we are approaching our goals with a healthy realism that recognises both sides of the coin rather than an uninformed optimism that leaves us disillusioned at the first sign of challenge.

INDECISION IS THE ENEMY

It is said that the best decision we can make in life is the right decision, the second-best decision we can make is the wrong decision and the worst decision of all is indecision.

When we make a big decision and things work out we breathe a sigh of relief and thank ourselves for leaning in. When we make a big decision and things don't go as we'd hoped we might temporarily feel a sense of defeat or failure but we have lessons, feedback and experience that will ultimately help us going forward. When we don't make any decision and stay stuck in limbo or living in our heads we gain nothing, only amplifying fear and worry.

There are moments in life in which the decisions we make play a huge role in shaping our future. This is evident when we look to our past. The decision to start a family, leave a partner, build a business or go back to college later in life are all big decisions that change everything. Of course, there are then dozens or hundreds of smaller decisions we make daily – what to eat, what to watch on Netflix, whether or not to check our work email after a certain time. The

Spectator character who sits back and watches the lives of others is one of those characters who encourages indecisiveness. They'd rather forgo responsibility than take full ownership in life. They might not be happy with their current position in life but will do anything to avoid the uncertainty of stepping into something new.

As you begin to shine light on your own potential for growth, contribution and purpose, what small decision might provide the first movement in a new direction for your life? Remember – indecision is the enemy.

Exercise: Clues in Your Past
(five-minute exercise)

Take five minutes to write about some of the things you are most proud of in your life up to this point.

Looking to the future we can often get caught in the fear of uncertainty and the thought of leaving our comfort zone. We can find ourselves refusing the 'call to adventure' and unwilling to step into the growth, fulfilment and purpose which can only be found in the unknown.

As you reflect on the notes you have taken of what you are most proud of in life you will no doubt have noted things in which you invested a large amount of work, energy and attention. This provides a good reminder that the things that are meaningful and purposeful in life are not supposed to be easy or free of challenge. They are in fact the opposite, filled with challenge that facilitates our growth and attainment of embodied wisdom.

Purpose – What to Remember

- Purpose is not to be found somewhere far off in the distance. Like happiness, confidence and success, it lives in what we do today. When we look back on our lives up to this point we can make sense of the steps that led us to where we are standing. It is impossible to accurately forecast where we will end up in time if we are willing to listen to our intuition as things change and so it is only in retrospect that we can see the path. With that in mind, purpose begins with listening, acting and taking a first step with faith, then watching the next part of the path open up.

- Indecision is the enemy. Our present-day life is a result of the decisions we made or didn't make up to this point. We'll have made countless decisions over the course of our lives, but it is the more consequential decisions we've made or failed to make that set the path of our lives. The worst decision in life we can make is indecision. The right decision gives us the result we hoped for, the wrong decision gives us lessons and feedback, but indecision gives us nothing at all.

- Purpose is often found in 'sharing our medicine', looking at areas of life in which we have struggled and sharing with those going through a similar experience. Joseph Campbell's framework of the hero's journey concludes with 'returning with the elixir', the hero's triumphant return as a different person with new levels of maturity and gifts to share with others who are beginning a similar path.

- Meaning and purpose can be found in fulfilling the two spiritual needs of growth and contribution. When thinking back to times in our life when we felt the most purpose, we will notice that these were times when we were experiencing personal growth in some area and/or making a meaningful difference to the lives of others.

● The external world and its polarising characters can be a perfect distraction from ourselves. In looking externally to the things we see in the world that inspire or upset us, we can begin to understand what we could bring to the world which would provide meaning and purpose in our lives.

● Much like the 'I'll be happy when ...' story, there is perhaps an idea that finding and living our purpose is a one-sided coin made up of only the positive. In reality, as the Buddha thought in his first noble truth, life is suffering. Following and living our purpose will be difficult, uncomfortable and hugely challenging. So, too, will living a life that ignores our purpose. For this reason we've got to figure out what is worth fighting for in life.

ARC EXERCISES

Begin by completing the following sentence stems in your journal:

- If money was no object I would spend my days ...
- If I had a year left to live I ...
- I would experience more growth in my life if ...
- I could contribute more to life by ...
- I am most inspired by ...
- An area of life where I need more decisiveness is ...
- If I could offer the world one gift it would be ...

Illumination Exercise:
Purpose – External and Internal Audit

If we think of the external world as a mirror to ourselves we can begin to recognise areas in which we can grow and contribute in a way that brings meaning and purpose to our lives.

Looking outwards, consider the three things that upset or disturb you the most in the modern world. Where do you find yourself pointing the finger? Perhaps it's the government's lack of leadership or indecisiveness. Maybe it's environmental issues or social inequality. Maybe you are disturbed by bullying in schools or in the workplace.

Looking at these issues, consider how you can use them as a source of inspiration for the impact you want to have on the world. Assuming no one else in this world can have the same impact as you, how can you take back the energy of these frustrations and use them as fuel in creating a life of meaning? Maybe in pointing to a world that lacks leadership you can commit to becoming a greater leader in your own life, making more courageous decisions and not passing responsibility to others. Perhaps you are disturbed by the disconnection and loneliness in the world and use that as fuel to create some kind of community or social hub.

Next, consider the three things that inspire you the most in the modern world, the beacons of light or best of humanity. What is it about these people, these movements or these organisations that restores your faith in humanity? Maybe it's the creativity of your favourite artist, the philanthropic efforts of your favourite entrepreneur or the selflessness of a mentor who has supported you in your life. How can you bring more of these traits into your own life?

Looking at a world of over seven billion people it would be easy to think our efforts are not enough, but as the Dalai Lama said, 'If you think you are too small to make a difference, try sleeping with a mosquito.'

What is it that the world needs most and how can you be a part of that inspiring change you want to see?

Journalling Prompts:
Purpose

1. What did you love to do when you were younger that you don't do any more? How can you bring more of this back into your life now?

2. What role do growth and contribution play in your day-to-day life?

3. What advice would your older self give you at this point in your life?

4. Can you recognise a time in your life in which you went through your own hero's journey and stepped from your 'ordinary world' into the unknown? Write about this experience. What did you learn? How did you grow? What challenges and internal or external resistance did you overcome?

5. What 'medicine' could you share with your tribe? In other words, what challenges have you overcome that have given you experience and wisdom that could help others going through something similar?

6. Write about three times you have made big decisions that have positively impacted the direction of your life. What can you learn from these experiences and how can you carry these lessons forward?

7. If you only had a few years left to live what would you do or create?

Meditation of the Week:
'I am'

For this week's meditation we will be doing a mantra-based meditation using the mantra 'I am'. A mantra gives us an anchor that brings us back to the present moment and helps us to reduce wandering thoughts.

You can repeat the mantra 'I am' either aloud or in your mind for the duration of your ten-minute meditation. Whenever your mind wanders, which it will, simply notice and bring yourself back to the mantra. Every time you return you are strengthening your capacity to be in the present moment.

Some people find it useful to match their breath to the mantra. You do not need to breathe in any particular way, but it is best to breathe through your nose to induce relaxation. As you settle into the meditation and focus on your mantra, you will relax and find a natural rhythm with your breath.

PART THREE

Building Your Self-Care System

Building the Base: The 2/5/10 Routine

'We don't rise to the level of our expectations, we fall to the level of our training' – Archilochus

'I fear not the man who has practised 10,000 kicks once, but I fear the man who has practised one kick 10,000 times' – Bruce Lee

YOU CAN'T TRANSCEND THE BASICS

'To be honest, Pat, the first session when you discussed this idea of "building your base" I thought I'd wasted my money signing up to the course. It all seemed very obvious and like nothing I didn't know or hadn't heard before. However, looking back over the last few months, I can feel that principle alone has become something I'll lean on for the rest of my life. In fact, if I had a euro for every time I've reminded myself to come back to the base over the last while, I'd be rich!'

It's the end of a twelve-week online course. On this call I'm asking participants to share their biggest learning, highlights or insights from the three months working together. All members of the group took part for their own personal reasons, some hoping to overcome addictions, others trying to work through big challenges in relationships, some seeking more meaning and purpose and others just looking for some little pointers that might help them reach their next level of 'high performance'.

Without fail, the base comes up in every client's reflections as something that's been advantageous in their personal and professional lives. Most agree that it did seem too obvious, too basic and nothing they hadn't heard before. At first they saw the 'build your base' training as some filler content before we got to the 'good stuff'. However, everyone agreed that the constant repetition of 'build your base' throughout the programme changed their way of seeing their habits and daily practices for ever.

I hope by the end of this chapter that 'build your base' proves a powerful mantra for you too, one that can bring you back to a sense of certainty and groundedness in a world that can so often feel overwhelming and chaotic.

Simply put, the base relates to the daily practices that we embrace to protect our most valuable assets in life – our energy and our perspective.

There are things we do that contribute to great levels of physical, mental and emotional energy in our lives; and there are things we do that do the opposite. In other words, there are the energy gainers, which build our base; and the energy leakers, which retract our base. When so much of our life is spent looking outwards, our attention drawn to external noise and distraction, it can be easy to become wrapped up in what is happening 'out there' and allow it to dictate the thoughts, feelings and behaviours happening 'in here'.

Our ability to recognise the stories we are telling ourselves and challenge those stories which are disempowering is largely dependent on our energy levels. When physical energy is low or we are living in a constant state of stress (fight/flight/freeze) we can find ourselves in 'survival' mode, constantly on the lookout for threats and struggling to find perspective and separation between what is happening and what we are telling ourselves about what is happening.

Without a conscious effort to consistently down-regulate the nervous system and manage stress and energy, the government, our boss, the economy, what we see on social media and how others react to us can dictate how we feel about ourselves and about the world.

The external world and a focus on things often outside our control can leave us feeling like cogs in the wheel, with life happening to us and us being at the mercy of our experiences.

Remember, all experiences contain two triggers, one external and one internal. When our base is there we can identify the situation and separate the story we are telling ourselves about the situation. The stress is in the story we are telling ourselves about how things 'should' be and not in the actual experience.

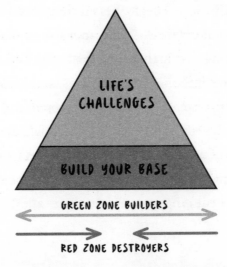

When our energy is low, we're caught up in stress or worry or we lose perspective. First something happens (external), then we give it a meaning (internal). Without developing a base through self-care practices it can be very easy to live on autopilot, forgetting that the meanings we give to our experiences are within our control and will ultimately dictate how we feel in life.

Compare how we might react to constructive criticism at work after a sleepless night versus how we might take the very same feedback after a great night's sleep and a morning meditation to centre ourselves before work. Without the space and capacity to pause it's easy to lose sight of the second trigger, the internal 'choice' of how we respond to the external world.

Everything is harder in life when our energy is diminished. Even the most positive person in the world would find it exhausting and unsustainable to stay positive when their energy is absent.

There's a reason trainee soldiers endure sleep deprivation as part of their initial training. When we're tired our decision-making abilities are compromised, and poor decision-making can lead to a cycle of stress and overwhelm. Once caught in the cycle it can be difficult to escape and come back to a feeling of certainty and control.

I could relate to my clients' initial thoughts of 'Really? I paid for someone to tell me this?' Two years earlier I'd signed up to yet another personal growth course in the States and been 'accepted' into an 'exclusive' group of people who would work together on developing their physical, mental, emotional and spiritual practices over the course of twelve months. 'Exclusive' and 'accepted' are usually good marketing words to make you feel lucky to get to pay a premium fee to be included, but nevertheless I was excited about the year-long journey of personal growth.

After paying my initial instalment in October to reserve my place on the course I counted down the days to January when the journey would begin and we'd be sent the first of our weekly training and challenges. A big price tag surely meant there would be some magic included on the course. As the start date got closer my excitement grew until at last the first challenge landed in my inbox.

'This week your challenge is to drink at least two litres of water a day.'

I quickly did the calculations in my head. 'I've just paid someone a lot of money to tell me to drink more water!'

A week later, I checked my inbox again.

'This week your challenge is to meditate for ten minutes daily.'

'There's more money down the drain,' I thought. But then I stopped and got honest with myself.

These things are obvious, fundamental and nothing new, but was I doing them consistently and without fail? The answer was no. I was out searching for more and overlooking the basics that seemed too simplistic, seduced by the thought of magic tricks, hacks and shortcuts.

We have never had so much access to resources and information but though we're often drowning in information we've become thirsty for knowledge. Just how much would be possible for us all, if we only did what we know we need to do?

In my early teens my parents gave me a set of dumbbells and a barbell for my birthday. As an avid professional wrestling fan I was excited to pump some iron and look like my heroes! Included with that set of vinyl York weights was a poster showing a full body workout plan that was to be completed three times a week. You'd complete the workouts and add a little weight to the bar every couple of weeks as your body got stronger. I stuck rigidly to the plan and took huge confidence from the little improvements I was seeing every week.

Though I never did end up looking like my favourite wrestling superstars, in my first two years lifting weights I saw more progress than I think I've seen since. Part of that will certainly come down to the fact that our initial efforts will always bring about some big results followed by some level of diminishing returns, but I'm convinced that the biggest contributor to my progress was the simplicity of my plan and willingness to execute what I knew and not seek out more bells, whistles, fancy exercises and distractions. These initial years of weight training proved the start of what would eventually become my career and I spent the remainder of my teens obsessively studying training, nutrition and recovery.

As the growth of the internet opened me up to a world of resources and information my own training plans evolved from the simple one-page workout poster to complicated and ever-changing plans based on the latest article I'd read online or seen in a magazine.

I think these patterns can show up for us in all areas of life.

- We start something new with a focus on the basics.
- After achieving some initial success and learning some new ways of doing things we add some bells and whistles.
- As we add more and more bells and whistles we begin to overthink and drown in the resources and information that were once beneficial.
- We wake up overwhelmed, having drifted far away from the basic plan that had yielded such positive results.

Just as I lost sight of the simple exercises that got me started with weight training and became distracted by shiny lights and possibilities, the same thinking can be applied to all areas of life. We see it in business when business owners start with a great product and customer service, then add bells and whistles, make things more complicated than they need to be and lose the magic they had at the start. We see it in relationships where the base that was built on date nights fades away as the presence, fun and curiosity that were there at the start are forgotten about.

Look at any area of life and there are a small number of fundamentals that yield the biggest results and impact. The best athletes in the world still practise the fundamentals. The best actors, singers and performers come back to the fundamentals and master them.

When it comes to the foundations of physical, mental and emotional wellness, we can't ever transcend the basics.

THERE IS NO FINISH LINE

We often fall into the trap of attaching end dates to certain things. We like the idea of completion, of ticking boxes and of feeling the temporary relief that comes with getting something done. The reality of life and the practices that keep us well tell us that it isn't over until it's over – none of us reaches the point where we can just kick back and relax, live hedonically for the rest of our life and leave our days of self-care in the past.

I'd see this time and time again when I worked in the fitness industry. A client would down-heartedly tell me that 'the diet plan didn't work'. They'd then explain that they'd followed the plan and cut out the junk food, lost the weight and then went back to eating 'normally' (re-integrating the junk foods they'd cut out), only to put the weight back on.

Though our practices and priorities may change over time it's essential that we recognise that in a world where so much is beyond our control, our certainty can only come by finding discipline and routine in what is within our control.

It might seem exhausting to think that for the rest of our lives we've got to invest daily in ourselves with empowering practices and habits. But it's also empowering to know that even though it sometimes feels that life and its challenges are happening *to* us, in reality they are happening *for* us. When we have prioritised our self-care we are in a position to embrace whatever cards we are dealt and choose the meaning of our circumstances.

I once heard an analogy of the stresses of life being like different taps on a bath that has no drain. One tap is the stress from our work, another the stress from our relationships, another still a stress from our worries about the future, and so on and so forth. As life gets busy and the stress from one area of life triggers stress in another, we've suddenly got all the taps on and the bath is filling fast. With no drain in sight, at some point the bath's going to overflow.

While we often seek self-esteem or self-confidence in external achievements, affiliations or possessions, we forget the importance of the word 'self' in self-esteem and self-confidence. Confidence and esteem come from the 'self' and from our willingness to give ourselves the time, presence and love that show us that our own physical and emotional needs matter and hold value.

Ultimately our goal in building the base and practising self-care is to change from reacting to responding. When we react in life we create more of the same and stay stuck in our existing behaviours, habits and patterns, living unconsciously and unable to separate ourselves from our disempowering thoughts as we go through our day on busy autopilot mode.

To create something new in life and move towards a new version of ourselves we've got to move to 'responsive'. Here, we can encounter the same external experience, but create space between stimulus and response so that rather than going to our autopilot familiar reaction, we can instead move to a conscious response intended to keep us on track towards what we want.

THE TRIUNE BRAIN

The 'triune brain' theory and understanding of the different parts of the brain, their functions and roles in our lives can help us better understand our behaviour. This is particularly true in understanding our actions that seem 'self-sabotaging', or counterintuitive to what we say we want in life. This theory rests on the idea that three primary aspects of our brain have developed over time as we have evolved as humans. These levels are:

- Reptilian brain (survival state)
- Mammalian brain (emotional state)
- Prefrontal lobe (executive state)

The reptilian brain (the brain stem) is the oldest part of the brain and is focused on survival. When we feel threatened or endangered, we are pulled into this reptilian brain through the fight or flight response. This part of our brain focuses on our most primal needs, so it pulls us into reactionary behaviours – which are not thought out or conscious of our long-term wants – to ensure survival. When our brain feels under threat, there isn't enough time to analyse and form a considered response, and so instead it prompts us to react quickly in its effort to keep us 'safe'.

Here's a case in point. It's Christmas and I've decided that my new year's resolution is to lose a bit of weight and train for my first marathon. With a bit of time on my hands over Christmas I feel relaxed and get to tap into the human mind of logic and creativity, thinking about how I can thrive in life and not just survive. I set some goals, form a plan and I'm filled with enthusiasm and excitement about the year ahead. Fast-forward three weeks. A few nights of poor sleep and stress at work throw me off course and I find myself 'out of my mind' and operating with my reptilian brain, relying on old habits to 'keep me alive'. Before I know it my ability to respond and think or act logically just isn't there and I'm reaching for takeaways and beers, despite 'knowing better'! With a build-up of stress and a lack of sleep, I have regressed to a more primitive part of my brain that isn't concerned with goals or the future, and only wants physical safety and survival.

The second level of the brain, the mammalian or limbic brain, is also focused on survival. It relates more to our survival within the context of our 'tribe' or group, and focuses largely on emotions and our feelings of safety within a social environment. As we evolved in groups or small tribes we were of course completely dependent on the protection and acceptance of the tribe. Separation from the tribe would have meant certain death. In the modern world, this part of the brain is what seeks to keep us attached and accepted by those around us, triggering fears of abandonment or rejection if we do or say 'the wrong thing'. To continue the analogy of my new year's resolution, in this case the mammalian brain would be responsible for me being dissuaded from my goal by a few sarcastic comments from loved ones – leading to me fearing being ridiculed or 'exiled' by the tribe. The result is the same; I again lose sight of the goal that was formed in my human mind, and fall back to prioritising my 'survival' within my social group.

Finally, the prefrontal cortex, the human brain, enables us to think of the future and past and to be creative and logical. It is this part of the brain that can plan, make decisions and problem-solve. In moments of stress or overwhelm, however, we lose our ability to use this logical part of the brain and drop back to the more primal and survival-based levels of the reptilian and mammalian brains.

Our ability to change from someone on autopilot, living out patterns, to someone who is responsive and conscious of what they are creating doesn't happen by accident. It is a skill governed by our willingness to invest in our self-care system daily. As mentioned in the Happiness chapter our goal is not to have a life devoid of challenge, but instead to lean into new inspiring challenges every few months that promote growth and not remain trapped in the patterns that leave us feeling stuck and frustrated.

As we take on bigger challenges over time our commitment to our base and expanding that base becomes of key significance. It is this commitment to our base and to looking after the needs of our reptilian and mammalian levels of the brain that allows us to come from a place of thriving and not just surviving. If we do not look after these basic needs, our lives will be run from these parts of the brain, and we will find ourselves stuck in the same loops and patterns. Understanding, acknowledging and supporting the need to feel safe (reptilian) and connected (mammalian) allows us to move into a place of greater evolution.

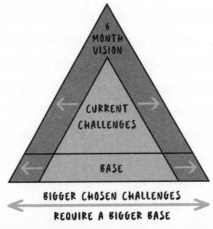

THE 2/5/10 ROUTINE

Throughout the book we've explored journalling practices and meditation techniques that enable you to bring awareness to your patterns and shine light on where you might be living life on autopilot.

Assuming you've taken the time to go through some of the prompts and techniques shared in the preceding chapters, you'll have increased awareness of your 'default settings', outdated beliefs and existing stories about yourself and the world. With this increased awareness comes the chance for some reflection on how these stories have been impacting your life.

This increased awareness also allows for greater choice going forward and helps you to step out of autopilot and become more conscious in your thoughts, feelings, actions and behaviours. The ARC method of promoting awareness, reflection and choice is what we have used in the eight-week programme outlined in this book.

The **2/5/10 routine** is a simple way of continuing your practices for increased awareness, reflection and choice every day and making an ongoing commitment to understanding and getting to know yourself on a deeper level beyond your unconscious patterns, beliefs, assumptions and habits.

Twice daily, in the morning and at night, you'll take pen and paper and answer five questions after meditating for ten minutes.

It's that simple.

The things that are easy to do are of course also easy not to do, so it is important to remember why you are taking this time for yourself. Without a conscious practice of looking after myself mentally and emotionally daily, I know I am rolling the dice with how I will feel and I'm relying on 'hope' as a strategy for feeling in a good place mentally and emotionally.

Maybe the same is true for you?

You might think of the 2/5/10 routine as your mental and emotional fitness programme, your chance to put little daily deposits in your mental and emotional fitness accounts, so that when there are more challenging times in life you will have saved for a rainy day and have something to fall back on. These investments allow you to come from a responsive and proactive level of the human brain and avoid being caught up in the survival patterns of the reptilian or mammalian brain.

The 2/5/10 routine, alongside your other self-care and your lifestyle factors, contributes to 'building your base'. We know that we improve at the things we practise consistently, and our 2/5/10 routine is a commitment to consciously practising relaxed concentration and the ability to find perspective from stressful thoughts.

Do your ten minutes of meditation and five journalling prompts first thing in the morning, before plugging into the matrix of your day and becoming reactive to the external world, and then again last thing at night as a means of rounding out your day before bed.

Your two ten-minute meditations in the morning and at night might be one or more of the techniques we've covered in the book, or perhaps it's a completely different style of meditation. It's important to find a style that works for you. There are countless free apps and resources; explore and find the right fit for you. The best meditation for you is the one you can stick to daily, so experiment with different forms until you find the practice that you find most useful. Like dating, it might take time to find the 'right one' for you, or the 'one' might change over time, but remember that your meditation practice is an essential part of slowing down to the speed of life and 'seeing' yourself and your patterns with some perspective.

After your ten minutes of meditation in the morning and evening you have your five 'morning prompts' and 'evening prompts'. I'm going to outline these prompts for your first thirty days of your 2/5/10 routine. After the first thirty days, I would encourage you to personalise them a little more, where appropriate, to ensure that you get maximum benefit from the practice.

For the first thirty days the five morning questions are:

1. What three things am I most grateful for today and why?
2. What am I most excited about today?
3. What are my top three priorities for the day?
4. What feeling would I like to experience today?
5. What am I willing to do to create that feeling?

For the first thirty days the five evening questions are:

1. What were my three biggest wins for the day and why?
2. Who did I positively impact today?
3. What did I learn today?
4. What feeling did I experience most consistently today?
5. Why might that feeling have been most present for me today?

Each prompt serves a purpose and builds on the practices we have explored throughout the book. The beauty of prompts, or questions, is that they open the mind, unlike statements, which close the mind.

A little creativity is needed to go beyond our current worldview and it's important that we look to be present each day to the questions and not make it another autopilot behaviour where we find ourselves writing the same answers every day!

Let's look at the purpose of these initial ten questions for your first thirty-day challenge.

What three things am I most grateful for today and why?

This prompt brings us from expectation to appreciation. We see what we have to be grateful for in life. In moments of stress our mind goes to what is missing or lacking in our life or what is outside our control, so this question around gratitude helps us find perspective.

Remember, too, that gratitude appreciates; when you see your world through a lens of appreciation you will find more to be grateful for. Seeing the world through a lens of lack will just show you more of what is missing.

The 'why' part of the prompt is a means of really feeling the appreciation. So rather than simply saying, 'I am grateful for my family,' you might say, 'I am grateful for my family *because* they have been and continue to be an incredible support system to me.'

What am I most excited about today?

When life gets busy it can be easy to feel the days are rolling into one another and we are running in a hamster wheel of work and external expectations. Prompting yourself to find something to be excited about in your day can provide inspiration and energy beyond the usual daily routines.

This could be something simple like catching up with a friend or taking time to try cooking a new recipe; or maybe you're excited about a date or a new class you are taking online. If you struggle to find something to be excited about, that's okay and it's normal. Like all these prompts, it's a practice and a call to get creative.

Stick with it and don't fall into the trap of fighting for your limitations. I have heard it said that 'When you fight for your limitations you get to keep them.'

What are my top three priorities for the day?

This question provides a focus and a chance to be proactive and choose the behaviours that will best serve you in life, rather than being reactive and caught in work that makes you feel you are only just keeping your head above water.

Of course your to-do list might have a dozen or more things on it, but this question is about really being honest about what three priorities would best support where you are trying to go in life. Another way of thinking of this question is to ask yourself, 'If I were to go to bed tonight feeling proud, accomplished and fulfilled, what three things would need to have happened in the day?'

What feeling would I like to experience today?

All goals in life tie in to a feeling we would like to experience. For example, the person wanting to run a marathon might believe that crossing the finishing line will make them feel 'accomplished'.

By asking the question of how we want to feel daily we can make these feelings a part of our journey rather than the end destination. Rather than wait until the end of their marathon journey to experience this feeling of having 'accomplished', they can choose to make it a daily experience.

What am I willing to do to create that feeling?

When we are reactive in life we allow our feelings to dictate our actions. Perhaps we feel unmotivated and so decide it's not the right day to go and exercise. This can unfortunately become a vicious cycle. When we move from a reactive to a responsive state we recognise, conversely, that the actions we take can impact how we feel.

After identifying a feeling you would like to experience today, follow up by recognising an action that would support feeling that way. You might identify 'calm' as a feeling you would like to create and then commit to an action that will support this objective of 'calm', perhaps a walk in nature.

What were my three biggest wins for the day and why?

In a fast-paced and over-stimulating world we can find ourselves spending a great deal of our lives in the future thinking about what's next. There is a tendency to have a story that assumes our happiness, confidence or feelings of success live somewhere in the future.

Taking some time each evening to reflect on our wins is actually where a great deal of our confidence can be found. We have to learn to press pause and reflect on our progress if we are to positively reinforce our efforts and build self-esteem.

For each win, include the 'what' and the 'why'. For example, 'Today's first mini win was a 5 km run (*what*) because it set me up for a productive day and got me energised before work (*why*).'

Who did I positively impact today?

In many western countries individual success is celebrated and encouraged, which is perhaps part of the reason so many people experience feelings of loneliness, isolation and disconnection from a tribe. Individualism focuses on the goals and experience of the individual person, while collectivism focuses on the goals or experience of the group. This question asks you to reflect on how you went beyond yourself to connect with and impact someone else.

The law of reciprocity, a basic law of social psychology, states that in many social situations we will look to pay back what we received from others. You could think of this as the law of karma – what I put out comes back – but at its most basic level there is a sense of meaning and purpose that is hard to match. It comes from knowing we went beyond ourselves to help someone else.

What did I learn today?

In my martial arts training, coaches have often shared the philosophy with me that we either win or we learn. This question ensures that every day truly is a schoolday.

Without reflecting on this type of question you will perhaps spend weeks, months or years repeating the same frustrating patterns and feeling caught in a loop of unconscious behaviour. Sometimes what you learnt in the day might be something very practical, like how to play a song on the guitar, how to bake a new recipe or how to operate a new system at work.

At other times the lesson from the day might have been how to improve your communication with a loved one, how to better schedule your day, how not to leave your workout until the end of the day when your willpower is at its lowest.

We learn from our experiences, but we learn a great deal more from reflecting on those experiences.

What feeling did I experience most consistently today?

We talked about emotional check-ins earlier in the book and about the importance of consistently bringing awareness to how we feel.

We have probably all had the experience of being caught up in living like 'human doings' rather than 'human beings', moving so fast through life that we become disconnected from our feelings until they become debilitating or lead to burnout or overwhelm.

There's a saying, 'If you listen to your body when it whispers, you won't have to hear it scream.' Similarly, if we check in with our emotions on a consistent basis we can listen to their feedback and learn from their wisdom in real time, rather than feeling the overwhelming discomfort of a backlog of unprocessed emotions spilling over into our lives.

Why might that feeling have been most present today?
Perhaps the feeling that was most present for you today was 'happiness' and on reflecting on your day you see that you spent less time on social media, practised a great morning routine and met a good friend for lunch.

Or maybe the primary feeling you experienced today was overwhelm and on reflection you see that you have a tendency to overcommit to meeting too many people on your day off and then struggle to be present and engaged.

There is a great deal to be learnt by checking in with and being curious about the thoughts or behaviours that may have influenced your feelings during the day. Our feelings so often point to the unconscious and, as we've said throughout the book, making our unconscious conscious is a key part of self-understanding.

2/5/10 Routine: 30-day Tracker

Flip to page 314 to use a simple tracker as a means of visually capturing your progress as you log your morning and evening journalling and meditation sessions. Remember, these small investments of time, energy and attention create a compound effect that will create positive ripples across all areas of your life.

Habits and Behavioural Change

'LESS' IS MORE

The whole area of habits and behavioural change could fill hundreds of books, but in this section I would like to help you gain a greater understanding of how and where you can find more consistency in continuing the self-care practices outlined in this book. If you have gone through the eight-week programme, or plan to, I hope that this is just the start of a journey that will open new doors for you.

The simple structure and exercises laid out in this chapter will ensure that the 2/5/10 system for building your base goes from a nice idea on paper to something that is a non-negotiable part of your everyday life.

In a world where so many opportunities, resources and ideas are readily available it is easy to dabble in different hobbies, habits or routines and jump from one thing to the next without ever truly reaping the rewards of a given practice. In an age of distraction our ability to focus our attention is undoubtedly one of the greatest powers we have. Willpower is finite and tends to diminish as old stories, emotions and stresses resurface and trigger old habits and reactions. To move from an over-reliance on willpower to setting yourself up for a sustainable practice of self-care I will use the acronym LESS to outline four simple exercises that will support your new habits and efforts in behavioural change. LESS is:

- Leverage
- Environment
- Scheduling
- Stretch zone

LESS – Leverage

Why is it that we sometimes say confidently that we are ready to implement a positive change in our lives, but then find ourselves self-sabotaging just days later when willpower seems absent? Earlier in the book, in our Communication and Conflict chapters, we looked at the deeper meanings behind the words we hear in our interactions with others. As a reminder, we identified that in communication there is always the 'what', the 'how' and the 'why'.

- *What* someone says relates to the words they use.
- *How* they say it relates to their tone and body language.
- *Why* they say it comes down to their values and fears, which act as unconscious emotional drivers in their lives.

Similarly, to come to a greater understanding of our own behaviours and any struggles we have around consistency or behavioural change we must come to a greater understanding of our 'why', our unconscious drivers. In doing so we develop leverage, which is the thing that pulls us through the messy middle and helps us move from mindless reactions to empowering actions. In developing leverage we become less reliant on willpower and motivation and are able to instead tap into inspiration.

We can think of motivation as an external force that prompts us to take action. Maybe we watch a motivational video or attend a seminar and feel the urge to get up and make things happen. There is value in being motivated, but the feeling is often short-lived, temporary and not always dependable. It comes and it goes and thus doesn't make for an adequate success strategy all by itself. Inspiration, meanwhile, comes from within rather than from an external prompt or push. At some times it feels stronger than at others, but it is always there at some level, even when motivation is not. Inspiration is found in connecting to what we value most in life and then in tying our actions to those values.

To develop leverage around the 2/5/10 system and move from relying on willpower and motivation to tapping into inspiration, I will invite you to explore the following prompts, which will help you to connect this daily practice to your internal emotional drivers. After completing the prompts I will encourage you to complete your 'leverage statement', a short statement designed to help you stay connected to your 'why' and stay on track when willpower is waning.

Going beyond the 2/5/10 system you can of course connect these questions to any behavioural change you are looking to implement to tie it to your values and drivers.

Six Questions for Your Leverage Statement

1. What benefits will you see in your life from practising the 2/5/10 system (or whatever other change you are looking to make) on a consistent basis?

Consider how it will impact on your own health, your relationships, your confidence, your work and all other areas that are important to you.

2. Looking at this list of benefits, explore 'why' each of these benefits is important to you.

Once you have written your 'why' for each benefit, ask 'why' a second time to go a layer deeper. If your answer doesn't feel compelling enough, go one layer deeper by asking 'why?' a third time. Your second or third 'why' usually points to the emotional drive below the logical reason for taking or not taking action. We all know logically that it makes sense to practise self-care, but it is the emotional connection that will bring about consistency and long-term change. Here is an example:

A benefit of practising the 2/5/10 system is it will help me to be more present with my kids.

Why that matters:

Because I notice I am finding it progressively more difficult to connect with them as I balance different stresses and worries in my head.

Why that matters:

I want them to know that however busy I am, they are my greatest priority.

Why that matters:

Growing up, I didn't feel I was a priority to anyone and didn't feel I had anyone I could go to when I was struggling. I don't ever want my kids to feel that way.

The answer to the third 'Why?' provides a strong compelling drive beyond the logical thought of 'It will help me present with my kids.'

3. What are the negative consequences of not staying consistent with the 2/5/10 system (or whatever other change you are looking to make)?

    What consequences will there be for your health, confidence, career, relationships or to any others areas that are important for you?

4. Looking at this list of consequences, explore why each of these consequences is a drawback in your life.

    Again, ask 'why' two to three times for each consequence. Your second or third 'why' usually points to the emotional drive below the logical reason for taking or not taking action. For example:

    A drawback of not following through with the 2/5/10 system is that I know I will be rolling the dice with how I feel and not proactively looking after my mental and emotional wellness.

    Why that matters:

    I have been caught in cycles of anxiety for the past three years and it is becoming overwhelming.

    Why that matters:

    I feel I have a lot of great things happening in my life but cannot fully enjoy anything as I find myself constantly living at an exhausting pace in which life feels as though it's passing me by.

    Why that matters:

    I am sick of feeling guilty for my inability to be present to myself, my experiences and the people in my life.

5. Who else in my life benefits when I stay consistent with the 2/5/10 system?

    When I practise the 2/5/10 system I feel calmer and more fulfilled. I am more present with my family and friends. I am less reactive with my partner and am better able to communicate with everyone around me. I communicate more authentically with my colleagues and because I am fulfilling my own needs I remove any expectations on others to fulfil my needs. This means I can love people without expectations. In short, all my close relationships are positively impacted when I do this work.

6. Who else in my life is negatively impacted when I do not stick with the 2/5/10 system?

When I do not take care of myself, at some level I have an expectation of those closest to me to fulfil my needs. This is not fair on me or them and builds resentment from both sides. Not looking after myself also has a negative impact on my partner and kids as I am less present, more snappy and more reactive.

Now, having explored these six prompts and gone a few layers deeper to understand your emotional drivers and your 'why', write a short leverage statement, about three to five sentences, taking the most compelling insights from your answers to the six prompts.

Include the benefits of following through, the consequences of not following through and the relationships that are positively or negatively affected as a result.

This short statement is one that you can read to remind yourself of the importance of this change you want to make. You can read this statement aloud daily to stay connected to your 'why' or have it as a tool to fall back on when motivation is dipping and you feel the need to tap back into inspiration.

LESS – Environment

The power and role of your environment should not be overlooked when it comes to creating sustainable changes in your day-to-day life. In much the same way as I would encourage a client who was looking to eat healthier to 'audit' their kitchen and ensure it was conducive to a healthier way of eating, I will invite you to consider how your internal and external environments support the goal of improved self-talk and emotional awareness in the long term.

Without a sense of intention in how you set up your environment it can be easy to fall into autopilot behaviours and slip back into habits that do not support your desired outcomes.

When thinking of the environment we can consider both our internal and external environments.

Our internal environment relates to what we are consuming, not only food but also media.

We all know that the foods we eat have an impact on how we look, feel and perform. Our bodies are constantly using the nutrients we consume to replenish, rejuvenate and repair. We are most likely also aware that in our bodies' digestion process our foods are digested, absorbed and utilised by the body.

Our focus in this book has been on mental and emotional wellness, but of course our physical wellness, nutrition and lifestyle choices are essential to our overall health. Without physical energy and recovery it is near impossible to think clearly and be at ease in body and mind. For this reason it is essential to ensure that we are providing our internal environment with what it needs to support us.

It is also worth considering that the same 'digestion' process is true of the media we consume. Have you ever watched a horror film and found yourself experiencing nightmares that night?

Although we might see our media consumption as just the few hours in which we are consuming the information, there is also the 'digestion' process and the after-effects on our psyche. In auditing the type of content we are currently giving our attention to on our phones, TVs or laptops, we reflect on whether it is supporting the type of outlook and experience we want to have in life or is creating overwhelm, fear and comparison.

The internet has opened us up to an incredible amount of content, but it is important that we are intentional in how we use it and recognise the profound effects our media consumption can have on our mental health. While years ago we would have had to travel to meet mentors in areas of interest we now have access to podcasts, courses and audiobooks that can share content that inspires, educates and informs.

I won't ever forget hearing a cassette by motivational speaker Jim Rohn when I was fifteen. He suggested turning your car into a 'mobile library' by listening to tapes while commuting to and from work. He suggested that studying a topic for just one hour a day could equate to nine forty-hour work weeks' worth of study in that specific area over the course of a year! I think for many of us it would be a conservative estimate that we spend an hour on our smartphones every day. Again, by auditing what we are paying attention to in our media consumption we can make some very healthy improvements to our internal environment.

Alongside our internal environment, our external environment, including our physical space and social circle, can have a profound effect on our ability to create lasting change in life. Those looking to get into the habit of exercising in the morning before work are often encouraged by their personal trainers to leave their training gear next to their bed so they are 'ready to go' upon waking.

I invite you to take a similar approach for your journalling and meditation practices by considering how you can set up your home environment to make completing the practice as 'resistance-free' as possible. In my experience clients who state when and where they will complete the practice tend to be much more consistent than those who skip over the step of thinking about the time and location in which they'll practise. Consider setting up a specific place in your home that encourages a calming and zen feeling, perhaps using candles, incense and music to create an atmosphere that you enjoy.

Finally, the company we keep can have a great impact on our ability to find consistency in new habits. Look to find people or groups, whether online or in person, who are interested in similar practices to those you are looking to develop. Perhaps consider hiring a coach or completing a programme in which you will meet like-minded people and be supported in your efforts.

Take a little time to write about how you might set up your internal and external environments to best support you with the changes you are looking to make. Consider (but don't limit yourself to):

1. Nutrition and diet
2. Media consumption
3. Your physical environment/home
4. Your social circle/support team

LESS – Scheduling

Management guru Peter Drucker is quoted as saying, 'Tell me what you value and I might believe you, but show me your calendar and your bank statement, and I'll show you what you really value.'

We all have one hundred and sixty-eight hours in the week with a variety of roles, goals and responsibilities to fulfil in that given time. It is worth considering whether our self-care has been given a consistent slot in our busy calendars or has been nudged out and overlooked in place of 'more important things'.

Some see self-care as a hot bath with scented candles or a bottle of wine on a Friday night. Others see it as something that can happen sometime in the future when we get to the end of our never-ending to-do list. For me, self-care has become a daily non-negotiable and an honest commitment to maintaining and improving my physical, mental and emotional wellness. I recognise its importance, so it goes in the calendar before anything else. There are times I could lie to myself and say, 'I don't have time,' but having seen the leverage it provides to improve all other areas of my life, I always ensure I make the time, even if it's just fifteen minutes in the morning and the same again in the evening. Sure enough, if I fail to put it in the diary, more often than not it'll fail to happen.

There's an old story I've always liked as a reminder to keep life simple and remember what matters most.

A lecturer walks into a classroom holding an empty jar and tells the students that today he'll be teaching them an important lesson. From under his desk he takes out a bag of rocks which he places one by one into the jar until it's full to the top. 'Is the jar full?' he asks the students.

They all agree that it's full. Grinning from ear to ear, the lecturer takes a second bag from under his desk, this time filled with smaller pebbles and stones. He pours them among the rocks, filling the jar right to the brim.

The class laugh and one student says, 'Okay, now it's definitely full.' The lecturer again smiles to himself and pulls out a bag of sand from under the desk, pouring it into the jar, gently allowing it to fall between the rocks, pebbles and stones, until now the jar is completely full.

He explains that there's a lesson in this little exercise. The bigger rocks, he tells the students, represent the things that are most important in our lives – our family, our kids, our health and self-care, our passions, and the people and activities we love the most.

The smaller stones represent the other things that matter in life – our work, our car, our home.

And the sand represents everything else – the busyness, the noise, the distraction, the gossip, the worry about what other people are doing and the fears of not being good enough.

'If I were to fill the jar with sand first, there wouldn't be any room for the stones or rocks, in the same way that if I fill my life with busyness, noise, distraction and overthinking there won't be any room for the stuff that really matters.'

This is a reminder that your self-care is the most important thing in the world. It can't be an afterthought or something that happens 'when you have time'. You've got to make the time and make this a priority. When you look after you, everyone around you benefits. When you decide you are too busy to look after yourself, everyone around you suffers. I use the word *decide* intentionally, because it is a decision.

You are the most important person in your world, as I am the most important person in mine. When we are tired, lacking in energy, overly stressed and not meeting our needs it has an effect on everyone in our life.

With that in mind, I am going to really reinforce this message that when you give yourself the time and space to check in and be with yourself in a caring way daily, everyone in your life benefits. When you skip over these practices of true self-care, everyone suffers.

I don't think any of us sits down in the morning and says, 'I'm going to give three to four hours of my valuable attention, time and energy to social media today,' but without being intentional in how we spend our time or energy it can just seem to happen. We look back on the day wondering where the time went and why we didn't have time for ourselves and we feel a little guilty about the hours spent aimlessly scrolling. What if instead we were intentional with activities like our phone usage, which would not only free up our time, but also allow us to enjoy that time guilt-free?

At the end of each week I would invite you to sit and schedule the week ahead, being intentional and prioritising what you deem to be important, remembering that without intention and a plan for our week 'life' just seems to come up with its own plans for us. Use a digital or physical diary or calendar and write in the times when you will practise your self-care rituals. Sticking with the framework outlined in the last chapter I will of course encourage you to schedule fifteen minutes each morning and evening to complete your 2/5/10 system.

Your schedule might look something like this:

Meetings with the Most Important Person in Your World
- Time and location (the when and where)
- Purpose (the why)
- Agenda (the what and how)

For example:

Daily Self-Care Morning Routine

- **Time and location**

  7.30 a.m. at the kitchen table.

- **Purpose**

  Set my intentions for the day and take some time to meditate and practise calm before the kids get up.

- **Agenda**

  10 minutes of meditation using a guided meditation and five minutes to answer my journalling prompts. Play some relaxing music, light a candle and enjoy a cup of good coffee!

Date Night

In addition to scheduling your daily practices I would strongly encourage you to set a little challenge for the next four weeks.

I want you to schedule one hour for yourself every week to 'date yourself'.

As with daily practice, this needs to go in your diary or calendar and be treated as sacred time, an appointment with the most important person in the world and not an afterthought.

Intentionally block off an hour when you will spend time with yourself doing something you enjoy, whether it's an existing hobby or activity or something you have always wanted to try.

The date night hour and daily practices equate to 4.5 hours of your 168-hour week. Make a commitment to this for the next 30 days and watch the impact it has on your levels of clarity, calm and compassion for yourself and others.

LES<u>S</u> – Stretch Zone

'We often overestimate what we can do in a day, but underestimate what we can do in a year'
– ANONYMOUS

The fourth part of the LESS model for behavioural change comes back to the 'stretch zone' concept that we talked about in the Confidence chapter. We said that we can often find ourselves falling into comfort zones in life, ruts disguised as routines. Our comfort zones are a result of slipping into a place where we are not challenging ourselves in life beyond our current skill sets. As outlined in the Happiness chapter, growth and challenge are an essential part of finding meaning in life, with happiness and confidence coming as a by-product.

If you were to think back to the times in life in which you consistently felt the most happy, confident and fulfilled, I would be willing to bet there was challenge and growth happening in your life during those times and in a sustainable way. Perhaps it was the growth of a new relationship, or the challenge of starting a new job. Maybe you were in flow with your fitness routine or working on a project that excited you.

A mistake that is often made when it comes to behavioural change is in taking on too much too quickly, falling into a panic zone and then retreating back to the safety of the comfort zone when things get overwhelming. We often repeat this cycle every year, but with less confidence each time, remembering all the times we have 'fallen off the wagon' in the past. We want to avoid this and find the sweet spot between comfort and panic, the stretch zone, where we are stretched a little beyond our current skill set or habits, where we can gain confidence in seeing our progress, growth and consistency.

When we find the sweet spot of the stretch zone and are willing to stay in this place consistently, it is incredible the progress that can be made in any area of life in a few short months. Perhaps the 2/5/10 routine I laid out in the last chapter feels like too much for you right now and you feel paring it back a little will be more reflective of your current stretch zone. Or maybe you're already meditating consistently and have a journalling practice and will need to mix up the 2/5/10 routine to add a little challenge and put you in your stretch zone. Stretch zones are unique to the individual, but it is really about being honest with yourself about what your edge for personal growth looks like.

After a number of weeks or months completing your journalling prompts in the morning and writing down your morning priorities and gratitude list it could be easy to fall into routine and write down the same responses to the prompts every day. This would be falling into a new comfort zone, with growth becoming stagnant. In this case the encouragement would be to ask yourself, 'What would this exercise look like if I were challenging myself a little bit beyond what is currently comfortable?'

Remember, our confidence and growth comes from going just a little beyond our comfort zone, not from staying in it or jumping way outside it! To ensure you are in a place of sustainable growth on a consistent basis you might consider checking in with these three questions each week while scheduling the week ahead.

1. What worked really well this past week?
2. Where did I fall short or struggle last week?
3. What did I learn from last week that I can implement this week?

LESS is More

To recap these four suggested steps and exercise the LESS model for consistent change I invite you to:

1. Come up with your **leverage statement** based on the six journalling prompts shared above.

2. Perform an **environmental audit** and consider how you can create an internal and external environment conducive to the habits you are looking to form.

3. Allow thirty minutes each week to reflect on the week gone by and **schedule** all your priorities for the week ahead.

4. As part of your weekly reflection, check in with your progress and reflect on whether you have been spending time in the **stretch zone**.

Your Next Chapter

'*The world is full of magic things, patiently waiting for our senses to grow sharper*' – W.B. YEATS

'*We must be willing to let go of the life we planned so as to have the life that is waiting for us*' – JOSEPH CAMPBELL

A SOULFUL LIFE

There is an old story of a westerner visiting Africa and being accompanied by a group of porters as he travels through the local region. The porters accompanying him carry machetes and cut through a trail of thick vegetation, working tirelessly as they move swiftly on their travels.

Keen to see as much of the land as he can, the westerner is grateful for and impressed by the speed at which the porters work and move. Starting early in the morning, within a few hours they make incredible progress crossing rivers, climbing hills and moving through difficult terrain.

Then, all of a sudden, despite looking fresh, the porters stop and sit down.

Surprised by the change of pace and the fact that they have stopped after just a few hours of walking, the westerner asks if they were tired having set off too quickly in the morning.

'It's not that we are tired. We have just been moving very fast all morning and have left our soul behind. Now it's time to allow our soul to catch up with us again.'

How often do we find ourselves moving at a pace that feels unsustainable and overwhelming? If not in body, we can in mind find ourselves longing to 'slow down to the speed of life' and be in the present moment. We are often so keen to improve things or get somewhere in life that we forget to actually live and enjoy our lives. The sense of a soulful life comes from an appreciation for and presence to what is rather than a story of or expectation of what 'should' be.

On two trips to Tanzania to climb Kilimanjaro, Africa's highest mountain, I was exposed to some more African wisdom. As with all higher altitude mountains there is an acclimatisation process in which the body slowly gets used to being at altitude where there is less oxygen in the air. With less oxygen, hiking, walking, sleeping and all other functions are of course more difficult and so it is key to ascend the mountain gradually and then rest well.

It is a slow process and one that the porters on the mountain are very familiar with – they escort thousands of clients to the summit each year. If you ever get to Tanzania to make the trip up Kilimanjaro you will become very familiar with the phrase 'pole, pole' (pronounced polay polay) which means 'slowly, slowly'. This is a mantra shared by the porters throughout the expedition.

Throughout the five- to eight-day ascent of the mountain, and particularly when you near the summit, this reminder, 'slowly, slowly', is repeated countless times. It's a reminder that if you move too fast, you'll burn out, fall ill and will fail to reach the summit.

It also, however, reminds us that we must keep moving in the right direction and not stand still in life. The feeling of 'soul' becomes absent in our lives when we're moving too fast and trying to keep up with those around us. Remember, this life is your own and you do not need to keep up with anyone. It is often our efforts to keep up that lead us down the wrong paths or up the wrong mountains.

Coming towards the end of this book I would like to leave with you one final exercise I have found hugely beneficial in my own life. It is an exercise that will enable you to get clear about the direction you hope to go next, allowing you to enjoy the journey while moving 'slowly, slowly' in a way that brings more 'soul' to your life. Treat it as a little ceremony, not just another journalling prompt.

In a fast-paced world where we tend to roll from one task to the next, the importance of ceremony has been largely lost. Be present with and give your full energy to this exercise and it could provide the insights that open a new chapter and direction in your life.

Give yourself at least an hour for this exercise if you can. Light a candle, put on some relaxing music and get comfortable in your environment. Turn off your phone, take a few deep breaths and get ready to take back the pen.

TAKE BACK THE PEN

Reading this book you will perhaps have come to see some of the unconscious beliefs, patterns, values, stories and drivers that have influenced your actions and decisions in life up to this point. If we are not aware of our stories and beliefs it can feel that we are living a 'life script' written by someone else. With increased awareness, we can 'take back the pen' and consciously choose the direction of the next chapter of our life.

To begin, consider what title and subtitle you would give to a book written about your life up to this point in time.

Write a few sentences about why you have chosen this title and subtitle.

Next, divide your life story into six chapters, the first chapter being your earliest years, the sixth chapter being the most recent years, right up to today, and the second, third, fourth and fifth chapters making up the rest of your life.

For example, if I were forty-two years of age I might divide my chapters as follows:

- **Chapter 1:** 0–7
- **Chapter 2:** 8–14
- **Chapter 3:** 15–21
- **Chapter 4:** 22–28
- **Chapter 5:** 29–35
- **Chapter 6:** 36–42

Now give each chapter a name and write a brief description of the plot. Include the main characters or influences in each chapter. Keep the language simple and short as if you were describing the story to a child.

Once you have written out the chapter titles and described the plot and characters in each chapter, reflect back and see if you can notice any recurring themes in your life.

1. Have there been similar recurring challenges or obstacles in your life?

2. Have you met the same types of people?

3. Have similar beliefs or stories appeared which have supported or held you back?

4. What can you see when you reflect back on the different chapters of your life up until today?

Spend a little time writing about any recurring themes or patterns that jump out for you. As we have said throughout this book, we often mistake 'remembering' for 'thinking' and so can find ourselves recreating the same experiences in different scenarios or relationships.

After writing about any themes or recurring patterns you see, go through each chapter and extract the lessons and wisdom. What have you learnt from your experiences so far? Look for and reflect upon your wins to nurture confidence. Look to the challenges you have overcome to recognise your resilience and strength.

Now, after writing about, reflecting on and extracting the lessons from your journey so far I would like you to write about chapter seven, the chapter that starts today.

- What title will you give to this stage of your life?
- What will the plot for this next chapter be?
- How will you grow?
- What challenges will you overcome?
- What will you bring into your life?
- Who will be the main characters in this next chapter?
- What traits and values will you demonstrate?

Write in detail about how you would like this next chapter to look and when you feel ready, highlight any key phrases or words that stand out to you.

This exercise can begin to act as a map or compass for decisions, actions and behaviours going forward.

Afterword

INNER MASTERY

Before stepping on stage to give talks for corporate clients or appearing in media features I am often asked how I would like to be introduced or what title I would like to be given. The phrase 'life coach' always makes me squirm because it conjures up images of someone who claims to have all the answers and have life figured out.

Years ago, when I worked solely in the fitness space, it was easy to label myself 'the fitness guy', but as I have pursued studies in meditation, breathwork, CBT, tantra, shamanism and a host of other areas that interest me, it has become increasingly difficult to give myself a short and snappy professional title.

In corporate environments I keep it simple by saying that I used to share physical fitness strategies and now share mental and emotional fitness strategies. For media I just go with 'speaker and coach'.

However, except when absolutely necessary, I avoid giving myself a label and hope that the people who'll read this book or listen to my podcasts will get a sense of who I am and what I'm about.

I'm not quite sure how I ended up doing whatever it is that I do now. It started with the move from physical fitness to workshops on goal-setting and time management. The goal-setting stuff didn't keep my interest for long and felt too methodical and 'heady'.

As I spoke more vulnerably from the heart about my struggles and areas that needed improvement, people seemed to connect a lot more and see their stories in my story.

Though it might not be the catchiest of titles, 'wounded healer' would perhaps be the title that resonates most deeply with me in terms of what I try to do now. All my own struggles have been the source of my greatest growth and gifts in life. Efforts to heal the parts of myself that I struggle with have given me the lived experience to share with others what I have learnt. You won't ever hear me giving anecdotal advice on things I haven't experienced. Ask me about stocks, parenting or politics and I won't have anything to offer. But ask me about loneliness, isolation, impostor syndrome, being stuck in one's head, struggling with confidence, riddled with anxiety or lacking in purpose and I can confidently share the 'medicine' of my lived experience, challenges, growth and 'wisdom'.

I feel we all have the opportunity to be 'wounded healers' and come to better understand and connect with ourselves and one another. It starts with bringing awareness and compassion to our challenges and struggles and seeing them as gifts in disguise. I hope this book has helped you to begin to do this. I am grateful for the challenges and struggles I have had and continue to have as they point to areas of potential growth, healing and acceptance.

As these challenges wake me up to new ways of living, my life expands. When I close my eyes to or turn away from my challenges and struggles, I 'go back to sleep' and my life contracts. In a world where we spend so much time looking outwards it isn't surprising that we compare our experience of life to what we see in others. Most of us tend to show our 'light' and hide the 'dark' parts of ourselves that seem unlovable; and it can be easy to fall into the trap of thinking that the struggles we feel internally are unique to us.

We all struggle in life sometimes and thus perhaps the greatest gift we can offer ourselves and one another is a little more patience, curiosity, tolerance and compassion. A great deal of life is spent in the head where our assumptions, beliefs, stories and judgements live. As with anything, coming from a place of living in the head to living from the heart is a practice. When we find ourselves caught in these judgements towards ourselves and others we can come to see it as an invitation to come back to the heart and practise living from a place of compassion, curiosity and appreciation.

Patience, tolerance, curiosity and compassion can feel tricky in a fast-paced world, but I hope that some of the ideas, meditations and journalling practices that I have shared with you offer some ideas as to how you come home to yourself and slow down to the speed of life.

Thank you for being a part of my journey and for allowing me to be a small part of yours!

Grá Mór,

Pat

Eight-Week
ARC Tracker

1/56   2/56   3/56   4/56   5/56   6/56   7/56

○   ○   ○   ○   ○   ○   ○

8/56   9/56   10/56   11/56   12/56   13/56   14/56

○   ○   ○   ○   ○   ○   ○

15/56   16/56   17/56   18/56   19/56   20/56   21/56

○   ○   ○   ○   ○   ○   ○

22/56   23/56   24/56   25/56   26/56   27/56   28/56

○   ○   ○   ○   ○   ○   ○

29/56   30/56   31/56   32/56   33/56   34/56   35/56

○   ○   ○   ○   ○   ○   ○

36/56   37/56   38/56   39/56   40/56   41/56   42/56

○   ○   ○   ○   ○   ○   ○

43/56   44/56   45/56   46/56   47/56   48/56   49/56

○   ○   ○   ○   ○   ○   ○

50/56   51/56   52/56   53/56   54/56   55/56   56/56

○   ○   ○   ○   ○   ○   ○

2/5/10 Routine – 30-Day Tracker

MORNING DEPOSITS

DAY 1   ◯

DAY 2   ◯

DAY 3   ◯

DAY 4   ◯

DAY 5   ◯

DAY 6   ◯

DAY 7   ◯

DAY 8   ◯

DAY 9   ◯

DAY 10   ◯

DAY 11   ◯

DAY 12   ◯

DAY 13   ◯

DAY 14   ◯

DAY 15   ◯

DAY 16   ◯

DAY 17   ◯

DAY 18   ◯

DAY 19   ◯

DAY 20   ◯

DAY 21   ◯

DAY 22   ◯

DAY 23   ◯

DAY 24   ◯

DAY 25   ◯

DAY 26   ◯

DAY 27   ◯

DAY 28   ◯

DAY 29   ◯

DAY 30   ◯

EVENING DEPOSITS

DAY 1	DAY 2	DAY 3	DAY 4	DAY 5
◯	◯	◯	◯	◯

DAY 6	DAY 7	DAY 8	DAY 9	DAY 10
◯	◯	◯	◯	◯

DAY 11	DAY 12	DAY 13	DAY 14	DAY 15
◯	◯	◯	◯	◯

DAY 16	DAY 17	DAY 18	DAY 19	DAY 20
◯	◯	◯	◯	◯

DAY 21	DAY 22	DAY 23	DAY 24	DAY 25
◯	◯	◯	◯	◯

DAY 26	DAY 27	DAY 28	DAY 29	DAY 30
◯	◯	◯	◯	◯